◀ **The Critical Thinking Companion** ▶

◀The Critical Thinking▶ Companion

THIRD EDITION

Jane S. Halonen
University of West Florida

Cynthia Gray

WORTH
PUBLISHERS

A Macmillan Education Imprint

New York

Publisher: Rachel Losh
Associate Publisher: Jessica Bayne
Senior Acquisitions Editor: Christine Cardone
Executive Marketing Manager: Katherine Nurre
Assistant Editor: Catherine Michaelsen
Media Editorial Assistant: Nicole Padinha
Managing Editor: Lisa Kinne
Senior Project Editor: Jane O'Neill
Director of Design, Content Management: Diana Blume
Cover Designer: Diana Blume
Text Designer: Lee McKevitt
Art Manager: Matthew McAdams
Photo Editor: Robin Fadool
Senior Production Supervisor: Sarah Segal
Composition: codeMantra
Printing and Binding: Edwards Brothers Malloy
Cover Image: DrAfter123/Digital Vision Vectors/Getty Images

Library of Congress Control Number: 2015949000

ISBN-13: 978-1-319-03049-0

ISBN-10: 1-319-03049-1

Printed in the United States of America
First printing

Worth Publishers
One New York Plaza
Suite 4500
New York, NY 10004-1562
www.worthpublishers.com

It is with the pain of personal loss that we dedicate the third edition of *The Critical Thinking Companion* to the memory of our Alverno College mentor, colleague, and friend, Sister Austin Doherty. Our own friendship at Alverno was made all the richer against the backdrop of the institution where Sister Austin served willingly in so many different roles. She was a remarkable woman whose talents in listening, inspiring, challenging, and celebrating modeled for us what women in psychology could and should become. She passed away in early 2015 after a long bout of illness. If there is a college in heaven, then Sister Austin has probably already drafted some plans for how the mission could be improved. We will miss her enormously.

About the Authors ▶

Jane S. Halonen has been a Professor of Psychology at the University of West Florida for over a decade. She has been fortunate also to have great professional families at James Madison University and Alverno College where she was lucky enough to cross paths with the talented Cynthia Gray. Jane's most recent research emphases have been on helping good departments become great ones as well as trying to help legislators understand the true nature of psychology in tough economic times. Jane has been involved over the course of her career with helping the American Psychological Association develop guidelines or standards of academic performance from high school through graduate levels of education. In 2000, she received the Distinguished Teaching Award from the American Psychological Foundation, and the American Psychological Association named her an "Eminent Woman in Psychology" in 2003. She served as the Chief Reader for the Psychology Advanced Placement Reading from 2004 to 2009. A self-identified "teaching conference junkie," Jane served on the National Institute on the Teaching of Psychology (NITOP) Board and has presented at nearly every regional teaching conference in psychology. With Peter Seldin, she also codirected the International Conference on Improving University Teaching from 2001 to 2008.

Cynthia Gray spent six years as Director of Institutional Research, Assessment, & Planning at Beloit College (Beloit, Wisconsin) until her retirement in 2013. Prior to her role in Institutional Research, Cynthia taught in the Department of Psychology at Beloit College and also at Alverno College (Milwaukee, Wisconsin), where she was fortunate enough to meet and work with Jane Halonen. Cynthia currently lives in Quincy, Massachusetts, where she uses her critical thinking skills to organize a household comprised of her husband Doug, their three children ranging in age from middle school to graduate school—Caleb, Hannah, and Morgan—father-in-law David, and the clueless family Chihuahua, Watson. Cynthia received her Ph.D. and M.A. from The Johns Hopkins University (Baltimore) and her B.A. from Earlham College (Richmond, Indiana).

Contents ▶

Preface   xi

Introduction   1

Chapter 1
THINKING CRITICALLY WITH PSYCHOLOGICAL SCIENCE   12

Exercise 1.1   The Case for Interference   13
Exercise 1.2   Stats-R-Us   15
Exercise 1.3   You Need an Operation   16
Exercise 1.4   Consumer Safety   18
Exercise 1.5   Psychology's Perspectives   20
Exercise 1.6   Critiquing Experimental Designs   21
Exercise 1.7   Animal Advocacy   24
Exercise 1.8   What May Come   24

Chapter 2
NEUROSCIENCE AND BEHAVIOR   26

Exercise 2.1   How Do You Do That?   26
Exercise 2.2   Call 911!   27
Exercise 2.3   The Split-Brain Problem   28
Exercise 2.4   The Neurotransmission Doctor   28
Exercise 2.5   Phantom Pain   29
Exercise 2.6   Caring for Phineas   30
Exercise 2.7   The New Superheroes   30
Exercise 2.8   The Addicted Brain   31

Chapter 3
STATES OF CONSCIOUSNESS   33

Exercise 3.1   Conscious Control   33
Exercise 3.2   To Sleep, Perchance to Dream   34
Exercise 3.3   A Midsummer Night's Dream   34
Exercise 3.4   The Light at the End of the Tunnel   35
Exercise 3.5   Jobs and Drugs Don't Mix   36
Exercise 3.6   Rock-a-bye Baby   37
Exercise 3.7   Remedies for Jet Lag   37

Chapter 4
THE NATURE AND NURTURE OF BEHAVIOR   39

Exercise 4.1   It's All Academic   39
Exercise 4.2   Nature or Nurture?   40
Exercise 4.3   Who's to Blame   41
Exercise 4.4   Keep on Truckin'   41
Exercise 4.5   Brother, Can You Spare a Dime?   42
Exercise 4.6   Your Personal Honor Code   43
Exercise 4.7   Character Building   44
Exercise 4.8   Seeing Double   45

Chapter 5
THE DEVELOPING PERSON 47

Exercise 5.1   When Bad Children Aren't Bad   47
Exercise 5.2   The Sitter's Dilemma   48
Exercise 5.3   On Death and Dying   49
Exercise 5.4   Piaget Meets Santa Claus   50
Exercise 5.5   Teen Pregnancy   52
Exercise 5.6   Developmental Delights   52
Exercise 5.7   The End of the Story   53

Chapter 6
SENSATION 55

Exercise 6.1   Crossing the Threshold   55
Exercise 6.2   Occupational Design   56
Exercise 6.3   Reach Out and Touch Someone   59
Exercise 6.4   It's a Matter of Taste   59
Exercise 6.5   Parts Is Parts   60
Exercise 6.6   Do You Hear What I Hear?   61
Exercise 6.7   The Eyes Have It   62

Chapter 7
PERCEPTION 64

Exercise 7.1   Cliff Hangers   64
Exercise 7.2   The Big Picture   65
Exercise 7.3   Context Cues   66
Exercise 7.4   Chaos Control   67
Exercise 7.5   The Case Against ESP   68
Exercise 7.6   Breaking the Code   69
Exercise 7.7   Assembling the Assembly Line   69

Chapter 8
LEARNING 72

Exercise 8.1   Powerful Consequences   72
Exercise 8.2   The Classical Connection   75
Exercise 8.3   Chemical Engineering   77
Exercise 8.4   Self-improvement Revisited   77
Exercise 8.5   The Discriminating Dachshund   78
Exercise 8.6   Little Albert Revisited   79
Exercise 8.7   Reinforcing Rhymes   80
Exercise 8.8   A Working Hypothesis   81

Chapter 9
MEMORY 82

Exercise 9.1   Thanks for the Memory   82
Exercise 9.2   Story Time   84
Exercise 9.3   The Magnificent Seven   85
Exercise 9.4   Roseanne's Dilemma   86
Exercise 9.5   Making Memories   87
Exercise 9.6   Too Much of a Good Thing   88
Exercise 9.7   Looking Ahead   89
Exercise 9.8   Creating Context   89

Chapter 10
THINKING AND LANGUAGE 91

Exercise 10.1 Basic Communication 91
Exercise 10.2 If We Could Talk to the Animals 92
Exercise 10.3 Heuristically Yours 93
Exercise 10.4 There's Good News and There's Bad News 94
Exercise 10.5 Money in the Bank? 95
Exercise 10.6 Seeing Is Believing 96
Exercise 10.7 Poor John and Mary 96
Exercise 10.8 Alex, the Accountant 97

Chapter 11
INTELLIGENCE 100

Exercise 11.1 Einstein's Theory of Intellgence 100
Exercise 11.2 "Character"istics of Intelligence 100
Exercise 11.3 Brave New World 101
Exercise 11.4 Challenging Questions 103
Exercise 11.5 It's All Good 104
Exercise 11.6 When to Test 106
Exercise 11.7 Just Too Cool 107
Exercise 11.8 To Retest or Not to Retest? 107

Chapter 12
MOTIVATION 109

Exercise 12.1 Theories of Motivation 109
Exercise 12.2 Now Hiring 110
Exercise 12.3 The Weight-loss Counselor 110
Exercise 12.4 You Don't Have to Be Lonely 111
Exercise 12.5 Humanistic History 112
Exercise 12.6 Chicken or Egg? 113
Exercise 12.7 The Creative Consultant 114
Exercise 12.8 The Diet Riot 115

Chapter 13
EMOTION 117

Exercise 13.1 Tourist Trap 117
Exercise 13.2 Pinocchio's Legacy 120
Exercise 13.3 Forget Your Troubles 121
Exercise 13.4 Express Yourself! 122
Exercise 13.5 'Cause I'm Happy 122
Exercise 13.6 A Rousing Walk in the Woods 123
Exercise 13.7 Honesty Is the Best Policy 124
Exercise 13.8 What Is This Thing Called Love? 125

Chapter 14
SOCIAL PSYCHOLOGY 127

Exercise 14.1 Pride and Prejudices 127
Exercise 14.2 Dear Abby 129
Exercise 14.3 The Sour Grapes Principle 131
Exercise 14.4 For the Sake of the Children 133
Exercise 14.5 People Were Stupid Back Then 134
Exercise 14.6 But My Teacher *Made* Me Do It! 136
Exercise 14.7 How Can I Help? 137

Chapter 15
PERSONALITY 139

Exercise 15.1   Freud Meets Mother Goose   139
Exercise 15.2   Matchmaker, Matchmaker   141
Exercise 15.3   Maslow's Decline   142
Exercise 15.4   Me on the Rise   143
Exercise 15.5   You Can't Cheat an Honest Man   143
Exercise 15.6   Rorschach's Fate   144
Exercise 15.7   Hopeless—Or Not?   144
Exercise 15.8   Pseudoscientific Personality Explanations   145

Chapter 16
PSYCHOLOGICAL DISORDERS 148

Exercise 16.1   How Much Crazy?   148
Exercise 16.2   And the Winner Is…   149
Exercise 16.3   Love and Work   150
Exercise 16.4   The End   151
Exercise 16.5   I'm Just Not Myself Today   152
Exercise 16.6   The Labeling Controversy   153
Exercise 16.7   The End Is Near (Again)   154
Exercise 16.8   All I Need Is an Agent!   155

Chapter 17
THERAPY 157

Exercise 17.1   How Does That Make You Feel?   157
Exercise 17.2   Even Domestic Engineers Get the Blues   158
Exercise 17.3   Flag on the Play   161
Exercise 17.4   Not So Clever Hans   162
Exercise 17.5   Who's Who Among Therapeutic Professionals   162
Exercise 17.6   There Must Be 50 Ways to Leave Your Shrink   164
Exercise 17.7   Who's Got the Check?   164
Exercise 17.8   Out, Damned Spot   165

Chapter 18
STRESS AND HEALTH 167

Exercise 18.1   Between a Rock and a Hard Place   167
Exercise 18.2   My Screw-up Profile   169
Exercise 18.3   Step on the Gas   170
Exercise 18.4   Customized Stress Assessment   171
Exercise 18.5   The Game of Life   172
Exercise 18.6   Healthy Living   174
Exercise 18.7   Enhancing Immune Function   175
Exercise 18.8   Healthy Executives   176

Answer Key 179

Preface ▶

Ralph Waldo Emerson once said, "A friend is one before whom I may think aloud." It is in that spirit that the original *Critical Thinking Companion* was written and published in 1995. Although the term "companion" may sound a bit old-fashioned, the term conveys an attitude of friendly support to students embarking on their first adventure in the formal study of psychology. Teachers also deserve friendly support in their attempts to make the introductory psychology classroom a stimulating and welcome place to be.

Students often begin their first psychology course overconfidently in that they believe they already understand human nature. They are frequently surprised—and sometimes disappointed—to find that the real science of psychology is not what they had in mind. Teachers must challenge these erroneous notions both knowledgeably and patiently to communicate the core of the discipline that they know and love.

The best teachers of psychology—and we are fortunate to have met and worked with hundreds of remarkable, talented teachers—not only assist students in understanding and applying psychology's principles, concepts, and related skills; they also instill or reawaken curiosity, a sense of wonder, for the puzzle that is human behavior. Encouraging active learning and student engagement accomplishes that goal. Critical thinking activities that encourage discovery are much more likely to lead to meaningful learning than dutiful reading and memorization. Meaningful learning—thoughtful, engaged, and reflective reading and application—takes effort, but is far more likely to have enduring effects on knowledge and thinking skills. Teachers who invest class time in active learning and critical thinking are bound to cover less psychology content than those who practice more content-oriented methods; however, we are convinced that the trade-off is worth it. Students who do psychology in their introductory course emerge with a better orientation to the discipline, a better foundation for using psychology in their lives, and improved thinking skills.

About the New Edition

The third edition of *The Critical Thinking Companion* retains much of what was helpful in earlier editions. We have transformed the original framework proposed in the first edition to clarify different kinds of critical thinking in psychology by aligning with the revised Bloom's Taxonomy (Anderson et al., 2001)[1]. We modernized some of our more outdated strategies and added a few new ones in each chapter. We focused on developing new strategies that would particularly help with the disciplines' "bottlenecks," meaning concepts that appear to be the most difficult to master (see Meyer & Land, 2006)[2]. The best way to get through a bottleneck is to wrestle with the content using solvable problems; our exercises fit that need nicely. In this edition, we devote more emphasis to higher-order skills including evaluating and creating. The third edition also retains the focus on the articulation of student learning outcomes. Every chapter includes different levels of cognitive effort that can be adapted to meet targets of student learning outcomes. Reinforcing the learning goals of each exercise will help students develop their metacognitions (that is, how they "think about thinking").

---

[1]Anderson, L. W. (Ed.), Krathwohl, D. R. (Ed.), Airasian, P. W., Cruikshank, K. A., Mayer, R. E., Pintrich, P. R., Raths, J., & Wittrock, M. C. (2001). *A taxonomy for learning, teaching, and assessing: A revision of Bloom's Taxonomy of Educational Objectives* (Complete edition). New York: Longman.

[2]Meyer, J., & Land, R., Eds. (2006). *Overcoming barriers to student understanding: Threshold concepts and troublesome knowledge*. London: Routledge.

How to Use this Book

Fans of earlier editions have suggested that the *Companion* can be used in multiple ways. Teachers can insert selected exercises into lectures and class sessions to enliven the experience. They can also assign specific exercises that highlight and assess areas that may be difficult to learn. For those interested in providing intensive experience in writing within an introductory psychology context, teachers can direct students to "pick one" from the roster of available strategies in each chapter. Their selections can reveal a lot about their cognitive comfort zones. Teachers can urge students preferring to demonstrate less risk to get out of their comfort zones and attempt more difficult cognitive challenges. Another side benefit of the *laissez-faire* method of choosing individual writing assignments is that this strategy reduces the boredom attendant to the teacher having to grade the same answer repeatedly.

We were eager to undertake this revision after a 15-year hiatus because we believe the *Companion* represents a unique opportunity to serve the greater community of psychology teachers who are dedicated to transforming the lives of their students. We recommend that you turn to the introduction to learn in more detail how to get started in improving students' critical thinking skills through active learning strategies.

Acknowledgments

We need to acknowledge several individuals who have been instrumental in the evolution of this book. Ludy Benjamin inspired and supported the first edition. David Myers provided robust support for the original manuscript and generously facilitated introductions to Worth Publishers, a relationship we have come to cherish over the years. Our colleagues in our various home institutions (for Jane: Alverno College, James Madison University, and University of West Florida; for Cynthia: Alverno College and Beloit College) have been the kind of individuals who make department meetings stimulating and beneficial. The larger teaching community (regional and national teaching conferences, Council of Teachers of Undergraduate Psychology, Advanced Placement readers, the Society for the Teachers of Psychology, and Teachers of Psychology in Secondary Schools) reliably reinforces our enthusiasm about our calling.

We owe a great debt to the remarkable Chris Cardone. She remains the most trusted person we know in publishing. Very few editors can fill the bill as taskmaster/companion. She manages that role with elegance, grace, and good humor while she simultaneously attends to all the details that can make authors proud of what they have created.

We remain indebted to our patient family members who put up with the necessary family absences required when we are in self-imposed writing prison. Jane's husband Brian is looking forward to her eventual retirement when he might be able to recapture more of her personal attention. His loving patience and enthusiastic support provide just the right climate in which her creativity flourishes. Cynthia's family (husband Doug and children Morgan, Hannah, and Caleb) continuously prove that learning is constant, exciting, and delightfully messy. They help Cynthia not just accomplish her dreams but experience hope for the full range of life's challenges.

Good companions make life richer. Although we no longer are companions who live and work in close proximity, our friendship endures. Whether you are a teacher or a student, we welcome you into our circle and hope you find the adventure ahead will be a transforming one.

Jane Halonen

Cynthia Gray

◀Introducing Critical Thinking▶

What is "critical thinking"? Long before you picked up this text you had probably heard the term and may have wondered what it meant. Although experts disagree about exactly what critical thinking entails, in this text it means *the special kind of thinking skills that promote conscious, purposeful, and active involvement of the thinker with new ideas.* Observing carefully, inferring accurately, building connections among ideas, asking questions, making decisions, analyzing the quality of evidence, and generating new ideas are all skills that comprise aspects of critical thinking.

All of us regularly manage to do simple acts of critical thinking of a practical nature. You engage in a simple form of critical thinking when you decide which cereal to eat for breakfast. Your choice of college was probably the result of a longer, more complex chain of critical thought and decision-making. When you have an argument with a close friend, you use critical thinking skills to try to determine what went wrong and how to fix it. So rest assured—you already have had a great deal of practice in certain kinds of critical thinking.

Your collective thinking experiences have already developed your unique perspective on the world and your personal theories about how things operate. By observation and direct experience, you have become skilled at establishing meaningful explanations for why things happen the way they do. You naturally develop hypotheses (that is, good guesses) about how behavior patterns fit together to assist you in navigating the challenges of your life. Sometimes your guesses are right; at other times, behaviors don't fit your expectations quite so neatly. You will discover big differences between how you expect the world to operate and how it truly does. These discrepancies are likely to leave you feeling confused or uncomfortable until you can develop new sets of expectations that fit with and explain them. Psychologists have a name for this discrepancy—"cognitive dissonance." You'll learn more about the effects of experiencing cognitive tensions that have to be resolved when you study social psychology later in the course.

Once you can explain what you encounter, you no longer need to think critically about that circumstance. Your knowledge base develops and helps you adapt to a more complicated world. You can revisit your conclusions and allow your knowledge base to help you navigate life's challenges until you encounter situations where that revised theory no longer works. Then it is back to the drawing board to rethink your personal theory to accommodate new information.

HOW COLLEGE WILL CHANGE YOU AS A CRITICAL THINKER

In contrast to the practical critical thinking you do each day, a college education will teach you how to think about the world from different vantage points using different kinds of thinking skills. Studying a particular discipline offers an opportunity to develop your critical thinking skills systematically in a specialized area. You will quickly discover that each discipline tends to define what it means to think critically in different ways. Even within a single discipline, no single definition of critical thinking prevails. Such richness of definition within a discipline as well as across disciplines can be a source of confusion to any new student trying to become a better critical thinker.

One overarching framework that educators across many disciplines use to foster critical thinking is called Bloom's Taxonomy (Bloom et al., 1942). Originally, Bloom and his colleagues described a framework that helped students identify and understand the more complex thinking that college requires. They generated six categories of thinking skills, differentiating those skills involving less effort as "lower-order thinking skills" (for example, memorizing, comprehending) from those that require more cognitive processing from the learner (such as analysis, synthesis, evaluation). In 2002, David Krathwohl, an original member of the Bloom research group, reconvened a new set of educators to review and revise Bloom's Taxonomy. Ultimately, they retained the structure of six categories, but revised some of the concepts and reordered their relationships. Figure 1 illustrates the scaffolded approach taken in the new Bloom's Taxonomy that distinguishes higher-order thinking skills (HOTS) from lower-order skills (LOTS). As you move from one level to the next, you will notice each level builds on skills learned in prior levels. For example, *Create* (the most advanced level in the taxonomy) depends on accurate understanding, applying what you have learned in new situations, analyzing how essential parts interrelate, and evaluating how well potential solutions will work.

The nature of the cognitive demands your professor will make in your courses depends on many factors. Professors who primarily lecture or who teach very large classes may feel stuck testing your knowledge of course content at the lowest levels of Bloom's Taxonomy. You can demonstrate your knowledge very effectively on multiple-choice tests and other objective testing forms (like true/false or fill-in-the-blank) using lower-level skills. Professors who have smaller classes or who focus on critical thinking skills will push you harder to show higher-level skills through essay questions, projects, and other assignments that require you to wrestle with the material.

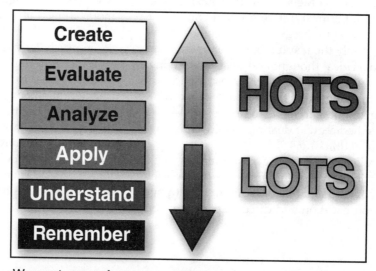

- We must **remember** a concept before we can **understand** it.
- We must **understand** a concept before we can **apply** it.
- We must be able to **apply** a concept before we can **analyze** it.
- We must have **analyzed** a concept before we can **evaluate** it.
- We must have **remembered, understood, applied, analyzed,** and **evaluated** a concept before we can **create.**

FIGURE 1 Lower- and higher-order thinking skills in Bloom's Taxonomy

HOW PSYCHOLOGY WILL CHANGE YOU AS A CRITICAL THINKER

In the third edition of the *Critical Thinking Companion*, we demonstrate that higher-order processing is not just possible but beneficial in a course that introduces you to the discipline of psychology. We borrow the basic organization of the revised Bloom's Taxonomy to explore how psychology students can improve their critical thinking skills as they relate to the science of mind and behavior. Psychology, like all sciences, strives to explain how things work. The science of psychology attempts to understand how human beings and other organisms behave, think, and feel. Although the focus of studies in psychology may be as diverse as the neural activity in the human brain, people's motivation in overeating patterns, the attachment styles of infants, and the migration patterns of birds, learning about each can involve the same type of critical thinking skills that promote the basic goals of psychology: describing, explaining, predicting, and controlling behavior.

In the *Critical Thinking Companion* nearly each type of thinking in Bloom's taxonomy is deployed in every chapter you will study in introductory psychology, not only to help you sharpen your ability to think critically but also to give you greater active engagement with the important concepts and theories of psychology. However, the first level in the revised Bloom's taxonomy—memorizing—is not addressed in the *Companion's* approach. The concept ***Remember*** involves rehearsing associations among concepts until you store the desired content to be retrieved and used at some later point. Although it is hard work and a valuable process that builds a strong knowledge base in any discipline, memorization tends to involve or engage you in a minimal way. Although you may use critical thinking skills to reorganize the elements of something to be memorized in some more meaningful fashion, critical thinking itself is not required for successful memorization.

As we explore the levels of the Taxonomy in the context of an introductory course in psychology we provide specific *student learning outcomes* that help define the focus of each level and provide exemplars of the different kinds of cognitive demands that characterize them. Some educators cluster related outcomes by category to communicate slightly different but related emphases within that category. A good example can be found in Figure 2. We will borrow from that structure to specify psychology-related outcomes.

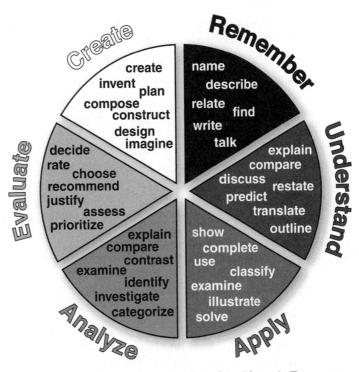

FIGURE 2 Learning outcomes related to Bloom's Taxonomy

UNDERSTAND

The first level of Bloom's Taxonomy that we explore in the *Companion* is **Understand**. As psychology's long history of memory research demonstrates, we can memorize connections between nonsense syllables and do so with remarkable efficiency. However, to understand concepts increases the cognitive demand on the learner. **Understand** imparts meaning and makes behaviors comprehensible. From a learning standpoint, *understanding* in psychology is apparent when students begin to identify, describe, and explain concepts about behavior with reasonable accuracy. They recognize patterns of behavior and become conversant in the concepts offered in psychology that capture the distinctiveness of the patterns. They can also accurately translate the scientific explanations in psychology into simpler language.

Student learning outcomes in **Understand** include the following:

- *Observe / Describe*—Report patterns of behavior.

Psychologists take pride in making sure that their descriptions are precise, objective, and parsimonious (that is, as simple as possible). They prefer describing behavior using "operational definitions" that leave little room for debate about what constitutes a target behavior. When clear operational definitions exist, psychologists can more readily count or measure behaviors, which makes them more amenable to statistical analysis. Although you usually think of description as a visual skill, it can technically include senses other than vision. For example, recognizing specific sounds, tastes, smells, and textures can also constitute an observation. You may be more likely to engage in observing behavior when a specific behavior captures your attention, and it doesn't quite fit with your expectations.

- *Explain*—Discuss behaviors using psychology terminology.

The discipline is rich in concepts that differentiate patterns of behavior. Accurately labeling behavior using psychological concepts simultaneously builds your understanding of behavior and the nature of the discipline by creating a strong conceptual foundation.

- *Translate*—Restate complex ideas in psychology in your own words.

This ability makes it easier to learn and remember concepts about behavior. As you study, translating the formal language of psychology in your textbook into your own words will make the key ideas more accessible and memorable.

- *Compare*—Note parallels between two examples.

This skill often represents one of the earliest activities that happens in the process of making decisions. You observe and describe specific similarities between two targets.

- *Infer / Predict*—Assign meaning to an observation.

You make inferences all the time. Behaviors come to have specific meaning derived from your experience. For example, as a child, you quickly learned to infer that when your mother raised her voice and called you by your first and middle name that you were probably in trouble. Inferences facilitate predictions about what will happen next. Unfortunately, inferences are prone to all kinds of errors so your predictions can be hit or miss.

APPLY

The next level of critical thinking in our model, **Apply**, involves trying out behavioral concepts or principles in new situations. Many educators refer to this critical thinking skill as "transfer of learning" and highlight that this capacity promotes adaptability. The examples we offer at this level of critical thinking should encourage you to move beyond simply understanding the concepts and frameworks of psychology to using them to solve simple problems related to behavior. You can speculate how changing conditions might influence a behavioral outcome. When you successfully apply psychology concepts to your personal life, not only can it encourage new insights into your situation, but it demonstrates your comprehension of the concepts as well.

Student learning outcomes in *Apply* include the following:

- *Illustrate*—Offer examples that accurately portray psychological concepts.

Identifying personal situations where you may have experienced hindsight bias ("I knew it all along") or déjà vu ("I have the feeling I've been in this situation before"), for example, reinforce your learning and enrich the understanding of the discipline.

- *Use*—Implement psychology concepts to enhance understanding.

Deploy psychological ideas to gain better insight into how behaviors develop or are maintained. When you read about new ideas in psychology, generating practical applications of those ideas strengthens your learning.

- *Solve*—Address simple problems by using psychology concepts.

Sometimes the content of psychology can be imported into your personal life to help address specific problems. A great example is applying what you will learn about human memory to make yourself more efficient and effective in studying for college-level tests. For example, there really is a science-based rationale for why cramming for tests is a bad strategy for long-term learning.

- *Classify*—Figure out how a behavioral concept is situated in relation to other similar ideas.

When you are able to identify the shared characteristics and qualities of settings and behaviors it becomes easier to predict the outcome of new situations. For example, once you comprehend how different areas of the brain specialize in specific functions, you can classify what kinds of losses might result in the aftermath of a stroke.

ANALYZE

Analyze, the third category of critical thinking in our framework, consists of applying the principles of psychology in creating, defending, or challenging arguments about behavior. We can identify all the component parts or variables that might influence the phenomenon we are exploring to develop a sound and defensible argument. We can break a larger stimulus into constituent parts and discuss how the parts interrelate. We can look for weaknesses and strengths in a psychological explanation. Analysis can include simple forms such as interpreting the factors that motivate behavior or more complicated processing that allows you to deduce a solution to a complex problem.

Student learning outcomes in *Analyze* include the following:

- *Infer*—Interpret possible meanings of the observed behavior.

You regularly draw inferences about behavior, distinguishing between the actual observed behavior and conclusions you make about the behavior, such as identifying the factors that prompted the behavior or predicting what future course the behavior might take.

- *Relate*—Make connections among the observations to improve insight into behavior.

Seeing potential linkages between ideas can improve comprehension and elaborate meaning to make your interpretation of behaviors more rich and complex. For example, recognizing the connections between situational factors (like the number of people in a given setting) and cognitive factors (such as an individual's perception of the similarities between herself and another) can help you understand how and why someone chooses to help or ignore a person in need of assistance.

- *Compare / Contrast*—Examine two ideas to identify their similarities and differences.

Professors often import "compare/contrast" strategies when they measure your learning using essay questions. For example, you could be asked to describe how classical and operant conditioning are alike and dissimilar. Identifying similarities and differences among targeted ideas illustrates your deeper comprehension of more complicated ideas.

- *Reason*—Develop conclusions about behavior through deduction or induction.

When you *deduce* a conclusion, you behave like Sherlock Holmes. You size up the situation, determine how all the parts work and interrelate, and ultimately generate a solution or put forward a plausible argument. For instance, you might deduce on hearing about a toddler's struggle with toilet training that she is experiencing significant challenges in resolving the anal phase of development (according to Freud). In contrast, when you *induce* a conclusion, you propose a larger principle that you derive from looking at the elements. For example, you observe that multiple professors appear to be more relaxed and easier to approach toward the end of the week compared to the beginning. You conclude that their jobs must be less stressful as the weekend approaches and generate the principle that you should negotiate with professors about grade corrections only on Fridays. Both kinds of "arguments" are relevant to the psychological reasoning you may use in an introductory course in psychology.

EVALUATE

When you *Evaluate*, the fourth category in our framework, you build on analytical insights to determine quality or make decisions or judgments about behavior or behavioral explanations. Evaluation can take the form of criticism or a review of strengths and weaknesses. Evaluation can involve comparing something to an adopted standard or applying criteria to make judgments about quality. Based on evaluative outcomes, you may take action, such as rejecting a theoretical claim or grading the quality of an argument. You can also adopt different theoretical frameworks as the basis of thinking through a psychological problem.

Effective evaluative behavior tends to support the following characteristics of good critical thinkers:

- *Objectivity*—Critical thinkers in psychology tend to prefer scientific evidence (especially controlled comparisons) over subjective experience as support for their beliefs about behavior. Psychological thinkers place great value on being able to distance themselves from their own thoughts, beliefs, and feelings in order to be as unbiased as possible in comprehending behavior and increasing their accessibility to different viewpoints.

- *Tolerance of ambiguity*—Many puzzles about human behavior may never be completely understood because so many variables (and perspectives) are involved. Our cause-effect conclusions are therefore usually tentative or temporary as we continue to increase our understanding of behavior.

- *Nonjudgmental attitude*—Because we cannot fully account for all motivating forces, psychological thinkers are inclined to uphold an ideal of reserving judgment on the actions of others.

Student learning outcomes in *Evaluate* include the following:

- *Assess*—Make judgments about quality or effectiveness of a behavioral explanation.

You are likely to encounter professors who use *rubrics*, specific behavioral schemes, to accomplish grading. For example, should you be assigned to deliver a short speech, your professor will assess how effectively you have met the expectations according to the rubric. In many course activities you may be asked to render a judgment about the quality of a behavior or behavioral claim. In most cases, you will assess the relative success of an effort based on previously established criteria, such as efficiency, elegance, comprehensiveness, and accuracy.

- *Decide*—Make an informed choice among behavioral alternatives.

You may be asked to choose which psychological framework (behavioral or cognitive) better explains the origins of a psychological phenomenon, such as procrastination. You deliberate on the advantages and disadvantages of both approaches, but ultimately choose a winner. Project assignments may involve lots of specific decisions. Each decision has consequences. Success involves making optimal choices and minimizing adverse consequences.

- *Justify*—Offer a compelling rationale to support your decision about behavior.

It is often insufficient to make a decision in the absence of a solid justification. People often make claims about behavior that can't be easily justified. For example, family superstitions (don't put a hat on the bed or something unsafe will happen to a family member) develop and are maintained in the absence of evidence. Your psychology professors are likely to ask, "What is the evidence for why you believe what you do?" to sharpen this skill. They will expect you to rely less on personal experience and more on science in developing your rationale as the course progresses.

- *Take perspective*—Adopt a particular point of view to enrich explanations about behavior.

One aspect of psychology that you may find a bit frustrating in the beginning is that there are so few hard and fast answers to the questions that you generate. There is no one unifying theory that pulls together all that you will learn about psychology. Instead, you will discover a variety of points of view, some articulated as formal psychological frameworks or orientations. Adopting a framework entails buying into the assumptions and values of that framework; however, effective evaluators also stay vigilant about the limitations or challenges that might transpire from exploring behavior from that particular perspective.

Perspective taking is a particularly important aspect of critical thinking in psychology. Our capacity to set aside or minimize our personal biases enhances our ability to understand human behavior. We can learn to understand what motivates behavior as we identify how people think and feel. We recognize that each individual's perspective is unique; his or her beliefs and value systems may not match those held by someone else.

- *Respect for differing realities*—Psychological thinkers recognize that individuals' perceptions (reality) are shaped by their genetic endowment, their culture, and their personal experience. As a result, no two people have exactly the same reality.

- *Appreciation for individual differences*—Psychologists maintain a humanistic regard for the uniqueness of each individual and use psychological methods and theories as ways of exploring and explaining differences.

- *Flexibility*—Because we can't ever reach complete objectivity, psychological thinking encourages the ability to shift viewpoints and to try out other points of view to gain a more complete picture of what we wish to understand.

CREATE

The fifth and final category reflecting our adaptation of Bloom's taxonomy is *Create*, being able to make a novel connection between previously unrelated or disconnected ideas. New developments in psychological theory often are the result of creative problem solving. In creative problem solving we may create new realities or reorganize assumptions in the process of developing a unique insight. Creativity is demonstrated in the design and execution of scientific research in which new insights expand our knowledge about behavior, although we don't necessarily have to design research to experience creativity in psychology. For example, later in the text you will have opportunities to make up rhymes, songs, and stories that have never been invented before to help you learn psychological principles. A willingness to be playful with ideas promotes this type of critical thinking.

Student learning outcomes in *Create* include the following:

- *Imagine*—Play with new possibilities.

Learning can be much more fun when you take a playful attitude toward enhancing the connections you make with the material. Cognitive psychologists know that wrestling with ideas and coming up with novel scenarios can deepen your understanding and appreciation of the content of the course.

- *Design*—Create research strategies that expand our knowledge about behavior.

You will learn about the variety of ways that psychologists gather information about behavior and will practice taking on a research question and employing sound methods to come up with valid conclusions. In beginning courses you may not have the time and expertise to execute a research study, but you can demonstrate your scientific skills by designing research strategies that help us eliminate alternative explanations or shed light on how variables interrelate.

- *Invent*—Generate new ideas or novel insights.

Psychologists use imagination when they try to develop a new way of looking at behavior patterns. Sometimes it can lead to the development of a new concept. For example, mindfulness, living in expanded awareness, emerged from finding out that seniors appeared to live longer when they took responsibility for caring for a plant. The creation of new concepts or theories is particularly exciting for psychologists, but you can also experience creativity when you come up with new strategies for doing tasks or insights that are new for you, even when others may have stumbled across a similar idea before.

- *Plan*—Target a goal, develop a strategy to achieve that goal, and then execute.

You will conduct an enormous range of planning as you pursue your education, from minor strategies like discovering where parking conditions on campus are best to the more complicated engineering of a project that meets your professor's expectations. You may discover that your peers might challenge your plans so you will have to engage in even more planning to prevail. Each planning assignment represents an opportunity to flex your creative muscles in producing a process or product that will not just meet but exceed expectations.

WHAT HAPPENED HERE? USING OUR CRITICAL THINKING FRAMEWORK ABOUT BEHAVIOR

We've outlined the critical thinking processes you will be working to develop. Now let's use an example to examine how you activate these processes when confronted with a stimulus that just doesn't make sense, according to how you have come to expect the world to operate. Suppose that some morning as you are hurrying to a final examination you find a young woman lying on the sidewalk, blocking your path, but others in the area continue to walk past her as if she were not there.

This example illustrates the basic role that critical thinking processes play in psychology. An event captures your attention because it differs from what you would normally expect in a given set of circumstances. This unusual event represents a *discrepancy* from your normal expectations or *personal theory* about how the world operates. If the discrepant behavior is compelling, you will observe it; interpret its significance; relate these ideas, sometimes using formal concepts in psychology; decide if you need to take action; and possibly resort to some creative strategies to reduce your confusion and understand the discrepancy.

UNDERSTANDING

At the outset, you have two elements pulling at your attention. The body in your way certainly begs your figuring out (understanding) what is going on, but the fact that others simply walk past her may also not fit well with the way you expect the world to operate. In fact, when you study social psychology later in the course, you will learn about all kinds of factors or *variables* that influence when people help and when they don't.

Perhaps you will formulate some follow-up questions in your search for additional clues that will help you to decide what to think and possibly what to do. In this case, you may gather extra information and pool as much information as possible as you try to make sense of the event and determine whether action is called for:

- Is she breathing?
- Does she appear to be conscious?
- Is she bruised or bleeding?
- Does she smell unusual?
- How is her hygiene?
- What is her general age?
- How is she dressed?
- Was she carrying any objects? Are these neatly stacked next to her or strewn about?
- Why is no one stopping to help?

With careful observation, you will assemble enough information to render an accurate description of what you have witnessed. Your target is well dressed, breathing, not bleeding. She is dressed like a college student and her hygiene is good. Her eyes are closed. She smells of lavender. Her books are neatly stacked at her side. At least ten people have walked past her.

APPLY

Problems generate discrepancies from an orderly, workable world. When we detect a discrepancy, we can apply principles and concepts in psychology to solve the problem and resolve the discrepancy.

The incident of the young woman lying on the sidewalk posed above allows us to recognize the pattern that urban settings may not produce the strongest altruistic or helpful response. You observe that no one stops to find out what's up with the fallen student. In fact, the "bystander effect" (Darley & Latane, 1968) explains very nicely why not many individuals attempt to help. When there are quite a few helpers available, they tend to engage in social comparison and, if others aren't acting as though the scene requires intervention, most individuals will accept the norm of not helping and continue walking. That pattern recognition—or application of a psychology concept—at least helps to explain what could be interpreted as potentially heartless inactivity on the part of the bystanders as lawful according to psychology principles.

ANALYZE

To solve this problem, we have to make accurate inferences about the behavior to interpret what we see. Our *inferences*—the interpretations or simple meanings we assign to what we see—and the relationships we draw among our inferences depend on our own experience and values. For example, if you just "pulled an all-nighter" to prepare for an examination, you might be more inclined to infer that scholastic despair is the reason for the woman's behavior.

Psychological arguments assume that behavior arises from complex causes. Consequently, when analyzing a behavior sample, psychologists strive to identify as many contributing variables as possible. When confronted with a cause-effect relationship, psychologically trained thinkers ask whether the conclusions are valid. They explore whether the same outcomes could be explained by different variables or using different relationships.

As you put all the clues together, you might relate your observations and interpretations, concluding that she is possibly a student with a melodramatic flair expressing despair over impending failure on her final exams. In this case, it is likely that only one conclusion will produce the most satisfying or accurate explanation. However, it is important to remember that not all forms of critical thinking reduce to one single, simple conclusion.

EVALUATE

Many interesting, compelling claims about behavior confront us in the course of nearly every day. Each occurrence provides an opportunity for exercising our critical thinking abilities. With each opportunity, we may actively examine, evaluate, and accept or reject some argument about behavior. The primary outcome of psychology-based critical thinking is to prompt us to ask, "What is your evidence?" for any particular position. Then we must determine if that evidence is sufficiently strong to influence us to maintain, revise, or reject our original ideas and beliefs. The fourth category of critical thinking, Evaluate, involves making judgments based on criteria and standards, which serves as a foundation for decision-making and offering criticisms.

Some resolutions of discrepancy require action. In the above example, you may merely construct some less compelling meaning to the discrepancy so that the event will make sense. *"This person is worn out from exam stress. I guess finals really can do you in."* In effect, you modify your personal theory to take into account the unusual event and to decide what to do. Driven by your personal experience, you may choose to involve yourself or walk on by, comparable to others you have observed. For example, if you live in a neighborhood where street people take refuge, finding a human form lying on the sidewalk might not be particularly discrepant with your experience. You would not regard this occurrence as very unusual from the events you expect to encounter under normal circumstances and might be less likely to take action. If you live where you rarely see a street person, however, this would be an extremely discrepant and probably quite disturbing event. You might be more inclined to take action. If you conclude further action is warranted, you will overcome bystander inertia to offer assistance. Knowing and applying the bystander effect principle can motivate a more constructive altruistic response. The value you place on being someone who *should* help will also help determine your actions.

CREATE

On the surface, the fallen college student scenario doesn't lend itself as readily to a creative response. However, the episode itself might spur creativity in other directions. For example, if finals really can induce semi-comatose behavior from stress, what might be some novel ways you could approach reducing stress during finals? For example, you could send flowers or cookies to those about to enter into this stress-filled period. You could stage a flash mob or impromptu exercise session with your peers. You could ask for a "freak out" zone in the library or see if Student Government could employ on-site massage therapists during finals week. The fallen figure can serve as a stimulus for all kinds of creative problem solving.

HOW THIS BOOK WILL HELP YOU DEVELOP CRITICAL THINKING SKILLS IN PSYCHOLOGY

As you learn the discipline of psychology, your knowledge of psychological concepts and theories will grow as will your ability to think critically about psychological issues and concerns. Your descriptions of behavior will become more specific and more efficient as you accurately apply psychological concepts, principles, and theories. You may discover that you pay more attention to behavior systems and variations and that you interpret them more cautiously and carefully. You will become more efficient and effective in solving problems related to behavior. You'll be more inclined to ask for evidence before you accept a new position. You may be more attuned to the values and assumptions that undergird your own and others' actions. You may recognize new possibilities with practice in creative thinking. However, all of these outcomes will take some time and some practice.

This book will help you expand your abilities to think critically as you actively learn about the discipline of psychology. Each chapter includes exercises that correspond to topics discussed in your psychology textbook. Each exercise emphasizes a particular category of skills designed to assist your overall development of critical thinking abilities throughout your studies. Exercises conclude with a list of critical thinking skills you will refine as you complete the exercise and learn the relevant psychological concepts. As you work your way through the exercises, you'll find some expanded descriptions of the categories of critical thinking in later sections of the book. These descriptions will help you polish your understanding and your ability to use critical thinking skills in psychology.

In this third edition, we also want to include some practice in *metacognition*, by which we mean the ability to evaluate the quality of your own thinking. Being a good critical thinker in psychology should confer important benefits that should make you more successful in your educational, professional, and even personal life. The Psychology Advantage section at the end of each chapter challenges you to reflect further on what changes might happen to individuals who exercise effective critical thinking skills specific to each chapter normally covered in a beginning psychology class. In this way we hope you will reap maximum benefits as you try out both the content and skills of Introductory Psychology. The reflection takes into consideration how psychology can help in other courses, in your personal life, and in the life you plan following graduation.

Chapter

◀Thinking Critically▶ with Psychological Science

The primary difference between personal and scientific explanations of behavior rests in the nature of acceptable evidence. Psychologists have learned to question observations based only on personal experience, because they know how biased or subjective human judgment is. This knowledge comes from their own research in perception, cognition, information processing, and social psychology. Psychology as a science promotes the belief that the sturdiest kind of evidence comes from *systematic* and *controlled* observation. This reliance on well-designed research leads to the most credible conclusions about behavior. Scientific critical thinkers try to support their ideas with evidence from controlled comparisons whenever possible, whether they design their own experiments or rely on the controlled observations of others.

Designing meaningful research that will increase our understanding of human behavior is a challenging but exhilarating enterprise. This enterprise relies on some key ideas and procedures. When researchers link concepts or variables to speculate about causes of behavior, they create *hypotheses*. Hypotheses are inferences that predict cause-effect relationships between behavioral variables. There are two kinds of variables in psychological research. *Independent variables* are factors that promote changes in behavior; researchers typically manipulate independent variables (causes) to produce a desired effect in experiments. The desired effect is called the *dependent variable*, because the effect *depends* on the various causes.

Suppose that we wanted to find out whether drinking coffee promotes anxiety. In our experiment

we could establish three different groups: one group would drink no coffee, another group would drink two cups, and the final group would drink four. In this example, the amount of coffee (none, two cups, or four cups) constitutes the levels of the independent variable that we think will lead to different intensities of anxiety. Our hypothesis could be that drinking coffee increases anxiety: The independent variable (coffee drinking) causes the dependent variable (anxiety). Or stated conversely, the level of anxiety (dependent variable) depends on coffee intake (independent variable).

Another important aspect of scientific critical thinking in psychology is defining and measuring behavior. Psychologists like to be as precise and as unbiased or objective as possible when exploring the meaning of a behavior. We often define the behaviors we wish to understand by describing the "operations" we go through to produce the behavior. These *operational definitions* promote objectivity in observation.

For example, how will we measure anxiety in our coffee-drinking subjects? We might measure each subject's anxiety response by counting nervous gestures, measuring blood pressure elevations, or requesting a self-rating of anxiety on a scale of 1 to 10. Each approach would give us a different way to quantify anxiety. Operational definitions provide the opportunity to measure behavior as precisely as possible. Researchers evaluate the precise measurements statistically to determine whether the experiment (or other research method) produces meaningful comparisons or patterns.

Competently designed experiments must have clear definitions of the variables in the research and acceptable methods of measuring behavioral responses. Effective *control procedures* are also essential to rule out alternative explanations. We want to make sure that we control all aspects of the experiment so that we can be certain a cause-effect statement is valid or truthful. Control procedures allow us to rule out all cause-effect explanations other than the one we intend to explore in the experiment.

In our coffee-drinking study, we would try to control other factors that might contribute to anxiety. For example, we might want to limit our subject population to people of a certain age. We would avoid conducting our experiment during a period when those people might be expected to be anxious for some other reason (for example, during final exam time). We would need to make sure that our subjects drank only the amount of coffee specified in their research assignment. And we would have to decide what to do with subjects who hate coffee. All these conditions represent threats to the valid construction of an experiment on the anxiety-producing effects of coffee. As psychologists, we would strive to produce an experiment in which any findings we obtain would be as free as possible from alternative explanations.

The exercises in Chapter 1 emphasize the importance of understanding and applying the principles of research design in scientific research and in consumer contexts.

▼Exercise 1.1   THE CASE FOR INTERFERENCE

UNDERSTAND: Explain

One of the first decisions that psychology researchers must make is *how* to study their target behavior. *Correlational methods* involve studying behaviors as they are. These approaches involve careful observation, measurement, and interpretation of behaviors to uncover relationships among the factors that influence behavior. Correlational methods can be employed in case studies, surveys, and field work.

In contrast, *experimental methods* involve procedures that manipulate the conditions surrounding the behavior being studied. In effect, the experimenter interferes with normal behavior to narrow down the causes of behavior. By establishing equivalent conditions and systematically varying a specific factor (the independent variable), the experimenter determines the impact of that factor. This is the chief advantage of experimentation; experimental methods allow us to determine cause-effect relationships in a way that correlational methods cannot. Experiments can be conducted using a single subject or many participants. The key to determining cause-effect conclusions is providing good controlled conditions and making accurate comparisons across conditions.

Read the following examples and judge whether the procedure described would be considered a correlational (non-interfering) approach or an experimental (interfering) approach.

The Problem of Child Abuse

Social scientists study the backgrounds of children who have been assigned to foster care. They discover that the majority of children who receive foster care have experienced physical punishment methods in their prior homes that would be severe enough to qualify as abusive.

Would this conclusion be derived from a correlational study or an experiment? Why?

_____

_____

Charlie's Weight Loss

Charlie is trying hard to lose his "spare tire" before his wedding. He has two months to get ready for the event. He decides to go about his weight loss systematically. The first week, Charlie exercises vigorously. The second week, he gives up meat. The third week, he drinks large amounts of water. The fourth week, he eats just bananas. He continues to vary his approach each week. At the end of his eight-week experiment, he concludes that his best weight loss comes from exercise.

Would Charlie's conclusion be derived from a correlational study or an experiment?

Why? _____

_____

_____

The Curious Teacher

Ms. Tucker decides that she wants to evaluate which of her teaching methods might make the biggest impact on her students. For the first half of the semester, she teaches using a lecture format. She evaluates what students have learned using a 50-point multiple-choice test. For the second half of the semester, she teaches using demonstrations and active learning exercises. She evaluates the second half using a 50-point multiple-choice test. She discovers that her students have better test scores when using active learning strategies.

Would Ms. Tucker's conclusion be derived from a correlational study or an experiment?

Why? _____

_____

_____

The Lucky Pen

Peter noticed that every time he used his special pen with green ink, something wonderful happened to him. First, he got an A on his history exam. When he loaned his pen to Amy, she later agreed to go out on a date with him. While he was carrying his pen, he bought a lottery ticket that later won $2,000. He decided that his pen truly had lucky powers, and he put it away so he wouldn't lose it.

Would this conclusion be derived from a correlational study or an experiment? Why?

_____

_____

The Best Neighborhood

The local newspaper publishes the results of a finding that produce a significant impact on the real estate market. The paper's researchers identify various neighborhoods in the city and compare the SAT scores of students who live in these different regions of the city. Based on their comparisons, they decide that the suburb of Suffolk has the best education. As a consequence, the real estate market in Suffolk booms.

Would this conclusion be derived from a correlational study or an experiment? Why?

_____

_____

Copycat Crime

A new popular movie depicts a grisly scene of teen violence against senior citizens. Although the criminals in the movie are caught and punished, city officials are dismayed to discover that similar acts of violence increase across the city shortly after the movie opens. A reporter decides to compare crime rates before and after the movie's release to determine if the movie has stimulated teen violence.

Would the reporter's conclusion be derived from a correlational study or an experiment?

Why? _____

_____

_____

Doctor's Choice

A physician is intrigued by a new medication that has been developed to treat sleep disturbance, but he is concerned about its expense relative to the medication he usually prescribes. He decides to evaluate the success of the medication. He determines that the next 20 patients who complain of sleep problems will help him establish the effectiveness of the medication. Once he identifies the complaint, the physician slips out of the room and tosses a coin. If it comes up "heads," he prescribes the new medication. If it comes up "tails," he prescribes the medication he previously prescribed. At the end of a three-month period, he asks his patients to report the degree of improvement on a ten-point scale. He discovers that the new medication provides no real advantage over the older, less expensive medication.

Would the physician's conclusion be derived from a correlational study or an experiment? Why? _____

_____

_____

After completing this exercise, you should be able to:

- describe the key features of correlational research.
- explain why correlational studies cannot confirm cause-effect conclusions.
- discuss the key characteristics of experimental research.
- distinguish between scientific and nonscientific explanations.
- identify how correlational studies differ from experimental studies.

▼Exercise 1.2   STATS-R-US

UNDERSTAND: Translate

Your friend Forrest is struggling in his required statistics class. He claims that he just doesn't have a feel for what statisticians do and is particularly puzzled when it comes to making sense of *correlations*. He is seeking your assistance in trying to figure out the meaning of some correlation coefficients—the conventional measurement used to assess correlation—that he produced from some data sets his stats professor provided.

Researchers use correlation as a statistical technique to determine the nature of the relationship between two sets of variables. Correlation coefficients reveal two important characteristics about the relationship. First, the correlation coefficient determines the *direction* of the relationship. A positive correlation means that the two data sets *covary*, meaning that higher values in one data set seem to correspond well to higher values in the second data set. A negative correlation establishes an inverse relationship between the two data sets. In this case, a higher value in one data set tends to be associated with a lower value in the second data set and vice versa. In some situations, a correlation coefficient reveals that there is no relationship between the two data sets, in which case the correlation coefficient hovers near .00. Therefore, the first type of information we need to examine in a correlation coefficient is the valence or sign of the correlation coefficient.

The second kind of information imparted by the correlation coefficient is the *intensity* of the relationship. Correlation coefficients range from $-1.0 \rightarrow +1.0$. Researchers tend to get more excited about strong relationships because these can sometimes be interpreted as "statistically significant." Decimals that are closer to either -1.0 or $+1.0$ would be indicative of a strong relationship between the two sets of data or variables. Decimals that approach .00 present weaker evidence that a real relationship exists between those data sets.

Forrest has mechanically executed the calculations he thinks he needs in his correlation homework assignment, but he is unclear about how to report his findings. He is turning to you for assistance in finding the right language to report whether there is anything exciting about the association between the two variables in each calculation.

Correlation:
1.   +.45 Reported hours of piano practice vs. ranking in the regional piano competition
2.   +.03 Number of phone calls made last week vs. number of phones owned
3.   −.88 Reported hours per week spent on social media vs. grade point average
4.   +1.33 Number of traffic tickets last year vs. dollars spent on gas during that same year
5.   −.26 Number of siblings vs. grade point average
6.   +.92 Blood alcohol level vs. number of drinks consumed prior to the blood alcohol test

What advice can you offer about the meaning he should attach to the number he calculated in each case?

After completing this exercise, you should be able to:

- describe the statistical purpose of completing a correlation coefficient.

- identify both the intensity and direction of information found in a correlation coefficient.

- interpret the statistical significance or meaning of specific correlation coefficients.

▼Exercise 1.3   YOU NEED AN OPERATION

APPLY: Illustrate

One of the distinguishing features of people who are trained in psychology is their concern for precision when confronting problems. Psychologists believe that you need to define behaviors in precise and measurable ways if you are going to make progress toward a solution. They routinely refine vague explanations to develop **operational definitions**. When an operational definition is successful, it sets the stage for more effective problem solving.

Let's look at an example to clarify. Suppose a teacher tells her struggling student, "Your work is awful!" That criticism is not only broad, it is potentially very damaging. What could be some operational definitions that would help the student embark on a more effective strategy? The teacher explicitly discloses one of the following:

- Your grade point average declined over the last six-week period.

- You seem to be on-task in class about 30% of the time.

- You have submitted only one of the last six assignments.

Notice that each of these operational approaches to the teacher's concern gets at the heart of the problem and gives the student an opportunity to focus on concrete ways of improvement.

Look at the following three problems in which behaviors are discussed in a vague manner. Try to imagine at least two possible ways to operationalize the behavior, setting the stage for more effective problem solving.

The Sloppy Roommate

Jack and Ed are roommates. Jack is tidy and Ed is not. After coming home from a hard afternoon at the library, Jack finds the living room in its usual shambles; Ed's clothes are strewn over the couch, floor, and tables. When Ed emerges from the messy kitchen, where he has been eating nachos next to a pile of dirty dishes, Jack explodes, "I can't stand living this way!" and runs from the room.

What are two ways we could operationalize the problem ("living this way") to help the roommates get back on track? Remember to address observable behavior, precision, and measurement where you can. _____

_____

_____

The Surly Boss

Joe was having problems with his supervisor at work. Although he was doing his work on time and seemed to get along with everyone, the supervisor rarely gave him feedback of any kind. The supervisor seemed to look at him strangely at times. Sometimes Joe thought the supervisor might be talking about him and laughing behind his back. Joe asked for an appointment and then challenged the supervisor, "Why don't you like me?"

What are two ways we could operationalize Joe's concerns to help him have a more productive relationship with his supervisor? Remember to address observable behavior, precision, and measurement where you can. _____

_____

_____

Bonnie's Worry

Bonnie had been working at the day-care center for three months. All of the children were a lot of fun, but Bonnie had some concerns about Emily. Emily preferred solitary play. She occasionally stayed focused on one or two objects for a long time. She also regularly talked to herself. Sometimes she would grab the other children inappropriately and would steal toys from others. When Emily's parents reported for a conference at the day-care center, Bonnie told the parents that she thought Emily was "slow."

In what two ways could "slow" be operationalized to help the parents better understand the nature of the difficulties that Bonnie was noticing? _____

_____

_____

After completing this exercise, you should be able to:

- identify the impact of vague behavior concepts.

- formulate operational definitions to improve problem definition.

- illustrate precision and measurement as important characteristics in operational definitions.

▼Exercise 1.4   CONSUMER SAFETY

ANALYZE: Reason

One sophisticated form of critical thinking applies the principles of psychology in creating, defending, or challenging arguments about behavior. Without effective critical thinking abilities, we could easily fall prey to questionable claims about the causes of behavior, such as this simulated sampling of headlines from tabloid papers over the last few years:

"Wiggling Your Ears Makes You Smarter"

"Woman's Head Explodes During Psychic Trance"

"Belly Button Shape Reveals Your Character"

"Eating Bananas Increases Your Bust Size"

"Elvis Spotted . . . "

Psychological reasoning is an important intellectual ability, whether we are selecting a product for purchase or exercising our citizens' rights by deciding which candidate will get our vote. The positions we create and defend on important issues will determine the kinds of actions we take. Understanding the principles of critical thinking in psychology should enable us not only to create and defend our opinions more effectively but also to challenge behavioral arguments that are invalid.

The primary emphasis of this type of thinking is one question: "What's your evidence?" Psychological research design teaches us to examine claims about behavior and to consider alternative explanations. What other variables might account for the relationship being claimed? By applying the following experiment-based principles of psychological reasoning, we can protect ourselves against invalid claims.

1. *Don't expect simple cause-effect relationships.* They rarely exist in relation to behavior, so a skeptical or disbelieving stance is generally the safest response to simplistic claims about the causes of behavior.

2. *Don't settle for cause-effect statements without sufficient evidence.* Remember that question: "What's your evidence?" Is the evidence *objective* (derived from systematic, unbiased, and well-controlled observation) or *subjective* (influenced by personal experiences, characteristics, and biases)? Personal testimony is particularly problematic, especially when the enthusiastic advocate is being paid for it.

3. *Don't confuse interpretation of behavior with behavior itself.* People often embellish their observation of behavior with statements about the meaning of the behavior. They then report their conclusions about the behavior instead of describing the behavior they observed. For example, on witnessing a professor's late arrival to class, we might leap to the conclusion that she is busy or disrespectful or scatter-brained rather than sticking to the facts. The observable behavior is arriving late to class. Invalid claims may report interpretations or judgments about a behavior rather than focusing on a description of behavior without interpretation.

4. *Don't mistake correlation for causation.* It is easy to come to the wrong conclusion about what causes behavior. Sometimes what appears to be a strong cause-effect relationship may be an illusion. For example, let's examine the first statement in the roster of tabloid headlines—"Wiggling Your Ears Makes You Smarter." Digging underneath this headline, you may discover that the writer swears by ear wiggling as a method of increasing intelligence. His evidence? He wiggled his ears all the way through his college admission test and his score was in a top percentile. This

silly example demonstrates that the occurrence of two variables close together in time (for example, ear wiggling and intelligent performance during test taking) can sometimes be interpreted as causal. (Even smart people make this error!) Clearly, other variables could have led to the writer's performance on his admission test.

5. *Do look for experimental comparisons that involve control conditions.* Controlled comparison is the key to ruling out alternative explanations that make some claims implausible or unbelievable. We may never know the real cause for some effect unless we perform systematic study on the proposed relationship to determine whether there is any other way to account for observed changes in behavior. Psychological research is heavily biased toward experiments in which controlled comparisons can reduce alternative explanations.

6. *Do examine how behaviors are defined or operationalized.* Definitions can be very slippery, as anyone who has gone to a hair stylist and asked for "just a little" hair trimming knows. Precision in definitions is even more important in psychological research. Some cause-effect claims may seem very compelling until you require precise definition of the terms used in the claim.

We describe eight consumer and civic claims. Your job is to decide how well each of them stands up to the principles outlined in this chapter. First identify the principle that is involved. Then decide whether the claims should be challenged or accepted, based on the six principles reviewed in this chapter.

The Tanned Rock Queen

A famous female rock star encourages you to join a new tanning salon and shows you her tan marks to prove the salon's effectiveness.

Principle(s) Involved

_____

The Moralizer

A local politician suggests that heavy metal music is responsible for increasing violence among teenagers and proposes that all such music be banned.

Principle(s) Involved

_____

The Laundry

A photogenic child wallows in a mud puddle in a TV advertisement. The smiling (and rich) mom who wants to try out the effectiveness of her new detergent rips the child's shirt in half and launders one half in her old detergent and the other half in the new detergent. The half laundered in the new product is substantially cleaner.

Principle(s) Involved

_____

The New Car

A toothsome announcer promises you that your social life will have lots of pizazz if you buy his company's new car—the Pizazz-mobile.

Principle(s) Involved

_____

Halloween Wisdom

A psychologist strongly endorses the traditional children's practice of trick-or-treating at Halloween. In a video produced by a leading U.S. candy company, he suggests that trick-or-treat rituals help children overcome common childhood fears. The psychologist also mentions that chocolate candies are probably the most beneficial treats to give, because they contain a chemical that promotes the release of neurotransmitters.

Principle(s) Involved

_____

One Bad Apple

The president of the most successful company in town has developed some strong preferences in her hiring practices. She had a bad experience with a graduate of your college three years ago. As a result, the company will no longer employ anyone graduating from your college, even though the legality of this practice seems questionable.

Principle(s) Involved

_____

The Blind Date

Your friend sets you up on a blind date. He describes your date as someone who has strong interests in the environment. At the start of the evening, your date proposes a walk along the beach and during that walk, picks up cans and shoves them into a backpack. You conclude that the rumored interest in environmental issues is valid.

Principle(s) Involved

_____

The Burglars

A newspaper reporter recently speculated that a full moon may have an enhancing effect on criminal behavior because crimes, especially breaking and entering, seem to increase dramatically when the moon is full. The reporter cited interviews with several leading mental health specialists who have noted a "full moon effect" in other areas of mental health management. (See Answer Key.)

Principle(s) Involved

_____

In most situations in which a compelling cause-effect relationship is presented, your best reaction is to ask, "What's your evidence?" Psychologists believe a skeptical stance (a general attitude of disbelief) may provide the greatest protection until objective, controlled evidence supports a claim.

After completing this exercise, you should be able to:

- identify some principles that will help you evaluate claims made in commercials.

- describe why clear definitions are so crucial in making fair claims.

- recognize why psychologists may not accept personal testimony as valid evidence.

- apply principles of experimental design to claims about behavior to judge whether the claims are valid or should be challenged.

- see why it is important to ask, "What's your evidence?" when someone is trying to "sell" you on a cause-effect relationship.

▼Exercise 1.5 PSYCHOLOGY'S PERSPECTIVES

EVALUATE: Take Perspective

The field of psychology is a broad one. Although all psychologists explore issues of behavior and mental processes, researchers in the field can approach these issues from multiple perspectives. The perspectives addressed in your text—neuroscience, evolutionary, behavior genetics, behavioral, cognitive, and social-cultural—are complementary. Each contributes to our understanding of how organisms think, feel, and act. As you work to think critically about psychology, understanding the different perspectives and their respective limits and strengths will help you make accurate judgments about what you are reading and learning.

Below are some of the issues that are of interest to psychologists working from all perspectives. For each of these examples, describe how psychology's six perspectives would approach the area of study. What are questions that psychologists from these perspectives might ask?

Issue: Drug Abuse

Neuroscience: _____

Evolutionary: _____

Behavior Genetics: _____

Behavioral: _____

Cognitive: _____

Social-Cultural: _____

Issue: Love

Neuroscience: _____

Evolutionary: _____

Behavior Genetics: _____

Behavioral: _____

Cognitive: _____

Social-Cultural: _____

Issue: Intelligence

Neuroscience: _____

Evolutionary: _____

Behavior Genetics: _____

Behavioral: _____

Cognitive: _____

Social-Cultural: _____

After completing this exercise, you should be able to:

- describe the focus of all six of psychology's current perspectives.

- link appropriate concepts with their corresponding perspectives.

- recognize that any psychological event can be explored from multiple perspectives.

- evaluate what type of questions are of particular interest to psychologists working within a specific perspective.

▼Exercise 1.6 CRITIQUING EXPERIMENTAL DESIGNS

EVALUATE: Assess

Scientific problem solving has four components:

- *Forming hypotheses*—We develop tentative predictions about the causes of behavior; hypotheses represent an attempt to resolve a discrepancy in our formal knowledge about the causes of behavior.

- *Defining variables operationally*—We define research components in terms of operations in order to promote objectivity in observation and precision in measurement.

- *Conducting systematic or controlled investigations*—We strive to reduce cause-effect explanations to their simplest possible forms. We often emphasize experimental comparisons as a preferred method for developing the sturdiest and most truthful cause-effect explanations. We carefully use control procedures to eliminate alternative explanations for any obtained results.

- *Interpreting results statistically*—We use statistical analysis to help determine whether we have isolated the most important variables.

The following three badly designed experiments and the questions accompanying them will help you to recognize research concepts and sharpen your ability to detect flaws in experimental design to establish how you would plan to execute the study if it were your responsibility. Assume you are serving as a consultant to each client who badly needs your understanding of good experimental procedure to get valid answers to the questions they pose. After you complete all the questions, compare your answers with those in the Answer Key at the end of the book.

The Colorful Boss

Arlene wanted to increase the productivity of the clerical staff in her plant. She thought painting their cubicles blue (her favorite color) would increase their rate of work completion but that painting the cubicles yellow (a color she thought was harsh) would have no effect or might even slow down the clerical staff's rate of completion. To test this idea she painted the work cubicles in the Sales Department blue and those in the Public Relations Department yellow. Then she kept track of how many projects each department completed in the next three months. For the two-month period following the painting, the sales clerical staff dramatically outperformed the public relations clerical staff in the number of projects completed.

Research Design Elements (See Answer Key.)

What is the *focal behavior* of the study and how is it *defined operationally?* _____

_____

What is the *hypothesis?* _____

What is the *independent variable?* _____

How is the *dependent variable* measured? _____

What variables are controlled? _____

What variables are not controlled? _____

Did the research measure what Arlene thought she measured? Justify your answer.

The Bad Driver

John is intrigued by the relationship between frustration and aggression. He proposes to study whether socioeconomic status is a factor in how drivers express aggression when they are frustrated. John decides to employ a high-status car (a shiny new Mercedes) and a low-status car (a dented, rusty 1983 Volkswagen) as the stimuli in a "field" experiment on the roads near his home during a sunny April afternoon. He plans to drive the high-status car from 1 to 3 P.M. and the low-status car from 3 to 5 P.M. During these periods, he will linger when he has to stop for red lights and will move forward only when the driver behind him honks. His research assistant, riding on the passenger side, will time how long it takes the driver of the car behind the experimental car to honk. John believes drivers will take longer to honk when they are behind the Mercedes than when they are behind the Volkswagen. He thinks frustrated people will suppress their frustration and aggression when the person causing the frustration is of high socioeconomic status.

Research Design Elements (See Answer Key.)

What is the *focal behavior* of the study and how is it *defined operationally?* _____

What is the *hypothesis?* _____

What is the *independent variable?* _____

How is the *dependent variable* measured? _____

What variables are controlled? _____

What variables are not controlled? _____

How can the experiment be improved? _____

Going for the Gold

Rita, a sports psychologist, has applied for a huge grant sponsored by the American Olympiad Organization. She wants to identify variables that will produce more winners in the next international competition. She plans to build a special camp where the athletes can train for two weeks each summer with other athletes. She will fly all the volunteer athletes to the camp and will randomly assign each of them to one of three conditions. Rita will host only one type of group at a time. In Condition 1, which meets during the first two weeks of the experiment, the athletes get no special treatment beyond the opportunity to train in the specially designed camp. Athletes assigned to Condition 1 are control group members. In Condition 2, during the second two weeks, the athletes will receive a well-regulated diet and low-dose steroids. In Condition 3, during the last two-week period, the athletes will sleep with a self-esteem training tape under their pillows. Rita believes that unconscious sleep preparation will be superior to other forms of training in producing winning athletes. She plans to measure her success by contrasting the number of medals the three groups of athletes win in their next outing.

Research Design Elements (See Answer Key.)

What is the *focal behavior* of the study? _____

What is the *hypothesis?* _____

What is the *independent variable?* _____

How is the *dependent variable* measured? _____

What variables are controlled? _____

What variables are not controlled? _____

Would you fund this proposal? If so, give your reason. If not, describe some ways in which the study could be improved: _____

All three experiments have flaws of sufficient magnitude that their findings would be invalid or at least questionable. However, even in well-designed and published research, you may encounter subtle problems in design, control procedures, and variable definitions that will challenge the interpretation of the results described by the researcher. As you continue to read about scientific experimentation, look for flaws. All those who publish their results expect criticism. Effective criticism helps the literature of psychology—and our knowledge about human behavior—to grow.

After completing this exercise, you should be able to:

- recognize the experimental design elements (such as hypothesis, independent and dependent variables, and so on) in a description of simple research designs.

- describe how control methods are used to rule out alternative explanations.

- understand the importance of careful operational definition in experimental design.

- make some overall judgments about the quality of an experimental design.

▼Exercise 1.7   ANIMAL ADVOCACY

EVALUATE: Justify

The role that animals play in psychological research is controversial. Psychology has a long tradition of turning to nonhuman animal species to conduct research that would not be deemed appropriate or acceptable with human populations. Although humanity may be spared using this approach, many people are highly critical of the practice of using animals for research.

Which side of the controversy do you fall on and why? _____

_____

_____

Now in order to practice taking the perspective of others (and to give you some practice in anticipating arguments that could be used against your position), marshal the best arguments you can in favor of the position that opposes your own.

_____

_____

_____

_____

After completing this exercise, you should be able to:

- describe both sides of the controversy regarding the use of nonhuman animal species in psychological research.

- report the status of current practice with regard to safeguarding animals in research.

- present a more defensible private position on animal rights.

▼Exercise 1.8   WHAT MAY COME

CREATE: Imagine

You have learned about a variety of ways in which psychologists are currently employed. The vast majority of psychologists have found meaningful employment as clinicians, experimentalists, or academics. However, career scholars routinely point out that individuals who are in college today may engage in occupations that have not yet materialized. Changes in social, political, climate, or spiritual conditions may lead the way toward the development of new psychological specialties. Try to project yourself ten years into the future and speculate about the kind of new position in which a psychologist might find gainful employment. Offer a rationale for why you think this new psychologist's position is viable.

_____

_____

After completing this exercise, you should be able to:

- identify traditional avenues for employment for psychologists.

- speculate about how living conditions may change over the next decade.

- imagine new opportunities for which psychologists might be trained.

THE PSYCHOLOGY ADVANTAGE

A friend of ours likes to say, "The reason you should take psychology is so you won't be a jerk!" We concur. Being able to understand and apply scientific principles in evaluating the legitimacy of claims about behavior should put experienced psychology students at a great advantage in dealing with other people, whether they are loved ones, friends, or coworkers.

First, let's talk about the workplace advantage of knowing how to evaluate claims. Knowing how to put fresh ideas through a test drive can potentially save a company time, energy, and dollars. Designing a pilot study to isolate real effects from desired or speculated effects can point the way to true reform and have important professional ripple effects, such as establishing a reputation for the researcher as someone who knows how to interpret graphs and plow through piles of data. No matter what the enterprise, those skills make invaluable contributions to a smoother functioning workplace.

Being a better critical thinker can also have important advantages in navigating life with friends and family. For example, understanding that precision contributes to clarity in communications in scientific enterprises can easily transfer to care in expressing yourself when you are trying to get personal needs met. When others present you with vague or global complaints, a few judicious questions that promote clearer articulation of the specific problems is more likely to produce a mutually satisfying solution. Crafting complaints that are specific and evidence-based will probably be more successful in promoting an interpersonal collaboration that may not only solve the problem at hand but also improve the quality of the relationship as well.

Chapter

◀Neuroscience▶ and Behavior

It weighs just a little over three pounds. It is covered with wrinkly gray matter and bathes in cerebral spinal fluid. At birth, it isn't capable of supporting independent function. As we age, experience influences its structure and integrity. It provides the grand stage on which we play out our hopes, dreams, fears, disappointments, and everything else that constitutes the human experience. The brain is a marvel of complexity as it processes incoming stimulation, governs a variety of simultaneous demands, and executes motor function from as minor as grasping for a rattle to as major as performing a triple axel on skates. Learning how the brain works is one of introductory psychology's greatest challenges.

▼Exercise 2.1 HOW DO YOU DO THAT?

UNDERSTAND: Describe

In this exercise you will develop a map that describes how the various parts of the brain collaborate to enable you to perform leisure activities. For this exercise, assume you play video games in your spare time—perhaps a strategy game like Minecraft. Using the following table, identify whether the specific brain sites in the list would be involved in the complex skills employed in playing Minecraft. Begin by identifying the general brain function of the specific site. (Consult your text if you need a quick refresher course.) Then determine whether that part of the brain is directly involved or is not essential in playing video games.

Brain Site	Function?	Involvement?
Hypothalamus		
Occipital lobe		
Reticular formation		
Cerebellum		
Parietal lobe		
Corpus callosum		
Medulla		
Temporal lobe		
Frontal lobe		
Thalamus		
Amygdala		
Hippocampus		

Obviously any leisure activity requires the collaboration of various brain functions. If you ever play video games in the future, you may have a new appreciation of the architecture of the nervous system that enables your behavior.

After completing this exercise, you should be able to:

- identify the function of the component parts of the brain.

- describe the differing contributions that each component part makes in a complex activity.

- appreciate the complexity of brain function.

▼Exercise 2.2   CALL 911!

UNDERSTAND: Compare

The human body is a remarkable system from an engineering standpoint. It manages to maintain a steady state through *homeostasis*, which means the body operates on multiple dimensions at once to maintain optimal functioning. You feel thirst when your fluid tank is low. You grab for the refrigerator door to graze when your stomach growls. You doze when fatigue and boredom entice you away from a less than stimulating lecture. However, the body's homeostatic process is best displayed by the toggle system provided in the autonomic nervous system that involves the *sympathetic nervous system* and the *parasympathetic nervous system*.

Under emergency conditions, the sympathetic nervous system kicks in and gears up your system to manage that emergency. In effect, it mobilizes behavior to overcome the challenge. Once the emergency is over, the parasympathetic system returns the body to a steady state and focuses on conserving and maintaining bodily resources. That toggle system is accomplished through multiple individual system actions. In this exercise you will compare what happens to the body in the sympathetic or emergency state versus what happens to those same systems when they return to normal operations.

Sympathetic Effect	System	Parasympathetic Effect
Speeds up	Heart rate	Slows down
	Respiration rate	
	Bladder integrity	
	Sweat gland activity	
	Pupillary action	
	Salivation	

After completing this exercise, you should be able to:

- discuss the role of homeostasis in optimal bodily function.

- distinguish the differences between the parasympathetic and sympathetic nervous systems.

- describe the general engineering principle of the toggle system applied to human anatomy.

▼Exercise 2.3   THE SPLIT-BRAIN PROBLEM
APPLY: Classify

Early studies in brain function led to the conclusion that the hemispheres of the cerebral cortex specialize in certain kinds of activities. Some reports have exaggerated the difference between the right and left brains' effects on behavior; a quick search for on-line right and left brain "quizzes" will demonstrate just how much people try to tie behavior and personality to hemispheric brain function. In reality, people use both hemispheres of their brain almost all the time, and most behaviors rely on an integrated functioning that causes both hemispheres to hum with electrical activity. However, we can explore the idea of hemispheric specialization by identifying the side of the brain that might be *primarily* responsible for certain behaviors. The discussion here assumes a right-handed person with no brain damage.

The left hemisphere is primarily responsible for matters of language, symbols, logic, and mathematics. The right hemisphere, sometimes referred to as the more creative or artistic hemisphere, responds to spatial, musical, and emotional kinds of stimuli. Designate each of the following behaviors with an *R* if it is a right-hemisphere specialization and an *L* if it is a left-hemisphere specialization. (See Answer Key.)

Studying concepts from psychology   _____

Drawing a map of your campus   _____

Daydreaming about your next holiday trip   _____

Listening to a piano concert   _____

Listening to rap music   _____

Thinking about your next "night out"   _____

Reading junk mail   _____

$6 \times 4 - 2 + 5 =$ _____

Redecorating your room   _____

Doodling   _____

Completing this exercise   _____

After completing this exercise, you should be able to:

- identify the kind of brain function implied by each activity.

- differentiate the primary functions of the right and left hemispheres.

- classify the targeted brain ability and relate it to the proper hemisphere.

▼Exercise 2.4   THE NEUROTRANSMISSION DOCTOR
ANALYZE: Solve

One of the most exciting arenas of neuroscience research is in neurotransmission function and malfunction. The variety of neurotransmitters facilitates intercellular communication. Each neurotransmitter functions at specific *synapses*, the gaps that exist between cells. A neurotransmitter can serve an *agonist* function, meaning that it speeds or facilitates the function of the specialized neurons that it serves. It can also serve an *antagonist* function, meaning that a neurotransmitter can impair or slow down the function of the specialized neural chain of which it is a central part.

Researchers have learned a great deal about neurotransmitters and how they function under normal circumstances, but insights are emerging all the time about the role neurotransmitters can play in behavior disorders.

In this exercise, you will identify how a neurotransmitter functions under normal circumstances in this first column. In the second column, you can speculate about what kinds of disorders have been associated with neurotransmitter dysregulation.

Normal Regulation Functions	Neurotransmitter	Disorders Implicated In Dysregulation
	ACETYLCHOLINE (ACH)	
	DOPAMINE (DA)	
	ENDORPHINS	
	GAMMA-AMINOBUTYRIC ACID (GABA)	
	NOREPINEPHRINE (NE)	
	SEROTONIN	

After completing this exercise, you should be able to:

- describe the general purpose of neurotransmitters in the nervous system.

- characterize specific effects of neurotransmitter function.

- recognize how dysregulation of normal function can result in a recognizable behavior disorder.

- identify specific behavior disorders that have been implicated in neurotransmitter dysregulation.

▼Exercise 2.5 PHANTOM PAIN

ANALYZE: Reason

Phantom pain is a curious phenomenon in which individuals feel pain in body parts that they have lost due to injury or because of congenital defects. Although psychologists initially believed that phantom pain and other phantom sensations were imaginary or "all in the head" of an amputee, current explanations of phantom pain focus on the motor and somatosensory cortex. The idea is that neurons from adjacent areas of the motor cortex branch and grow to areas where the neurons have been damaged or have died because they have not received stimulation. Those areas are still connected to the area of the somatosensory cortex related to the missing limb. When the motor neurons that have "taken over" send signals to the somatosensory cortex, they can be experienced as pain in the missing limb. For example, a woman loses her hand in an automobile accident. Motor neurons from the adjacent area controlling the eyebrows and eyes branch out to utilize this space. The stimulation from these new neural branches is perceived by the sensory cortex as pain in the missing hand. Because the eye and brow move almost constantly and unconsciously and uncontrollably, the woman's pain is constant and is not relieved by medication.

On April 15, 2013, two bombs exploded near the finish line of the Boston Marathon, killing three people and wounding hundreds. Sixteen of those wounded lost at least one leg as a result of their injuries. Using the above described theory of phantom pain, what would you expect to happen to those individuals who lost legs?

Given your understanding of the structures of the motor and somatosensory cortexes, from what areas of the body might new signals be coming? Would you expect there to be any difference in the experience of phantom pain based on the age of the victim?

Why or why not? _____

After completing this exercise, you should be able to:

- identify areas of the somatosensory cortex responsible for specific functions.
- describe how neural death and growth might account for instances of phantom pain.
- draw conclusions about the possible course of specific instances of phantom pain.
- recognize that explanations of experiences and behaviors are often complex because of the interconnectedness of the central and peripheral nervous systems.

▼Exercise 2.6   CARING FOR PHINEAS

EVALUATE: Take Perspective

Phineas Gage was a young railroad worker who was injured when an iron tamping rod was accidentally propelled up through his left cheek and out the top of his skull. Amazingly, he was able to sit up and speak immediately after the accident, but there was massive damage to his frontal lobes. Although this damage did not interfere with his memory or physical abilities, it did leave him a profoundly changed person. His personality became radically different; this formerly responsible, hardworking, and respectable person became aggressive, verbally abusive, and unpredictable. He ended up losing his job and leaving the country.

Describe how Phineas and his friends might have perceived these changes.

_____

If you were a social worker assigned to Phineas, what types of services might you

offer him? _____

What would be your expectations for the rest of Phineas's life? Why? _____

_____

Speculate about what other kinds of changes might have occurred in Phineas's recovery if the tamping rod had pierced the brain at a different location.

After completing this exercise, you should be able to:

- recognize that specific areas of the brain are responsible for particular functions.
- identify potential consequences of an injury to a specific area of the brain.
- discuss the long-term prognosis of an individual with a particular brain injury.
- speculate about treatments and support services that might aid in recovery.

▼Exercise 2.7   THE NEW SUPERHEROES

CREATE: Invent

Science fiction writers are always searching for good ideas for plots that will capture the interest of their readers. A common premise during one particular era of science fiction movies was that radiation somehow altered biological processes, transforming normal human beings into superhumans—some good and some evil. One such example is the Incredible Hulk, who, due to a laboratory accident, developed superhuman strength that manifested itself when he was angry.

Your task in this exercise is to create your own team of three superheroes by pretending that it is possible to magnify the abilities governed by selective sites in the human brain.

Identify the area of the brain that would have to be altered to accomplish the special skill of each superhero. Then create a simple story line in which the superheroes' special abilities could be useful. _____

In this exercise, you confront a rather novel discrepancy in thinking about brain functions. You take a familiar concept—superhero figures—and combine the possibilities of science fiction with brain function concepts to develop new heroes. You may find it helpful to begin by listing the component parts of the brain and their functions. Then give your imagination free rein as you explore the kinds of alterations that might fit the demands of a superhero's life. What challenges would allow your superheroes to demonstrate their exceptional abilities? Try not to limit your possibilities or to get bogged down by old ways of thinking. Finally, evaluate whether your novel combinations are satisfying. (See Answer Key for some examples.)

Name of superhero 1 _____

What superability does this superhero possess? _____

What brain structure is augmented? _____

What simple plot would encourage this superhero to come to the rescue? _____

How original or playful is your creation? _____

Name of superhero 2 _____

What superability does this superhero possess? _____

What brain structure is augmented? _____

What simple plot would encourage this superhero to come to the rescue? _____

How original or playful is your creation? _____

Name of superhero 3 _____

What superability does this superhero possess? _____

What brain structure is augmented? _____

What simple plot would encourage this superhero to come to the rescue? _____

How original or playful is your creation? _____

After completing this exercise, you should be able to:

- identify certain brain functions with specific sites in the brain.
- expand your thinking patterns to allow for playful thinking.
- use criteria to evaluate whether a creative product is adequate.

▼Exercise 2.8   THE ADDICTED BRAIN

CREATE: Design

The former college roommate of a long-term cocaine user is shocked when he observes some significant changes in his old friend. Instead of being outgoing and curious, his friend seems sullen and suspicious. The roommate suggests the addict seek help for his addiction. During the course of the conversation, the addict uncharacteristically becomes very suspicious and aggressive, accusing his friend of wanting him out of the way so that he can take all his money. Later that evening, the addict takes a large amount of cocaine and begins to have difficulty breathing. Although the roommate calls an ambulance, the addict continues in respiratory distress and starts having convulsions. He dies a short time later of cardiac arrest.

Given what you understand about the functions of the brain, list several brain areas that could be involved in the behaviors/experiences of the cocaine addict. Make sure you are explicit about which brain areas are responsible for which behaviors. Pick one of these relationships and state it as a clearly written hypothesis. Design and briefly describe a study, using rats as subjects, in which you might be able to test your hypothesis. Discuss whether evidence from a study with rats could generalize to human behavior.

After completing this exercise, you should be able to:

- identify brain areas responsible for specific drug-related behaviors.

- create a clear hypothesis statement.

- design an experiment that would allow you to test your hypothesis.

- discuss the generalization possibilities for animal analogue studies.

THE PSYCHOLOGY ADVANTAGE

An ability to think critically about the brain and its processes is probably one of the most important skills psychology has to offer. On a personal level, being able to connect the actions of specific drugs to areas of the brain and related impairments in cognitive function may guide the decisions you make about drinking or using drugs while driving, competing in athletics, or trying to take an exam. Recognizing the tremendous early plasticity of the brain may influence when you introduce your children to a second language. Understanding the functions of specific brain areas may help you predict the outcome when a parent or grandparent has a stroke and more effectively plan for their rehabilitation and recovery. Therefore, being familiar with how the brain works or falters can help you make life-enhancing decisions.

Beyond practical considerations, understanding brain processes is awe-inspiring. Every gesture, thought, and act are the result of a complex interplay of anatomy, physics, and chemistry. Our awareness that even the simplest of actions requires the orchestration of a dazzling interaction of components can help us develop a very keen appreciation for what our three pounds of brain tissue can accomplish.

In a larger sphere of influence, psychology's understanding of the brain shapes the work of other disciplines. Some of those connections—such as those between psychology and medicine—are fairly straightforward. Learning how and where trauma changes the chemical processes in the brain is helping doctors and psychologists predict who is most likely to develop posttraumatic stress disorder (PTSD) and how to treat it more effectively. Cochlear implants to restore or improve hearing were developed using information about both the brain structures and the perceptual processes that result in meaningful audition. The connections between areas like physics and computer science and psychology may be less obvious, but are no less important. For example, scientists are learning about creating effective computing structures and models for information processing from understanding the fluid and plastic nature of neural connections in the brain. Very recent research is also looking at the effectiveness of implanted stimulation devices in the hippocampus and other memory-related areas of the brain that might aid in the restoration or improvement of long-term memory damaged by injury or disease.

Chapter

◀ States of Consciousness ▶

You are driving down the highway. It is a lovely day for a drive, so you relax, roll the window down, and allow your mind to wander. Suddenly, you realize you are many miles down the road without having paid attention to how you got there. You don't remember passing familiar landmarks, although you obviously did in order to reach the place in which you now find yourself. Does this process sound familiar? Such trance states are regular occurrences in the course of our daily lives. We are capable of executing well-learned behavior without paying much attention. We are likely to experience many levels of consciousness during a single day. The following exercises explore aspects of conscious and unconscious experience.

▼ Exercise 3.1 CONSCIOUS CONTROL

PART 1: UNDERSTAND: Observe

Conscious experience comes in different forms. List at least 12 activities or experiences that demonstrate the variety of levels of consciousness you experience over the course of a single day. For example, maybe you are listening to music, studying for an exam, or practicing a new and difficult cello concerto.

PART 2: APPLY: Classify

As you created your list, you may have recognized that your experiences could be ordered along a continuum from "extremely alert and self-aware" to "out of it." Create a rank order of consciousness out of your list. Compare both your list and your rank order with those of your classmates.

After completing this exercise, you should be able to:

- identify how consciousness is involved in different daily activities.

- recognize different forms of conscious experience in your own life.

- organize your conscious experiences along a continuum of awareness and control.

- explain your position in a group discussion about categorizing conscious experience.

▼Exercise 3.2   TO SLEEP, PERCHANCE TO DREAM

APPLY: Classify

Although no one knows for certain why we dream, several theorists have offered theories regarding the origins of dreams. For example, Sigmund Freud proposed that dreams serve a *wish fulfillment* function. Any unmet needs during waking hours translate into unconscious activity that expresses those needs, often in symbols that require interpretation. Rosalind Cartwright's view of dreaming is more cognitive. She proposed that dreams represent *problem solving*, supported by the idea that creativity can flow in dreams because the normal constraints or logic and reality don't apply. Finally, J. Allan Hobson suggested the *activation synthesis model* in which dreams are byproducts of neural activity that transpires during REM sleep. Random signals originate from lower brain centers, and the cortex knits the signals into a narrative that understandably is not organized, coherent, or typically even plausible. All three approaches have fans, but let's see how you do in applying these frameworks to dream content.

Maria had an unusually hard day at work as a waitress and was exhausted when she fell asleep at the end of the day. When dreaming emerged in her first REM cycle, she was back at work. The restaurant was oddly decorated with images of the Eiffel Tower, the George Washington Monument, and the Leaning Tower of Pisa. In addition, the restaurant was filled with male bodybuilders who were exercising with barbells of different sizes. All the bodybuilders were demanding to be waited on at the same time, but they spoke in a language Maria couldn't understand. When Maria attempted to move toward them to take their order, her feet melted into the floor. As she was struggling to extract herself, church bells began to ring and everyone in the restaurant began twerking. Maria suddenly awakened to the sound of her alarm, which had been ringing for a while.

What elements would each theorist respond to in Maria's dream?

- What would Sigmund Freud say?

- What would Rosalind Cartwright say?

- What would J. Allan Hobson say?

After completing this exercise, you should be able to:

- describe the differences among the three most prominent dream theories.

- recognize the relationship between dream steps and REM sleep.

- classify forms of evidence in support of dream theories.

▼Exercise 3.3   A MIDSUMMER NIGHT'S DREAM

ANALYZE: Reason

Peter is a young man who lives in North America. Although normal in most ways, he is quite unable to sleep unless there is natural darkness. This is not generally a problem where he lives, because even though summer days are quite long, there are still enough hours of darkness for him to get sufficient sleep. One December, however, he has the opportunity to go to Antarctica. He is there for four days, during which time the sun never sets.

Describe what will happen to Peter's behavior and physiological well-being over the course of the four days. What can he expect when he returns to his home?

After completing this exercise, you should be able to:

- identify the role of sleep in recuperation and energy conservation.

- discuss the effects of sleep deprivation on behavior and emotional states.

- anticipate Peter's rapid return to health and normal behavior when he resumes his usual sleep patterns.

▼Exercise 3.4   THE LIGHT AT THE END OF THE TUNNEL

One unresolved controversy in the area of consciousness involves the explanation of the near-death experience. Some patients who survive cardiac arrest characterize the near-death experience as a pleasant journey in which lights and tunnels are prominent features. Some report encountering loved ones who have already died. Others report the sensation of being drawn out of their bodies, sometimes being able to look down on those who are administering their care. Many people report that their near-death experience is transformational: They retain a sense of peace and often report that death is no longer something to be feared.

Two conflicting explanations are offered for this experience of altered consciousness. The first, which we will call the *spiritual hypothesis*, proposes that near-death experiences verify that the body and soul are two distinctive components of human experience. According to this view, a near-death experience simply provides a preview of the experience the human soul will encounter after death.

The second explanation we will call the *physiological hypothesis*, because it is grounded in physiology. This explanation suggests that the light at the end of the tunnel is simply a hallucination. Physiologists know that challenges to the integrity of the brain (such as suffocation or injury) can produce hallucinations. They argue that many patients who have experienced the near-death experience have also been subject to harrowing medical conditions in which oxygen deprivation has occurred. According to this view, the perceived experience of the afterlife is merely a hallucination, not a promise of a life to come.

PART 1: ANALYZE: Infer

This particular controversy highlights very different values and belief systems. Given your understanding of the spiritual and physiological hypotheses:

What values and beliefs support the spiritual hypothesis? _____

What values and beliefs support the physiological hypothesis? _____

PART 2: EVALUATE: Justify

Psychological and religious explanations differ in their emphases. Preference for objective evidence derived from empirical research dominates psychological thinking. Religious thinking is primarily subjective; faith does not require objective evidence.

Decide which hypothesis has greater appeal for you, given our current state of knowledge. _____

What do you believe is the source of the near-death experience? Why? _____

_____

What values support your belief? _____

_____

_____

_____

After completing this exercise, you should be able to:

- identify at least two values involved in the conflict regarding near-death experiences.

- state your own preference for interpreting the near-death experience.

- trace the way your own belief system has developed from your values.

- distinguish some general differences in the values of science-based versus religious-based thinking.

▼Exercise 3.5   JOBS AND DRUGS DON'T MIX
EVALUATE: Assess

You are part of a drug prevention team that is trying to foster a campaign to help reduce illegal drug use in adults, similar to the Narcotics Overdose Prevention and Education (NOPE) program that police officers use when working with children. As a starting point, you have decided to create targeted anti-drug campaigns for different groups, based on the risks of impairment of performance inherent in their activities. For each type of specialized occupation or interest below, specify the illicit or illegal drug that would most dangerously impair the user's function and explain the likely effect of using the drug on the individual's preferred activity.

Profession or Preferred Activity	Riskiest Drug Substance	Performance Impairment
Bicycle messenger		
Marathon runner		
Artist		
Stay-at-home mom		
Sword swallower		
Teacher		
Tightrope walker		
Accountant		

After completing this exercise, you should be able to:

- recognize the impact of illegal drug substances on the performance of professionals' activities and on the preferred leisure activities of adults.

- articulate the impact of specific drugs on aspects of human activity.

- compare degrees of dangerousness among drug substances.

- formulate some reasonable ideas about how one might campaign to persuade a specific individual about the dangers of drug use.

▼Exercise 3.6 ROCK-A-BYE BABY

CREATE: Invent

How people sleep—and how well they sleep—is an issue for many. In the United States, advertisers present an almost overwhelming array of books, tapes, songs, foods, and drugs guaranteed to put anyone to sleep. The old sleep standby, however, is the lullaby. Adapt or create a lullaby to address some aspect of sleep and sleep schedules. We offer two adapted examples below. Because you won't be able to hear our creative melodies, we will leave crafting an original lullaby to your imagination!

Traditional Lullaby	Adapted Lullaby
Rock-a-bye baby, on the treetop, When the wind blows, the cradle will rock. When the bough breaks, the cradle will fall, And down will come baby, cradle and all.	Rock-a-bye baby, going to sleep, Alpha waves cease and delta waves peak. Then comes a dream with stage-one-like REM, And the next night it starts all over again.
Go to sleep, Go to sleep, Go to sleep, little baby. When you wake, we shall have cake, Go to sleep, little baby.	Go to sleep, Every night, The same time to bed, you will sleep tight. When you wake, refreshed and right, You will do it every night.

After completing this exercise, you should be able to:

- appreciate the essential qualities of lullabies in inducing sleep.

- apply sleep theories in a creative expression.

- put your sleep-starved friends at rest if you perform for them!

▼Exercise 3.7 REMEDIES FOR JET LAG

CREATE: Design

If you have ever traveled cross-country, especially from east to west, you have probably experienced the phenomenon of *jet lag*. This confused and overtired feeling supports the speculation that we have a *biological clock* that governs our sense of fatigue. We may experience the same disorientation when our weekend sleep schedules don't match the schedules we maintain on weekdays. For people with these mismatched schedules, Mondays are horrors.

Suppose you have just been given a research grant to identify effective treatments for minimizing jet lag. You have been exploring possible treatments and have come up with three suggestions—(1) preventive doses of vitamin B complex; (2) 10 minutes of meditation; and (3) 15 minutes of aerobic exercise. Each suggestion is complete with a reasonable physiological rationale. How might you discern which, if any, of those treatments would reduce or prevent jet lag?

Your task in this assignment is to design a simple experiment that will determine the relative effectiveness of those treatments. To do this, you will provide the important elements of the study by answering the following questions.

What is your hypothesis? _____

What is the independent variable? _____

How will you measure the dependent variable (jet lag)? _____

What other variables will you need to control? _____

After completing this exercise, you should be able to:

- standardize the experience you are studying in an experiment.

- develop some method for making the participants' experiences comparable.

- design simple studies that attempt to exclude alternative interpretations.

- recognize that experiments are an expensive and complicated means of gathering evidence.

THE PSYCHOLOGY ADVANTAGE

Consciousness is one of the areas of psychology in which students are often interested, and occasionally disappointed when they realize that a rigorous model of experimentation and empirical research are employed here as in other, more tangible areas of psychology. Such techniques don't seem to support or encourage talk about the mystery that is the human mind (as opposed to the brain) and human awareness. Why, then, should you be interested? What is the benefit?

In a very pragmatic sense, understanding consciousness can allow you to move more effectively through your life. Understanding sleep, for instance—what makes for good sleep, how much sleep is enough, the consequences of not getting enough—allows you to live a healthier and more productive life. Knowing the impact of drugs on the brain and behavior can enable you to make better decisions about how, when, and if you use certain substances that impair sensation, perception, coordination, and judgment. Even being aware of how to minimize jet lag while traveling is useful.

In a more subtle and perhaps meaningful way, however, understanding consciousness may encourage you to look at how you experience your life a little differently. Modern life is busy, complex, and ever-changing. As you worked through the first exercise in this chapter, you probably realized how much of the time you were multitasking, less aware of the actions you were completing, like listening to music, brushing your teeth, or walking to class. That makes sense when the things you are doing or thinking are rote activities where deep processing isn't required or where you aren't trying to make sense of new ideas. You probably also noticed that when you were doing things that required high levels of consciousness—like studying for an exam, driving someplace new, or maybe even talking to a new, quite attractive, person—that was *all* you were doing.

Consciousness is a limited resource, just like energy. In fact, it requires energy, and quite a lot of it. Studying is exhausting, as is driving or walking in heavy traffic. Knowing this reality, and knowing that multitasking makes one less aware of each task being attempted, can make you sensitive to the times when you want to be aware and to arrange your activities accordingly. Do you want to really understand that new concept in physics? Then don't have your textbook and notes open next to *Facebook* or while you are listening to music. Do you really want to get to know that new person? Ignore the cell phone while you are talking to him or her. Do you want to know who you really are and what you really want? Figure out how to listen to yourself, without all the distractions. Whether you meditate, pray, or just go for a quiet walk with your thoughts, you will be more conscious of yourself as well as the goals in your life that can lead to the greatest fulfillment. The things you are actively conscious of are the things you will remember.

4

Chapter

◀The Nature and Nurture▶ of Behavior

The exercises in this chapter focus on the ways human behavior is affected by two forces: the developmental processes that unfold in our lives from nature (our biological heritage) and the processes that are constructed in our lives through nurture (the social environment in which we live). The fundamental question inherent in explaining most developmental processes is to what degree biological factors cause behavior patterns and to what degree the environmental and cultural forces that surround us account for these patterns. Psychologists often refer to this issue as the nature versus nurture controversy. This designation is somewhat misleading because both forces are likely to be influential in the development of any human behavior.

▼Exercise 4.1   IT'S ALL ACADEMIC

UNDERSTAND: Explain

As you've learned, one of the longest-running debates in psychology is the nature-nurture debate: How much of who we are and what we do is genetically based (nature) and how much is a result of our environment (nurture)? Arguably the most important public demonstration of our changing understanding of the answer to this question is found in our educational systems. Until the late 1950s and early 1960s, the United States based its educational system on the assumption that we inherit intelligence (as measured by success in school and IQ tests). Then, in 1965, the federal government founded the Head Start program. Its purpose was (and still is) to provide basic health, social, and educational services to children in low-income families, in order to facilitate their success in school. Its premise is that by providing a safe and healthy environment, children will be better able to respond to intellectual stimulation and demonstrate academic proficiency. This program was in conflict with the earlier view that intellectual ability was primarily inherited and not susceptible to significant environmental enhancement. Although there is still much controversy about the efficacy of Head Start programs in particular, the vast numbers of both public and private programs that provide social and economic support to under- and poorly performing students suggests that there is considerable merit in this approach.

How might this preschool program have been different if the creators of the program believed the earlier premise that intelligence was strictly inherited? What might our educational system look like now?

The current "No Child Left Behind" legislation holds schools accountable for the academic performance of their students. Is that more supportive of the nature or nurture perspective on intelligence? Why? _____

_____

What do you believe is the role of genetics in intelligence? (You will be able to explore this more in Chapter 11.) _____

_____

After completing this exercise, you should be able to:

- differentiate between the nature and the nurture perspectives on intelligence.

- describe your understanding of the heritability of intelligence.

- identify the consequences for education of changes in our understanding of the heritability of a specific feature (intelligence).

- understand how public policy can be affected by scientific theory.

▼Exercise 4.2 NATURE OR NURTURE?
APPLY: Classify

You can almost trace the history of psychology by looking for changes in the way the field has viewed individuality and differences between people and groups of people. At times, psychology has assumed that we are a *tabula rasa* (blank slate); that everything we are and know is a result of our experience. At other times, it has begun with the assumption that we are a product of our traits and inherited features and that experience makes no significant modification to our personality. Modern research and thought suggests that, most of the time, the truth lies somewhere in between. As these different perspectives work their way into the common culture, they influence everything from literature to educational practices. Below are some clichés and popular sayings. Evaluate each one, deciding which represent the assumption that life history determines who we are (nurture) and which assume that we are shaped by our heredity (nature).

"Sugar and spice and everything nice, that's what little girls are made of . . ."

_____

"Handsome is as handsome does." _____

"The apple doesn't fall far from the tree." _____

"You can't teach an old dog new tricks." _____

"Early to bed and early to rise, makes a man healthy, wealthy, and wise."

_____

"Boys will be boys." _____

"You are what you eat." _____

"Blood will tell." _____

"All men are created equal." _____

What other examples can you think of? _____

_____

After completing this exercise, you should be able to:

- describe the approaches to understanding human behavior that are characterized by the terms "nature" and "nurture."

- classify common sayings using their underlying assumptions about nature and nurture.

- recognize that assumptions about nature and nurture can be found in many unexpected places.

▼Exercise 4.3   WHO'S TO BLAME?

ANALYZE: Infer

Any conversation about the role of genes and environment in the development of an individual seems to flow naturally to a discussion about the responsibility parents have for their children's behavior. Early in 2000, a 6-year-old girl in Michigan was shot and killed by a first-grade classmate. The young boy brought a loaded gun to school and shot her after a petty conflict developed during class. He later claimed that he had only intended to scare her but that the gun "went off." The bullet struck the little girl in the throat, and she died a short time later. No one was surprised to discover that the 6-year-old killer was being raised in neglectful and abusive circumstances, complicated by his caretaker's drug abuse. Amid reactions of shock and outrage, one question was repeated over and over: How could it happen? Was there something biologically wrong with the child, so that he didn't understand or couldn't control what he was doing? Did his life experience make him prone to violence?

Using the concepts from this chapter, provide your explanation of how the boy's development—both nature and nurture—might have led to this tragedy. Explicitly discuss issues of genetics and environment, explaining how each factor might, or might not, have contributed to his behavior. You might find it helpful to organize your discussion around specific topics, such as temperament, prenatal environment, peer influence, culture, and gender.

After completing this exercise, you should be able to:

- recognize that behaviors and behavior patterns are often the result of environment-gene interactions.

- identify potential environmental and genetic influences on violent behavior in a real-life situation.

- develop opinions about the influence genetic and environmental factors have on violent behavior.

▼Exercise 4.4   KEEP ON TRUCKIN'

You are a consultant asked to work with a company that has suddenly experienced a huge increase in the diversity of its workers. This trucking company has employed men almost exclusively for the last 25 years, but over the last 5 years they have hired increasing numbers of women. In fact, as of their last hiring blitz, 40 percent of their employees are now women and the vast majority of those women are experienced truck drivers or warehouse employees. Many of the men who have been there for a while are beginning to grumble. Some are hassling the women about their choice of career, targeting those actually driving or working in the warehouse, rather than those working in the office. In an effort to ease the transition for both old and new employees, the company's owners want you to help them design a program to make their current employees aware of the biases they bring to the workplace regarding gender roles. After much reflection, you decide that the best way to do this is to teach the employees about how people develop gender-based expectations for behavior.

PART 1: ANALYZE: Compare and Contrast

Describe how social learning theory and gender schema theory explain how the men at the company have formed their notions of appropriate male and female occupations. Give one example for each that is specifically related to this situation.

Social learning theory: _____

_____

Example: _____

_____

Gender schema theory: _____

_____

Example: _____

_____

PART 2: EVALUATE: Justify

Now, identify which of these explanations you think would be the most useful or relevant in explaining to the male truckers why they have the images of male and female occupations that they do. Why do you think that? How might you use this theory to

change the male truckers' perceptions and behaviors? _____

_____

_____

After completing this exercise, you should be able to:

- define social learning theory and gender schema theory and describe how each explains gender-typed behavior.

- recognize how these theories would lead to workplace problems as women and men move into occupations that are traditionally associated with the other gender.

- apply the principles of social learning theory and gender schema theory to a particular workplace situation.

- choose an explanation of behavior you believe best fits a particular situation and justify your answer.

▼Exercise 4.5 BROTHER, CAN YOU SPARE A DIME?

EVALUATE: Decide

In 2003, a group of researchers from the University of Virginia published research* in which they examined differences in measures of intelligence between twins. Some of

*Turkheimer, E., Haley, A., Waldron, M., D'Onofrio, B., & Gottesman, I. (2003). Socioeconomic status modifies heritability of IQ in young children. *Psychological Science, 14*(6), 623–628.

the twins had families with higher socioeconomic status, and others lived in families with lower socioeconomic status; all twins, however, were reared together with their twins. What the researchers found was that twins who were reared in the higher socio-economic contexts were *more* alike in their scores than were twins reared in the lower socioeconomic households.

How might you explain this outcome? _____

_____

What does this finding have to say about the nature-nurture debate in the area of intelligence? _____

_____

After completing this exercise, you should be able to:

- recognize the value of using twins in studies about genetic differences, even when those twins are reared together.

- interpret findings of a published research article to draw conclusions about the roles of genetics and the environment in the expression of intelligence.

- connect the findings of a specific research study to a larger psychological debate about the degree to which the environment and genes interact.

▼ Exercise 4.6 YOUR PERSONAL HONOR CODE

EVALUATE: Choose

One sad aspect of your college experience will be the likelihood that at some time during your studies you will observe one or more students taking advantage of cir-cumstances to cheat. Whether managing a subtle peek at your neighbor's answer sheet to help you decide on the best multiple choice alternative or buying a term paper from your friendly online vendor, the array of strategies people use to cheat runs from the mundane through the remarkably innovative. (A colleague of ours likes to say that if cheating students would just spend as much time studying as they do on trying to circumvent the rules, those students would probably be academically successful.)

Nearly every time you are in an academic performance arena, you have the oppor-tunity to game the system and cheat. Looked at from that vantage point, the vast majority of students do not cheat in the majority of situations where this is possible. Now let's look at the reasons why you do what you do. Which of the following most closely corresponds to your rationale for *not* cheating?

___ I'm afraid of what would happen if I got caught.
___ I believe my personal integrity would be damaged if I don't do my own work.
___ I want to follow the rules that have been laid out by the instructor.

Now let's look at some rationales for those who *do* cheat.

___ Everybody else does it and I don't want to lose ground to those who do.
___ The results of this specific challenge don't contribute much to my overall growth so cheating doesn't matter.
___ I can't afford to flunk.
___ Nobody gets hurt by what I do.
___ The instructor should be paying more attention so if I can get away with it, I will.
___ I am not personally defined by the results of any specific test.

There are clearly many more explanations or excuses that cheaters offer, but let's turn the discussion to the academic research.

Lawrence Kohlberg developed a stage theory to address the moral reasoning that people offer to justify their behaviors. In the first level, *preconventional*, people focus on the consequences of their actions. Regardless of the actual moral choices they make, the preconventional thinker wants to maximize reward and minimize punishment. In the second level, *conventional*, conforming to popular norms or conventions seems to be the driving force behind decisions. At the highest level of moral reasoning, *postconventional*, people enact their decisions according to a personal moral code. They don't care what other people think about their actions but must live up to their own high ideals.

Review the various rationales offered for cheating or maintaining academic integrity and try to classify which Kohlberg level best captures their development:

	Preconventional	Conventional	Postconventional
Rationales for those who maintain integrity			
I'm afraid of what would happen if I got caught.			
I believe my personal integrity would be damaged if I don't do my own work.			
I want to follow the rules that have been laid out by the instructor.			
Rationales for those who cheat			
Everybody else does it.			
I don't want to lose ground to those who do.			
The results of this specific challenge don't contribute much to my overall growth so cheating doesn't matter.			
I can't afford to flunk.			
Nobody gets hurt by what I do.			
The instructor should have been paying more attention, so if I can get away with it I will.			
I am not personally defined by the results of any specific test.			

One of the harder things to understand about Kohlberg's classification system is that postconventional reasoning doesn't always lead to the most defensible moral behavior. The key to classifying postconventional reasoning is adherence to well-defined personal standards rather than conforming to societal norms (conventional) or avoiding unpleasant consequences (preconventional).

After completing this exercise, you should be able to:

- characterize Kohlberg's stages of moral development.

- discuss why one can commit seemingly immoral acts and still be operating at an advanced moral development stage.

- justify why cheating is not a moral choice.

▼Exercise 4.7 CHARACTER BUILDING

CREATE: Imagine

You are a novelist writing a mystery. You begin with a marvelous plot and the realization that your detective needs certain traits and abilities to be successful. This person needs to be sensitive enough to deal with witnesses and victims; tough enough to stay alive in the face of bombs, hired killers, and guard dogs; intelligent enough to break secret codes and outwit the criminal mastermind; and witty enough to be interesting and to find the humor in devastating situations. Create a brief biography for this fictional character, in which you outline the heritable traits and life experiences that have allowed your detective to become this person. Which characteristics seem to be primarily "inborn"? Which ones were acquired by experience?

Biography: _____

_____

_____

_____

_____

After completing this exercise, you should be able to:

- articulate the interaction of genetic and environmental factors in the development of individual characteristics.

- weigh the potential contributions of genes and experiences for specific characteristics.

- construct a biography for a fictional character that speculates about the genetic makeup and life experiences that might lead to the development of that character's specific traits.

▼ Exercise 4.8   SEEING DOUBLE

CREATE: Design

As psychologists and other scientists grapple with understanding the roles that genetics and environment play in our development as unique individuals, the experiences of twins, particularly monozygotic twins, have been invaluable. Monozygotic twins are genetically identical, yet it is clear that they are unique individuals. Why? The environment must play a large role in these differences, but how? Temperamental differences in identical twins are noted from birth, so environments must be different in utero, even for individuals carried in the womb at the same time. Identical twins are also similar in many ways. Are these similarities the result of their shared genetic makeup? Maybe. It is also possible that they share enough of the same environment—a particular family and all the related social, economic, and educational correlates—to have been shaped by similar life experiences. This outcome is supported by the fact that non-twin siblings are also similar in many ways, even though they are genetically different.

One way in which these ideas can be teased apart is by looking at twins and siblings who have been raised in different environments since birth. Although current adoption practices in the United States do not encourage the placement of twins in separate families, it has happened in the past, both here and in other countries. Sometimes these twins find each other as adults, and scientists are presented with a wonderful opportunity: a chance to study differences in genetically identical (monozygotic) or related (dizygotic) individuals who have been raised in different environments. However, looking at existing situations only allows scientists to find correlations; it doesn't allow them to answer questions about cause and effect.

Imagine that you want to examine the role that environment plays in an individual's level of extraversion. Generate your hypothesis for an "ideal" twin study experiment, in which you ask and answer some questions of cause and effect. Outline the basic experimental design. What are the ethical issues that prevent you from actually conducting this experiment? Can you think of ethical ways to ask the same questions?

Hypothesis: _____

_____

Brief description of design: _____

_____

Ethical issues: _____

_____

Alternatives? _____

_____

After completing this exercise, you should be able to:

- describe the difference between monozygotic and dizygotic twins.

- recognize the ways in which identical twins have different environments.

- explain how studies of twins adopted or raised by different families provide scientists with insight about the role of genetics and environment in an individual's development.

- design an experiment using twins to examine the role that environment plays in extraversion.

- assess the viability of such an experiment in light of the ethical considerations.

- identify possible ethical alternatives to twin experiments.

THE PSYCHOLOGY ADVANTAGE

Understanding how biological predispositions interact with the social, economic, and physical environment to produce behavioral outcomes is invaluable. As a parent, this information could help you make choices about toys and activities to foster a broad understanding of gender roles and to raise children more likely to accept or tackle nontraditional roles and occupations. Knowing how the complicated concept of intelligence is a construct with both biological and environmental components might make you more able to work with your child's school to create an effective learning environment that recognizes your child's innate abilities and also provides the support necessary for your child to demonstrate those abilities effectively. Even if you are not a parent, this knowledge can help you make informed decisions about public policies related to educational spending and inform your vote for the allocation of public money for the abundance of programs affecting children and youth across the nation.

Although it wasn't addressed specifically in this chapter, there are also implications for the treatment of behavioral and emotional disorders. At one end of the conceptual "nature versus nurture" spectrum, people are the product of their environment, and thus changing the environment in meaningful ways would change patterns of behavior, cognition, and emotion. At the other, they are not, and treatment would logically focus on the management of the signs and symptoms that are biologically driven rather than real change. If, as is most likely the case, the real answer is that disorders arise out of both environmental and biological influences, then knowing how to separate and analyze those factors will lead to more effective treatments and more satisfying and productive lives for those affected by these disorders.

Chapter

◀ The Developing Person ▶

Life is a miracle. From the moment of conception to the moment you have "shuffled off this mortal coil" (something Shakespeare's character Hamlet was contemplating), you undergo continuous changes. Sometimes the changes are quite dramatic, such as the loss of your first tooth or the first appearance of pubic hair. At other times, the changes are subtle, so much so that you may not notice the little differences that suddenly become apparent. Developmental psychologists focus on the nature of those changes, emphasizing physical, social, cognitive, and emotional differences over time. In this chapter, we explore many of the concepts and frameworks that psychologists have used to describe, explain, and predict those developmental changes.

▼ Exercise 5.1 WHEN BAD CHILDREN AREN'T BAD

UNDERSTAND: Translate

No matter how charming the child, eventually parents find themselves exasperated with their child's behavior. Sometimes it is easy for a parent to assume intentional misbehavior when other motives actually may be at work. By watching his own children, Piaget gave us some cognitive concepts to reexamine what bad kids may really be up to. See if you can identify the cognitive concept from Piaget that explains each child's cognition.

- Although the parents spent $300 on holiday toys for their 1-year-old daughter, she spent more time playing peekaboo by sticking her head in and out of a box that one of the toys came in. Why should the parents have saved their money?

_____

- A well-meaning aunt talked with her 9-month-old nephew about meeting her new boyfriend. However, when he saw the young man, the child shrieked unconsolably. "It must be his mustache!" the aunt thought. _____

- "Stop doing that!" screamed the exasperated mother in response to her infant's irritating habit of throwing his bottle from the high chair to the floor. She must have stooped over at least 20 times during this meal alone, and her child just wasn't learning! Why should the child's behavior not be surprising? _____

_____

- An older brother and younger sister constantly fight when they are playing cards. No matter how many times the brother explains the rules to his sister, the sister spreads her cards out in a long line instead of a pile and declares, "I win! I have more cards!" What principle is keeping the sister from learning the rules?

  _____

- A 4-year-old girl walks into the kitchen and sees her mother pouring herself a glass of juice. The little girl asks for a glass too, so the mother reaches into a cabinet and pulls out a kid-sized cup. Her daughter screams and cries because she wants "more juice." She doesn't stop crying until her mother pours the juice out of the child's cup and into a larger container. _____

- Two-year-old twins were forever arguing about whose toy belonged to whom. The young father decided to put a stop to the arguing once and for all. He sat them both down and gave them a lecture about understanding the way the other twin felt. Although the twins nodded their heads, they were fighting again almost before the father had left the room. Why should the father have saved his breath? _____

After completing this exercise, you should be able to:

- recognize Piaget's key developmental milestones.

- translate Piaget's ideas to routine child-caretaking situations.

- describe how knowledge of Piaget's principles could increase your patience as a parent.

▼Exercise 5.2   THE SITTER'S DILEMMA

APPLY: Classify

As a college student, you are hard up for money. So when a nearby family advertises for a sitter two nights a week, you are very tempted by the thought of what you think should be easy money. After one night, however, you realize that this money is not going to be so easy. This family has gone through five babysitters in as many weeks because the children—ages 9 months, 2 years, 5 years, and 9 years—are energetic and difficult to manage. You need the money, however, so you decide to put your newly acquired knowledge about child development to use to create a plan to keep the children occupied and out of trouble.

List two activities that would appeal to each of the children, based on their ages. ____

_____

What activities might interest all of the children? _____

_____

Because of the differences in their ages, these children all have different bedtimes. The infant goes to bed at 7:00 P.M., the 2- and 5-year-olds at 7:30 and 8:00 P.M. respectively, and the 9-year-old retires about 8:30 P.M. How might your plan for the evening change as the younger children go to bed? _____

After completing this exercise, you should be able to:

- identify the cognitive, social, and physical abilities of children of these ages.

- use your understanding of these abilities to create appealing activities.

- demonstrate the ability to design differential plans by age.

- construct a classification system that reflects appropriate developmental expectations.

▼Exercise 5.3   ON DEATH AND DYING

ANALYSIS: Relate

After reading his own premature obituary in the newspaper, Mark Twain was reported to have said, "The news of my death is greatly exaggerated." Although most of us don't have a chance to read our own obituaries, some of us will have an opportunity to contemplate our own death when we are diagnosed with a terminal illness.

Surprisingly, death has been a taboo subject in Western culture, and as a result research in understanding the impact of terminal illness is comparatively recent. Elisabeth Kübler-Ross developed a provocative set of observations about the grief processes many people go through in coping with terminal illness. Many demonstrate *denial,* rejecting the bad news and assuming that someone somewhere has made a mistake. *Anger* becomes prominent when resentment brews about why they must struggle with this awful fate. Typically, terminally ill people often begin *bargaining*—either with God or with the attending physicians—for another alternative. *Depression* about impending losses and unpleasant ends can dominate the emotional life of these people. Some people discover *acceptance,* creating a feeling of peace about their fate. Kübler-Ross provides an interesting general description of how people adjust to terminal illnesses. However, her observations can also lead us to new ideas in our own research on death and dying.

In this exercise you will practice the characteristic of *variable-mindedness.* We may never be able to isolate—and therefore completely understand—all the variables that contribute to any behavior pattern. Psychologists expect behaviors to be hard to identify and complicated to explain. Being *variable-minded* means thinking very broadly about all possible factors that might influence some behavior.

Can you identify three factors or variables that might influence the emotional experience of the terminally ill? That will be your task in this exercise. You will be given three general categories—characteristics of the illness, characteristics of the person, and characteristics of the environment. For each category, you will identify one variable that might influence the way terminally ill people experience the stages of death and dying. Then you will speculate about the impact of that variable. In effect, you will be creating a hypothesis about the way each of these variables influences the terminally ill person's grieving process.

For example, under "characteristics of illness" rate of decline is an independent variable that might affect the nature of the emotions a terminally ill person experiences. Perhaps abrupt decreases in physical strength will prompt angry responses more quickly than more gradual losses of strength and well-being. A possible hypothesis might then be *"Diseases that produce more rapid deterioration may exaggerate the negative processes of grief."* Can you identify other characteristics of a terminal illness that might influence the ill person's grief processes? (See Answer Key for some examples.)

Characteristics of the illness

Variable: _____

Hypothesis: _____

Characteristics of the person

Variable: _____

Hypothesis: _____

Characteristics of the environment

Variable: _____

Hypothesis: _____

This task illustrates how difficult it may be to isolate the specific causes of behavior. Even if we were able to identify some hypotheses that we thought might be valid, we would be unable to set up experiments to demonstrate the differences we predict. Experiments require the experimenter to manipulate independent variables in experimental design. It would be unethical to experiment with humans in controlled procedures to answer most of the questions involved in our hypotheses. In such cases, we may instead substitute correlational studies in which we determine the strength of the relationship between two or more variables without directly manipulating them.

After completing this exercise, you should be able to:

- identify at least three variables that might influence the grief process.

- generate a simple hypothesis or prediction about each of those variables.

- describe what it means to be "variable minded" as a way of thinking about the behavior of others.

- develop meaningful research relationships.

▼Exercise 5.4   PIAGET MEETS SANTA CLAUS

ANALYZE: Compare/Contrast

Swiss psychologist Jean Piaget was a careful observer of the cognitive patterns of children. Through systematic observation and careful recording he was able to deduce stages of cognitive activity that became apparent as children interacted with their environments over time. One of his most well-established concepts is *conservation*, the ability to recognize that even though the shape of an object changes, its mass does not change. To demonstrate conservation, researchers may form shapes out of equivalent amounts of clay, perhaps rolling one mass of clay into a snakelike configuration and shaping the other into a ball. A child who can conserve recognizes that the physical masses of the two objects are the same despite their different shapes.

Although the conservation demonstrations of Piaget are interesting to watch, we demonstrate our ability to understand physical realities through the life span in other ways as well. An effective comparison contrasts how humans in different phases of development react to cultural symbols, such as Santa Claus.

Your task in this exercise is to develop the point of view of children who are dealing with Santa at various stages of their own cognitive development. As you assume their perspective, try to anticipate the kinds of observations and impressions an encounter with Santa would trigger. How would you react in each stage of development? What features of Santa would be most important? What would you believe about his existence?

To be successful in this task, you must develop an objective or unbiased way of looking at a concept you already know quite well. Chances are good that you are a formal operational thinker in relation to the existence of Santa Claus. But can you set aside what you know (and believe and feel) in order to describe an encounter with Santa from the perspective of a child at the stages targeted in this exercise? The characteristics of the stages as Piaget described them should help you to identify with experience, thoughts, beliefs, and feelings of those whose behavior you are attempting to explain. You may want to review the stages of cognitive development in your text before you predict the experiences of children in the different stages. (See Answer Key.)

What are the general characteristics of the *sensorimotor stage* child? _____

_____

_____

_____

On encountering Santa, what would the *sensorimotor stage* child

- observe?

- think and feel?

- believe?

What are the general characteristics of the *preoperational stage* child? _____

_____

_____

_____

On encountering Santa, what would the *preoperational stage* child

- observe?

- think and feel?

- believe?

The breakdown in belief in Santa Claus tends to correspond with a child's transition into the *concrete operations stage.*

What are the general characteristics of the *concrete operational* child? _____

_____

_____

_____

On encountering Santa, what would the *concrete operational* child

- observe?

- think and feel?

- believe?

How do these transitional experiences differ from the characteristics of the formal

operational child and adult? _____

_____

After this exercise, you should be able to:

- suspend your viewpoint as a formal operational thinker and assume the perspective of someone else at an earlier developmental stage.

- recognize the most probable characteristics and reactions of children in different stages of development.

- observe how the nature of beliefs, feelings, and cognition shift over time.

- identify changes in cognition that lead to changes in belief.

- generalize how children with different traditions change in their cognitive ability to evaluate cultural myths similar to Santa Claus.

▼Exercise 5.5 TEEN PREGNANCY

EVALUATE: Justify

Teen pregnancy has been a popular issue at the forefront of a variety of political and social forums. Many organizations have created programs designed to reduce teen pregnancy, but sometimes the outcome of these programs is uncertain. Some programs use traditional pregnancy statistics, such as "percentage of high-school girls who get pregnant," as a way to document reductions in the overall rate. Some program planners worry that these programs have limited impact on teen pregnancy rates. Your task in this example is two-part:

1. Deduce at least two ideas for additional steps that could be taken to reduce teen pregnancy. Be sure to think about the problem from the various dimensions of development (for example, biological, social, cognitive) as you generate your suggestions. Given what you understand of adolescent development, what might make such programs unsuccessful? How might you use this knowledge to create a program that has a high rate of success? _____

2. Identify one pregnancy statistic that you think would be the most persuasive in verifying a reduction in teen pregnancy that was related to the impact of a specific pregnancy prevention program. _____

_____

After completing this exercise, you should be able to:

- explain how the social, cognitive, and emotional abilities of adolescents influence teen pregnancy rates.

- generate some ideas for ways to decrease the pregnancy rate.

- advocate for a valid strategy for measuring the true impact of an important community mental health issue measure regarding teen pregnancy.

▼Exercise 5.6 DEVELOPMENTAL DELIGHTS

CREATE: Design

Play is an inherent part of human nature and part of the serious work of childhood. Most of us, when allowed to explore our environment and freed from concern with other tasks, play. And, despite what the advertisers would have you believe, one does not need expensive gadgets, bells, whistles, and lights to have fun. Given something as simple as a piece of fabric, an infant will play peekaboo, a preschooler will play dress-up, a school-age child might use it as a prop in a self-written play, and even an adult could have fun, perhaps creating a quilt or using it to help redecorate a bedroom. Below are some lists of everyday objects. Create a fun activity for children of the given ages, and use the objects to make toys.

Example:

Objects: string, empty thread spools, hanger, markers, paper

Children: 2 months: Using hanger and string, make mobile with shapes from paper, markers, and spool
14 months: Use all of above to make a pull toy
4 years: Use all of above to make a puppet for telling stories

Objects: drinking straws, cardboard, large plastic cups, string

Children: 6 months, 4 years, 7 years

_____

_____

_____

Objects: 4-quart pot, spoon, measuring cups, sinkful of water

Children: 9 months, 3 years, 10 years

_____

_____

_____

Objects: two chairs, pillows, several books, large blanket

Children: 12 months, 2 years, 9 years

_____

_____

_____

After completing this exercise, you should be able to:

- identify the cognitive, physical, and social abilities of children of different ages.
- use an understanding of these abilities to determine appropriate play activities.
- look at everyday objects in new ways to create "toys" that would be fun for children of various ages.

▼ Exercise 5.7   THE END OF THE STORY

CREATE: Invent

Erik Erikson conceptualized how people grow and change through the mastery of specific developmental challenges. For example, the fact that you are probably reading this book as part of a course assignment in college means that you have successfully made your way through Stages 1–2. You have successfully navigated the following:

- Trust versus Mistrust (First Year of Life)
- Autonomy versus Shame and Doubt (Second and Third Years of Life)
- Initiative versus Guilt (Fourth through Sixth Years of Life), and
- Industry versus Inferiority (Age 6 through Puberty)

So, congratulations! You've made it halfway through the psychosocial crises that correspond to maturation. Now what might the other half look like?

In this task, assume you have lived to a ripe old age, but you've been tagged to depart this life and now must make sense of the last half of your life. Before you go, write an obituary, in which you are careful to reflect happy resolutions of the final four stages:

- Identity versus Confusion (What can I become?)
- Intimacy versus Isolation (How will I address my need to affiliate with a significant other?)

- Generativity versus Self-absorption (Will I be a valuable and productive member of society?)
- Integrity versus Despair (Will I manage to live fully with few regrets?)

_____

_____

_____

_____

_____

_____

After completing this exercise, you should be able to:

- provide accurate descriptions of Erikson's psychosocial stages.
- apply the developmental tasks in later life to personal goals for the future.
- generate a creative scenario befitting a life well-lived.

THE PSYCHOLOGY ADVANTAGE

The content and skills related to Developmental Psychology may be among the most valuable an introductory course has to offer regarding the impact these issues can have on your personal life. Understanding developmental stages can make a big difference in family relationships. For example, knowing how cognition changes over time can influence how parents respond to their children from setting more reasonable expectations about what children can achieve to demonstrating greater patience with them when they are actually behaving like children. The standard expectation that adolescents will have a transition period that necessarily is filled with turmoil does not appear to be standard at all. Many adolescents report developmental years that are happy and productive. More important, the automatic strains that many parents anticipate simply do not come to pass. The advantages don't stop with just being a more effective parent. Understanding how values and priorities change as one ages can make a son or daughter much more effective in dealing with the needs of an aging parent.

On the professional front, individuals who are familiar with developmental stages have an advantage with workforce positions that emphasize human services. For example, background in developmental stage theory can make child care strategies more effective and efficient. Knowing the stages of grief can help in any position that involves health care delivery. Recognizing moral development differences can make you sturdier with regard to "doing the right thing" when confronted with professional moral and ethical dilemmas.

Chapter

◀Sensation▶

Human beings (and all animals) need certain information to survive and thrive. We need to be able to find the edge of a cliff, feel the temperature of the air, taste the bitterness of a particular poisonous plant, and detect the presence or absence of other creatures. This is the job of our senses: to take the world around us and turn it into neural signals inside our bodies. This process of sensation relies on several physiological systems that translate (or transduce) different kinds of energy. As you apply the concepts in this chapter, you will take the first steps in understanding how these systems prepare us to live in the vast and ever-changing world around us.

▼Exercise 6.1 CROSSING THE THRESHOLD
APPLY: Classify

Our senses provide the information that enables us to detect the presence of objects and then to distinguish different objects from each other. Each sense organ has the job of detecting the presence of a particular kind of energy (light, chemical, sound) and differentiating among different levels of that type of energy. We call the minimum amount of energy that the sense organ can detect the *detection threshold* or *absolute threshold*. The *difference threshold* or *just noticeable difference (jnd)* is the smallest change in energy that the sense organ can perceive; the amount of change needed to tell that two things are different. We use these abilities constantly as we perform our everyday tasks. There is also debate about how much we rely on information that is below our ability to detect. Energy that cannot be detected by a sense organ is called *subliminal* or *subthreshold*.

For each of the situations below, identify which of the following concepts is necessary to complete the task successfully: absolute threshold, difference threshold, or subthreshold. Then relate examples from your daily life to illustrate each of these concepts.

- A woman preparing for a trip to Mexico tries to learn Spanish using a "Learn While You Sleep" tape. _____

- A sentry on night duty notices a very soft noise and calls out for the thief to "Halt!" _____

- A father takes his children to the playground. During the visit, a child starts to cry. Without looking, the father can tell that it is not his child's cry.

- There is a sale on 5-pound prepackaged bags of russet potatoes. In order to make sure that you get the most for your money, you pick up several to see which is the heaviest.

- You help your friend look for her contact lens on her white kitchen floor.

- A music group records the phrase "Buy our tapes" backwards in one of their songs.

- It is late at night and you are trying to go to bed without waking your roommate. You want to find your favorite nightwear without turning on the light. After carefully and quietly opening your dresser drawer, you reach in and try to distinguish it from the four other things that are in the drawer.

- You are one of the judges in a chili-tasting contest and are trying to select the winner of the "Hottest Chili" award.

- In that same chili-tasting contest, you are asked to try to identify which of the chili samples contains cinnamon.

Your examples:

Absolute threshold: _____

Difference threshold: _____

Subthreshold: _____

After completing this exercise, you should be able to:

- define and differentiate among absolute threshold, difference threshold, and subthreshold.

- determine which type of threshold is being used to complete some everyday tasks successfully.

- apply threshold concepts to daily activities.

▼ Exercise 6.2   OCCUPATIONAL DESIGN

PART 1: ANALYZE: Reason

Humans differ in the quality of their sensory abilities. Whether by variations in genetic endowment or by deficits caused by environmental damage, human sensory abilities differ from person to person. These abilities also vary over time for each individual; when you catch a cold, for example, several of your senses are affected. Your stuffy nose and head cold may prevent you from smelling, may flatten the taste of your food, and may even interfere with your ability to maintain your balance. We also are subject to a decline in the acuteness of abilities as we age.

This exercise will cause you to think about how the range of sensory abilities could influence a person's choice of career—even your own. For example, think about the unique blend of sensory abilities that would be required for a successful career as a trapeze artist. The ideal combination of sensory abilities that would enable the trapeze artist to soar is reflected in the accompanying Sensory Profile of a Trapeze Artist. The senses of vision, touch, and balance would need to be especially acute. Hearing could be average because trapeze artists rely somewhat less on hearing. To perform their jobs, they really do not rely at all on taste or smell. Finally, a reduced capacity to transmit pain would probably enable longer hours of practice and performance without distraction, although this diminished ability could pose some danger for the artist who might not recognize or attend to serious injury.

Sensory Profile of a Trapeze Artist

	Diminished Abilities	Average Abilities	Heightened Abilities
Vision			X
Hearing		X	
Smell	X		
Touch			X
Taste	X		
Pain	X		
Balance			X

Consider the three occupational choices of garbage collector, dessert chef, and college professor. Construct your version of an ideal sensory profile for each job and explain your answer. (See Answer Key.)

Sensory Profile of a Garbage Collector

	Diminished Abilities	Average Abilities	Heightened Abilities
Vision			
Hearing			
Smell			
Touch			
Taste			
Pain			
Balance			

Explanation:

_____

_____

_____

Sensory Profile of a Dessert Chef

	Diminished Abilities	Average Abilities	Heightened Abilities
Vision			
Hearing			
Smell			
Touch			
Taste			
Pain			
Balance			

Explanation:

_____

_____

_____

Sensory Profile of a College Professor

	Diminished Abilities	Average Abilities	Heightened Abilities
Vision			
Hearing			
Smell			
Touch			
Taste			
Pain			
Balance			

Explanation:

_____

_____

_____

PART 2: EVALUATION: Justify

Consider the following sensory profile:

Sensory Profile

	Diminished Abilities	Average Abilities	Heightened Abilities
Vision		X	
Hearing		X	
Smell	X		
Touch			X
Taste	X		
Pain		X	
Balance			X

For what occupation might such an individual be well equipped? Why? _____

_____

_____

_____

Some jobs demand far more obvious abilities than others do. However, this exercise does suggest that our sensory abilities may play a subtle role in shaping our future choices.

After completing this exercise, you should be able to:

- use graphic strategies for communicating simple relationships.

- recognize that jobs vary in their sensory requirements.

- identify situations in which sensory deficits may confer performance advantages.

- offer plausible explanations for proposed sensory profiles.

- anticipate the kind of sensory profile that might be involved in your own occupational future.

▼Exercise 6.3   REACH OUT AND TOUCH SOMEONE

CREATE: Imagine

Think for a minute about how we communicate. Most of the time we use words, and although we write and read those words, much of our daily communication relies on speaking and hearing them. Talking is fast, easy and, with technology, almost unlimited by distance. About 20 years ago, there was a long-running and very successful ad campaign that encouraged people to use the telephone to "reach out and touch someone," by calling long-distance to talk with friends and family. Although the ad talked about touching, talking requires that we detect sound, the sense organ we use is the ear, and the instrument that allows us to do this long-distance is the phone. What would happen, however, if we actually did rely on touch to communicate? Communication would have an entirely different set of behaviors and requirements, because the skin detects a different kind of energy than does the ear. Using what you know about the sense of touch, try to invent a way to communicate using this sense. The following questions will help you think about the issues involved.

What sensations can the skin detect? _____

_____

_____

_____

How might you use the skin's sensory abilities to "talk"? (If you need an idea, think about individuals who have lost the ability to hear or see; how do they communicate?)

_____

_____

_____

What form might long-distance communication take and what kind of instrument might you use? _____

_____

_____

_____

After completing this exercise, you should be able to:

- discuss the skin's ability to sense pressure, pain, warmth, and cold.

- recognize the relationship between the energy that a sense organ can detect and the way that sense organ can be used to communicate.

- invent a novel form of long-distance communication using your knowledge of touch.

▼Exercise 6.4   IT'S A MATTER OF TASTE

CREATE: Design

As you learned in Chapter 1, Thinking Critically with Psychological Science, the scientific method is a process. You ask a question, design an experiment to find the answer, and find that often the answer leads to more questions. The result of this process is an ever-changing, and more accurate, understanding of the world around us and within us.

One area in which a fairly major shift in our understanding of how a sense organ works is the area of taste. You are probably familiar with the "tongue map" theory of taste. This theory suggests that specific areas of the tongue are sensitive to specific tastes: The back of the tongue senses bitter tastes; the sides and middle, sweet and sour; and the tip, salty. You may be surprised to find that this "map" is not included in your textbook. Modern research studies have demonstrated that this map is not accurate; rather, there are receptors for each taste all over the tongue.

Design an experiment in which you test a component of either the "tongue map" theory of taste or the idea that each of the four basic taste sensations can be detected all over the tongue. You don't need to test the whole theory; rather, decide on a single question that has variables that are easy to define operationally.

What is your hypothesis? _____

What is/are your independent variable(s)? _____

How would you define it/them operationally? _____

What is/are your dependent variable(s)? _____

How would you define it/them operationally? _____

Briefly describe the design of your experiment:

_____

_____

_____

What are some things you will need to be careful to control if you conduct this experiment? (Hint: What about the subjects or variables could change the results of your experiment?) _____

_____

_____

_____

If practical, why not conduct your experiment and bring the results to class? Even better, why not work on this exercise in groups or as a class and conduct the experiment together as a lab. Explore and have fun!

After completing this exercise, you should be able to:

- create a specific hypothesis giving a theory of taste.

- identify the independent and dependent variables within that hypothesis.

- operationalize variables.

- design control procedures to eliminate alternative explanations for your findings.

▼Exercise 6.5   PARTS IS PARTS

ANALYZE: Infer

Remember the last time you walked by one of those perfume testers in the mall, or opened the container that had been sitting in the back of the fridge for two weeks too long, and were overwhelmed by the smell? What about the time you were trying to study and the music down the hall was so loud you couldn't hear yourself think? How about those psychedelic plaid pants from the 1970s that your Uncle Frank insists on wearing for special occasions; you probably wish you didn't have to see those. And who wants to taste those nasty cough syrups? There are always times in our lives when we would rather our senses didn't transduce signals from the environment quite so successfully. It would be much easier if we didn't have to attend to all those inconvenient or uncomfortable signals. But what would be the negative consequences of turning off each sense's ability to transduce energy from the environment? You might not have to smell the moldy leftovers, but you also wouldn't be able to smell Mormor's Swedish coffee cake. No loud music, but no soft whispers of love.

Using the chart below, list the type of energy from the environment that the sense organ transduces to create the sensation, and identify three positive and negative consequences of turning off that sense organ. If you had to pick, which one would you turn off and why?

Sensation	Energy	Positive Consequences	Negative Consequences
Vision			
Hearing			
Smell			
Touch			
Taste			

After completing this exercise, you should be able to:

- identify the energy detected by each sense organ.

- describe the ways in which such detection is painful or inconvenient.

- articulate the value of the information detected by the various sense organs.

▼Exercise 6.6   DO YOU HEAR WHAT I HEAR?

EVALUATE: Take Perspective

Cochlear implants provide a potentially viable solution to problems surrounding hearing loss or total deafness. These devices use existing nerves and electronic signals to override damaged auditory nerves and restore some level of hearing to the recipient. Recipients of cochlear implants often show a variety of improvements in their hearing ability, including the ability to hear more easily and understand speech so they are able to listen to music and use a standard telephone. At first glance, it might appear that this would be a widely embraced technological and medical advance. However, as it has become more readily available, this technology has generated serious debate in the deaf community.

Many deaf people do not see being deaf as a handicap as it does not impact their ability to live a productive and full life. Additionally, the deaf culture is a powerful and significant subculture of American society, much like being Hispanic or Chinese-American, and members of this community are proud of this cultural identity and insulted by the intimation that deafness must be corrected or treated. Additionally, there are questions about both the safety and efficacy of the cochlear implant process. The surgery can destroy any remaining functioning auditory nerves near the surgical site, meaning that the person undergoing the implant procedure could lose the natural hearing they do have. Cochlear implants also fail, leaving a person in need of additional surgery and with, at best, no improvement in his/her hearing and often with less hearing than was present before the surgery.

Imagine you are considering cochlear implant surgery for yourself. How would you weigh the above considerations? What would be the questions you would ask before making your decision?

_____

_____

_____

Now imagine you are making this decision for your child. This question often creates conflicts between hearing and deaf parents, because deaf parents generally wish to raise their children in the deaf culture while hearing parents who live outside of this culture often want the surgery to correct or improve what they perceive as a handicap. Would you ask different questions or consider different issues? Why or why not?

_____

_____

_____

After completing this exercise, you should be able to:

- understand how point-of-view influences a moral or ethical position.
- describe risks and benefits associated with cochlear implant surgery.

▼Exercise 6.7 THE EYES HAVE IT

UNDERSTAND: Observe

Most of us take vision for granted, going through our lives depending on the accurate transduction of light into form, color, and movement. Imagine how your daily life might be different if something happened to change the way you experience your visual world. How would you adapt and how long would it take?

Select an activity that you can perform safely (with a partner) even with your eyes closed. Maybe you could play catch with something soft, fold laundry, put away the dishes, water the plants, or walk the dog. First, perform the activity with both eyes open. Then try covering one eye with a patch (be careful not to put pressure on the eye) and perform the activity again. After this, try the activity completely blindfolded. If you wear corrective lenses, why not try removing them? Finally, if you have access to upside-down goggles, try your activity while wearing them.

- What differences did you note in your ability to judge the shape, distance, speed, and direction of the objects with which you were working? _____

_____

- How did your attention change or focus differently in each situation? _____

_____

- Which situation was the most difficult for you? Practice doing your activity several times under these most difficult circumstances. Did you adapt? How long did it take? _____

_____

- Compare your answers with your classmates to see if their experiences differed from yours. If so, see if you can find patterns to the differences. Are some activities easier to perform completely blindfolded than with one eye covered?

After completing this exercise, you should be able to:

- describe accurately an activity and the aspects of vision that are involved in that activity.

- discuss how changes in vision influence the completion of a particular activity.

- identify which aspects of vision rely on binocular vision and which are monocular.

- compare your experience with those of your classmates.

- appreciate the complex role that vision plays in everyday activities.

THE PSYCHOLOGY ADVANTAGE

What exactly is the advantage of understanding about sensation and how the brain takes energy from the world and turns it into signals we can process? At least part of the answer to this question is obvious: knowing what energy we transduce and understanding which sense organs process that information can give us some control over how we perceive our world. By attending to specific clues in our environment, we can intentionally exercise more processing power to acquire more information or appreciate the results of the transduction. If there are sensory systems that don't work effectively, we are better equipped to enhance their function or substitute other kinds of information.

However, other parts of this answer are probably less obvious. There is a growing branch of psychology, sometimes called engineering psychology, in which psychologists use their expertise to help design or redesign objects to work most effectively with human functions. Sometimes these designs are as simple as more effective workstations or better wheelchair designs, but sometimes they include things like communications systems. Imagine a product like the Apple Watch being developed without the knowledge of detection and difference thresholds for vision and touch, or speech and voice recognition systems that don't take into consideration the need to distinguish the important signals in a noisy background. How many times have you been on your phone or trying to listen to music in a noisy environment? Engineering psychologists seek to solve this and other problems involving optimal function of the senses.

Chapter

◀ Perception ▶

Psychologist William James believed that the world starts out as a "blooming, buzzing confusion" for the newborn. Perception is the process by which we work to make sense of what can be a confusing array of sensations. Using expectations and experiences to help select, organize, and interpret important sensations, we turn the world around us into a meaningful, and meaning-filled, place.

▼ Exercise 7.1 CLIFF HANGERS

PART 1: UNDERSTAND: Explain

Evidence suggests that the ability to perceive depth is at least partly innate. Human infants less than a month old will turn away from objects with trajectories that would hit them, but they will not turn away from objects with trajectories that are angled away from them. In addition, human infants between 6 and 14 months (as well as day-old goats, newly hatched chicks, and young kittens) will stop when approaching a visual cliff (a drop-off covered by a stable, yet transparent, material). Even coaxing from parents is not enough to convince most of them to venture out "into space."

Identify two possible cues that the infants (and goats, chicks, and kittens) might be using to perceive the drop-off. Are the clues monocular or binocular?

1. _____

2. _____

PART 2: CREATE: Design

Pick one of the possible cues you identified above. How might you test to see if this cue is being used to identify visual cliffs? Given what you know about human development, what would improve or increase this ability to detect visual cliffs?

_____

_____

_____

After completing this exercise, you should be able to:

- identify the binocular and monocular cues essential for depth perception.

- articulate two hypotheses about how infants might be using monocular or binocular cues to perceive depth.

- create appropriate experimental designs for evaluating these two hypotheses.

- discuss what factors might influence an infant's ability to use cues to perceive depth.

▼Exercise 7.2   THE BIG PICTURE

APPLY: Illustrate

Gestalt psychology offers principles of good form and rules for grouping stimuli. Typically these principles are illustrated using two-dimensional stimuli; lines and dots create images orchestrated to demonstrate specific effects. However, the Gestalt principles can also be seen in operation in three-dimensional dynamic forms, as this exercise will illustrate.

Let's start with a group performance such as the work that might be performed by a marching band during the half-time activities of a football game. Think about a marching band performance you have seen (or look one up on YouTube) and try to think of it as a demonstration of Gestalt principles of good form and grouping.

Figure-ground. Marching in front of the band and waving a baton, the drum major stands out from the rest of the band, enhanced by more dramatic costuming and a central position in relation to the other band members.

Proximity. Certain band members may cluster together, particularly when their assignment is to create a visual impact distinct from the rest of the band. The minimal distance maintained within the cluster enhances the crowd's perception that this subgroup is a unit by itself. This principle is apparent when band members must form a particular letter of the alphabet or some other visual design; their proximity helps us to perceive that design as distinct from the activities of the other subgroups on the field.

Similarity. Band uniforms, musical instruments, and choreographed marching enhance our perception of the band as a group or as subdivisions that form meaningful smaller groups.

Closure. Even though there are gaps between individuals and the shapes and images being formed on the field do not have closed and connected edges, we are readily able to identify our school mascot or the shape of the flag being formed by the band members. Additionally, when the music and movement stop, we see the performance as a completed experience.

Continuity / connectedness. As band members break into smaller marching groups to develop a distinctive formation, their movements relative to each other and to members of other groups will cause the crowd to perceive them as subgroups. For example, the horn section, moving clockwise in a circle, will be perceived as a whole group because their movements cause them to appear to be connected with one another. In contrast, the drum section, moving counterclockwise, will be perceived as a separate group.

Now it's your turn. Apply the design principles to either a football game or a ballet performance. (See Answer Key.)

Selected performance:

Figure-ground: _____

Proximity: _____

Similarity: _____

Closure: _____

Continuity / connectedness: _____

The principles of good form are readily apparent in virtually every aspect of life. However, we would be distracted if we constantly attended to the components of good design rather than to the overall form itself. Although this exercise generally empha-sizes principles applied to visual stimuli, we could illustrate the Gestalt ideas in other sensory modes (such as hearing or taste).

After completing this exercise, you should be able to:

- recognize that perceptual images can be analyzed into specific design principles.
- apply Gestalt principles to perceptual stimuli.
- identify other group performances that illustrate Gestalt principles.
- speculate about how the design principles work in sensory modes other than vision.

▼Exercise 7.3 CONTEXT CUES
APPLY: Solve

One of the many concepts that you have learned in this chapter is that perception involves the interpretation of stimuli and can be influenced by various internal factors (like expectations and beliefs), as well as by external factors (like perspective or envi-ronmental context). Predicting how ambiguous stimuli will be interpreted in the real world is tricky business, because the possibilities are almost as varied as the number of interpreters! Nevertheless, it is possible to *design* stimuli in such a way that there are limited, and predictable, interpretations. The reversible figure-ground picture of the

Science Source

vase versus royalty provides a good example. A person could see either the vase, the faces of Prince Philip and Queen Elizabeth II, or alternate between the two. Notice how when you attend to one aspect of the image, you can't technically "see" the other. By shifting your attention to a different element of the figure, a different perception will "pop," and you will no longer be able to see the original image. Perceptional organization means paying attention to one focal object at a time.

Using what you know about setting context, speculate about the conditions under which a person would see only the vase, only the faces, or would alternate between the two.

_____

_____

_____

After completing this exercise, you should be able to:

- recognize the role of context and expectation in the interpretation of ambiguous stimuli.

- describe situations in which the same stimulus would be perceived differently.

- use an understanding of perceptual processes to predict people's response to ambiguous stimuli.

▼Exercise 7.4   CHAOS CONTROL

ANALYZE: Relate

Perceptual processes help us to maintain a sense of stability and control in what could be perceived as a chaotic environment. Two processes—habituation and perceptual set—are especially important in promoting our adaptation to complex environments. *Habituation* allows us to disengage from environmental stimuli that are redundant (that is, they don't offer us new information) or become boring. This process frees us to "attend" and respond to changing elements in the environment. *Perceptual set* represents our formulation of expectations about how the physical world and its inhabitants will behave. From each experience we extract a meaningful pattern so we can predict that similar procedures and outcomes will be part of that experience in the future.

In this exercise, imagine that your perceptual skills of habituation and perceptual set are "broken." Identify five probable effects of this malfunction as you go about a regular school day. (Hint: You may find it helpful to remember some of your feelings and experiences while visiting a new place, where your awareness might be heightened and your expectations might be few.)

What kinds of effects could you anticipate if your perceptual skills malfunctioned?

1. _____

2. _____

3. _____

4. _____

5. _____

After completing this exercise, you should be able to:

- identify the role that habituation and perceptual set play in organizing chaotic environments.

- revisit routine behaviors to examine why they become routine.

- appreciate the efficiency of perceptual processes in attending to important stimuli and ignoring unimportant ones.

- use your imagination to envision life with perceptual impairments.

▼Exercise 7.5 THE CASE AGAINST ESP
EVALUATE: Assess

Extrasensory perception (ESP) is the ability to obtain information that is independent of the information received through hearing, vision, touch, taste, or smell. Such abilities—including clairvoyance, telepathy, and precognition—are popular in science fiction. In fact, according to a 2005 Gallup Poll, 73 percent of Americans believed that at least some ESP abilities were real. Do such abilities actually exist? The scientific community may not have delivered a final verdict, but most psychologists would say "no." Why would scientists who express pride in their open-mindedness seem to have such a closed mind when it comes to such mysteries of the universe? Psychologists believe that the absence of objective evidence weakens the claims that support ESP.

As shown in the chapter exploring brain function, our brains actively make sense of the stimulation from the environment. Sometimes our brains distort incoming sensations to produce more acceptable perceptions. This creativity is just one factor that encourages skeptical psychologists to disbelieve claims of supernatural knowledge. Most psychologists would insist that there is a compelling alternative explanation for events that might be mislabeled extrasensory perceptions.

For each of the experiences and examples listed below, identify how persuaded you are by the example that ESP has occurred. Rate your level of persuasion on a scale of 1 (not persuaded at all) to 6 (persuaded without a doubt). Then, try to identify a reasonable *alternative hypothesis* for each of the experiences listed.

Example	Rating	Alternative Hypothesis
You are driving along in your car and find yourself humming a pleasant tune. You turn on the radio and that very song comes on. You smile to yourself and think your ability to predict music on the radio is just a bit uncanny.		
Brenda prides herself on being able to predict the gender of unborn children. Expectant parents eagerly sought her predictions until newer, less fallible medical technologies displaced her skills.		
Eugene is one lucky guy. Almost every month he wins something in the state lottery. His friends believe he must be clairvoyant.		
Pat hates it when she gets those "ooky feelings." Her heart starts to race, and she knows something terrible has happened, sometimes to a loved one but most of the time to a stranger whose bad luck is reported on television.		
Bruce hardly studies at all, and he gets superb grades. He claims he has a special ability to predict the kinds of questions instructors will include on exams. He brags that this ability saves him hours of study and earns him nearly a 3.5 grade-point average.		
A magician claims he can identify the most pressing concerns among audience members. He asks each person to fill out an identical index card, stating his or her most serious worry of the moment. He collects the cards, raises one index card to his head, and—without reading the card—voices a specific concern. Then he asks, "Whose worry is this!" A shy woman in the middle of the room raises her hand and claims, "It's mine!" He examines the card to verify her claim. One by one, the magician then accurately identifies at least five more pressing concerns for astonished members of the audience.		

Compare your answers with those of your classmates. Were there any similarities in your initial ratings? For which examples did you have the most trouble generating alternative hypotheses?

After completing this exercise, you should be able to:

- see the importance of objective evidence in challenging claims of ESP.

- identify how illusions can be used to create a powerful subjective argument for extrasensory perception.

- recognize how normal rates of occurrence of behavior influence reported successes of ESP.

- generate some alternative explanations for reported paranormal behaviors.

- understand why psychologists are skeptical of claims that cannot be verified objectively.

- justify saving your money rather than spending it on pseudoscientific claims.

▼Exercise 7.6   BREAKING THE CODE

EVALUATE: Critique

Magicians are masters of the principles of perception. They can be astonishing with tricks that involve "sleight of hand." How do they manage to make objects disappear? Produce rabbits out of hats? Pull a coin out of someone's ear? Magicians are particularly skilled at misdirecting attention. They know that human perceptual processes concentrate attention on a prominent "figure" against a backdrop referred to as "the ground." By violating figure-ground relationships, magicians are able to persuade you that they can accomplish impossible feats.

Magicians are not just skilled manipulators. They also consider themselves to be part of an important guild—the guild of magicians. Magicians don't give away their secrets. They are keenly aware that once you know how a trick works, the magical properties fade. However, the freedom of information on the internet makes keeping magicians secrets nearly impossible.

Find a magic trick about sleight of hand on the internet. With confidence in the properties of physics that objects don't really disappear, see if you can figure out how manipulation of the figure-ground relationship takes place.

_____

_____

_____

After completing this exercise, you should be able to:

- articulate how figure-ground relationships organize attention.

- propose alternatives for how a sleight-of-hand magic trick works.

- assess the effectiveness of the magic hypothesis.

▼Exercise 7.7   ASSEMBLING THE ASSEMBLY LINE

CREATE: Plan

A large manufacturing company is working to ensure that its new gidgit line has the appropriate quality control. (Gidgits are block-like toys with a very complex shape.) They hire inspectors to look at the items as they roll by on a conveyer belt and to pull off the ones that are not made properly. Using what you know about visual perception, how would you set up the situation so that the inspectors' jobs would be easiest? What could you do to facilitate their recognition of the correct shape and/or their comparison of gidgits?

_____

_____

_____

_____

After completing this exercise, you should be able to:

- describe the perceptual task involved in a real-life scenario.

- use an understanding of the visual system to identify essential elements necessary for completing the described visual perception task.

- manipulate the physical environment to facilitate successful completion of the given perceptual task.

THE PSYCHOLOGY ADVANTAGE

In a very pragmatic sense, knowledge of perception and the perceptual processes inherent in the human brain allow us to create an environment in which we can focus on the important things in our workplace and home. Gestalt principles, for example, may allow you to organize your counter, junk drawer, or desktop at work so you can see and identify objects easily and quickly note what is and isn't present. Understanding signal detection theory can help you organize your auditory world so that the important things don't get lost in the noise.

Österreichische Galerie Belvedere, Vienna, Austria / Bridgeman Images

The beauty of life, however, isn't all in the practical. These principles of cognitive organization that we call perception allow us to create rich, beautiful, and coherent works of performing and fine arts. Understanding them gives us a richer appreciation of the aesthetics of performance. Take a look at Gustav Klimt's painting "The Kiss." It is beautiful to look at, but when you look closely—even in the black-and-white version shown below—you can see how the use of similar shapes and shades defines the figures rather than true outlines (similarity and proximity); that the figures, while obscured, are still perceived as complete individuals (closure); and that the contrast between the static background and the movement created by the shapes and shades in the clothes of the individuals make those individuals the clear focus of the painting (figure-ground). The same principles work for music and most other art forms we appreciate and enjoy; understanding them makes us better artists and appreciators of art.

Finally, understanding how our minds give meaning to the world around us puts psychologists one step ahead of those who want to take advantage of the human inclination to see patterns, even where none exist. There are plenty of charlatans and misguided individuals who make incredible claims for everything from cures for cancer to ways to pick the next winning lottery numbers. Being able to identify alternative explanations for ESP and by understanding where patterns are meaningful and where they are illusory will make you less likely to be a victim of these kinds of scams.

Chapter

◀Learning▶

The basic ideas in the learning traditions of psychology can be difficult to master if your view of learning is too narrow. It is relatively easy to think of learning as only the kind of "book learning" we do in school. In psychology, learning generally refers to the learning of behaviors that help us survive better in some environment. The "learning" associated with the acquisition of concepts or ideas is more likely to be found in the traditions of memory research, which we will explore in Chapter 9.

There are three dominant traditions of learning theory in psychology. Ivan Pavlov accidentally discovered the principles of classical conditioning when he was examining the digestive processes of dogs. His approach helps us understand how we learn to attach significance to events associated with automatic, reflexive responses. Operant conditioning, attributed to B. F. Skinner, switches the emphasis from reflex-based learning to learning that is shaped by consequences. Observational learning grew out of Albert Bandura's experiment in which children imitated aggressive responses after seeing an adult model interact aggressively with a bobo doll. The exercises in this chapter differentiate the three kinds of learning and clarify some concepts that are especially difficult to master.

▼Exercise 8.1 POWERFUL CONSEQUENCES

OBSERVE: Translate

In operant conditioning, the consequences that follow a behavior determine whether or not that behavior recurs. We tend to repeat things that make us feel good (principles involving *reinforcement*), avoid things that make us feel bad (principle of *punishment*), and disengage from behaviors that have no impact (principle of *extinction*).

Any time consequences *reinforce* a behavior, it will be strengthened. For example, a builder who wants to reinforce a wall to make it stronger may add another stud, and a tailor who needs to reinforce a seam will stitch over the area again. Similarly, reinforced behavior is more likely to occur in the future. When you see the term *reinforcement*, expect that the target behavior will get stronger or increase in intensity.

* *Positive reinforcement* is relatively straightforward. When a good consequence follows some performance, you are more likely to repeat that performance in order to capture more of the good consequences that follow it. For instance, if you study hard for a test and receive an *A* for your efforts, you will probably expend the same energies on your next test because you have received this positive reinforcement.

- *Negative reinforcement* is a little trickier. Negative reinforcement is often confused with punishment, but they are not the same. In negative reinforcement situations, the target behavior is the one you can perform to help you escape some bad circumstance. When a behavior is negatively reinforced, the behavior has helped you escape some pain, some embarrassment, or some other negative situation. For example, if you live in a rainy climate, you may routinely carry an umbrella to prevent getting soaked by the rain. Your habit of carrying an umbrella would be negatively reinforced: You escape an unpleasant outcome by remembering to bring the tool that will keep you dry. When you see the term *negative reinforcement*, try to identify what is negative about the target situation. Will a specified behavior allow you to escape or avoid the unfavorable circumstance? If so, that escape behavior will be negatively reinforced. We rarely enjoy being in uncomfortable or painful situations. This explains why negative reinforcement situations are such powerful incentives to strengthen behaviors that will allow us to escape.

- *Punishment* tends to reduce the frequency of the behavior it follows. However, almost any parent can tell you that the effects of punishment vary. To be effective in reducing undesirable behavior, punishment should be swift, consistent, and sufficiently strong. Coordinating punishing consequences to meet those criteria can be a challenge. Even when punishment works, punishing practices may have undesirable side effects. For example, children associate the punisher with pain and may dislike or avoid the punisher.

- *Extinction* is also a process that reduces the occurrence of a behavior. When a behavior meets with no consequence, there is no incentive to continue the behavior. Although extinction is effective in reducing certain behaviors, the process may take a very long time.

Here is a fairly simple way to decide which of the four principles of operant conditioning are at work. Think of it as a simple multiplication problem between the *object* of the consequence, which can be good (+), bad (−), or nonexistent (0), and the *action* of the consequence, which can be getting something (+), having something taken away (−), or no action (0).

Reinforcement: Behavior is likely to increase when the outcome of the behavior is positive. In math, there are two ways to get positive numbers when multiplying; you can multiply two positive numbers OR you can multiply two negative numbers. Both yield positive products. The same is true here.

- When a behavior is followed by getting (+) something good (+), it is like multiplying two positive numbers; the result is *positive reinforcement*. The behavior is likely to increase.

- When a behavior is followed by having something bad (−) taken away (−), it is like multiplying two negative numbers. *Negative reinforcement* is also likely to increase the occurrence of the behavior in the future.

Punishment: When the outcome of a behavior is negative, the behavior is likely to decrease in the future. This can happen by either getting (+) something bad (−) OR by having something good (+) taken away (−). Both yield negative products and the behavior is likely to decrease. *Note:* Punishment is risky business. To ensure effectiveness, it must be done quickly, consistently, and with the proper intensity.

Extinction: When a behavior has no meaningful consequence (0), it is also likely to decrease in the future. This can happen either when the nature of the consequence is neutral (0) or when there is no noticeable action/outcome (0). The product of anything including zero is zero; the behavior is likely to go away.

The following scenarios describe some behaviors and their consequences. Your task is to apply the principles of operant conditioning to predict whether the targeted behavior (the underlined one) will reoccur. Read the short scenario, focusing on the underlined behavior, and identify whether the consequence for the person performing the behavior was good (+), bad (−), or none (0). Then specify whether the targeted behavior is likely to increase (↑) or decrease (↓) in the future.

	Object and Action of the Consequence	Likelihood of the Behavior Recurring	Operant Principle Illustrated
Example: A young man notices his neighbor's trash can still out by the curb. He brings it up and sets it next to the neighbor's garage. The next day, the neighbor comes by with homemade cookies.	Retrieving a trash can (+) and getting a cookie (+)	Increases	Positive Reinforcement
a. A student volunteers to answer a tough question in class, and the teacher comments favorably on the quality of the student's contribution.			
b. A wife brings home flowers to her husband because of the special dinner he had cooked for her.			
c. A child is sent to his room with no supper after presenting a bad report card.			
d. Dad and tot enter the check-out lane of the supermarket. When the child screams for candy, the dad pops a sucker in her mouth to quiet her down.			
e. A child spills milk all over the supper table, and Mom (having had a very bad day) swoops the child up from the high chair and spanks him.			
f. A student has a terrible headache after an intense preparation period for a test. He takes two aspirin, hoping to make it go away.			
g. Two children, who usually spend most of their time fighting, finally play peaceably over a coloring book. Dad peeks in and sighs, "At last, they are getting along." He returns to work without saying anything to them.			
h. As a spoiled child is being driven by a fast-food restaurant, she begins screaming that she must have french fries or she won't survive. The parents surrender and drive in for a large supply.			

Continued

	Object and Action of the Consequence	Likelihood of the Behavior Recurring	Operant Principle Illustrated
i. A teenager <u>whines</u> about having nothing to do. Dad gives him a lecture about all the stuff in his room and the good old days when he, the father, didn't have all that stuff but still managed to be happy.			
j. A terrorist applies an electric current to the feet of a spy to make her <u>confess</u>. She tells him everything she knows.			

After completing this exercise, you should be able to:

- describe the four principles of operant behavior.
- explain how reinforcement processes increase the likelihood of a behavior's recurrence.
- distinguish between negative reinforcement and punishment.
- demonstrate effective problem-solving processes to make accurate predictions.
- see how these principles might make you better at predicting behaviors in your own life.

▼Exercise 8.2   THE CLASSICAL CONNECTION

APPLY: Classify

In most classical conditioning examples, we should be able to identify an *involuntary response* at the core of the learning process. In Pavlov's original conditioning experiment, the dog's salivary reflex was the involuntary response. When food is presented to a hungry dog, the dog will salivate. This connection is natural and unlearned, or unconditioned. It is the brain's way of readying the digestive tract, and it assists in our survival. We might say that this is a "hard-wired" feature of dog design. Food is an *unconditioned stimulus (UCS)* and the salivation is an *unconditioned response (UCR)*—a natural and unlearned one.

If you present a neutral stimulus—one that has no particular meaning, such as a bell—to a dog just prior to presenting the food, and if you present this pair of stimuli often enough, you are likely to see a new learned connection develop. The bell will come to signify that the food is on its way. Because the bell had no effect initially, the meaning of the bell had to be conditioned. Therefore, it is called the *conditioned stimulus (CS)*. When the researcher has successfully conditioned the dog to respond to the bell, the dog will salivate in the absence of food. This salivation is called the *conditioned response (CR)*. Note that the unconditioned response and the conditioned response are virtually the same. They are likely to differ only in intensity. (Even dogs are smart enough to know you shouldn't eat a bell. . . .)

Now it's your turn. Four examples of classical conditioning are outlined in the following paragraphs. Each describes a situation in which an unconditioned stimulus, an unconditioned response, a conditioned stimulus, and a conditioned response occur. Can you identify the components in each example?

The Troublesome Shower

Martin likes to take a shower in the men's locker room after working out. During one such shower, he hears someone flushing a nearby toilet. Suddenly, boiling-hot water rushes out of the showerhead, causing Martin serious discomfort. As he continues the shower, he hears another toilet flush and immediately jumps out from under the showerhead.

What is the unconditioned response (UCR)? (The UCR is the *involuntary, "hard-wired" reaction* that does not need to be learned.) _____

What is the unconditioned stimulus (UCS)? (The UCS is the event that automatically *elicits the involuntary response.*) _____

What is the conditioned response (CR)? (The CR is the new behavior that is *acquired through learning.*) _____

What is the conditioned stimulus (CS)? (The CS is the event that *takes on new meaning through conditioning.*) _____

The Water Show

Jeanette was happy when she heard about her family's plan to go to a water sports show. Then she heard the weather report, which predicted temperatures exceeding 100 degrees. Jeanette suspected that the weather would be hard to bear, but she went to the show. As she watched the water skiers perform taxing routines to the blaring organ music, she got more and more sweaty and uncomfortable. Eventually, she fainted from the heat. After the family outing, Jeanette could never again hear organ music without feeling a little dizzy.

Unconditioned response (UCR): _____

Unconditioned stimulus (UCS): _____

Conditioned response (CR): _____

Conditioned stimulus (CS): _____

The Trouble with Tuna

Brian was really looking forward to lunch. His mother had prepared a tuna salad sandwich. Unfortunately, the mayonnaise she used had been left out too long and was tainted. Not long after eating, Brian felt extremely nauseated and had to rush to the bathroom. Thereafter, the mere mention of a tuna sandwich would send Brian scurrying to the bathroom with a rolling stomach.

UCR: _____

UCS: _____

CR: _____

CS: _____

Captain Hook's Time Problem

Captain Hook had a nasty encounter with a crocodile in Never-Never Land. As a result of the battle, he lost his hand to the croc, which also swallowed an alarm clock. Fortunately for Hook, the loud ticking warns him of the hungry croc's approach. Unfortunately for Hook, any clock's ticking now ushers in a full-blown anxiety attack. (Be careful here.)

UCR: _____

UCS: _____

CR: _____

CS: _____

After completing this exercise, you should be able to:

- isolate the behaviors involved in the classical conditioning process.

- relate the appropriate terms to the conditioning examples.

- recognize how classical conditioning procedures produce learned responses.

- use classical conditioning terminology to describe the process of learning.

- identify the involuntary response that is the origin of most classically conditioned responses.

- identify how classical conditioning processes can cause phobic reactions.

- describe how generalization extends the number of scary things that cause phobic reactions.

▼Exercise 8.3   CHEMICAL ENGINEERING

APPLY: Compare

Dr. Merrow, who teaches chemistry at the college level, reports being unhappy with how little her students read their assignments before classes. She has decided the solution is to turn to the old tried-and-true method of quizzing but wonders what the most effective strategy would be. She has heard that schedules of reinforcement produce different rates of responding and wonders what strategy would be the most effective. First, label each example with the schedule of reinforcement that most applies. Then determine which of the following conditions would make the most sense for producing the highest rates of responding among the students:

1. Require a quiz at the start of every class.

   _____

2. Require a quiz to be taken at any time online before each class starts.

   _____

3. Require a limited number of quizzes randomly throughout the semester.

   _____

4. Require a limited number of quizzes anytime before the end of the semester.

   _____

After completing this exercise, you should be able to:

- distinguish reinforcement from punishment conditions.

- recognize how individuals experience reinforcement variably from the same conditions.

- describe the effectiveness of various schedules of reinforcement.

- apply schedules of reinforcement to a common education problem.

▼Exercise 8.4   SELF-IMPROVEMENT REVISITED

ANALYZE: Contrast

Virtually everyone at some time or another attempts some self-improvement strategy. Maybe you are trying to lose the "freshman 15" or you want to stop smoking. Perhaps you've decided you need to reduce your speeding or the frequency with which you swear. Regardless of your objective, you have probably also experienced how incredibly hard it is to change behaviors that have become second nature.

In this exercise, revisit a behavior that you were unsuccessful in changing.

What was the target behavior? _____

What strategies did you attempt to change the behavior? _____

Now, let's reintroduce the different learning frameworks to understand why your plans went awry. Did the strategies for self-improvement you selected fit best with:

A. observational learning?
B. classical conditioning? or
C. operant conditioning?

Using language consistent with the framework, why did you fail? _____

_____

Finally, knowing what you know now, describe one thing you might do in each of the frameworks to promote a more successful intervention.

A. observational learning
B. classical conditioning
C. operant conditioning

_____

_____

_____

After completing this exercise, you should be able to:

- describe fundamental types of learning that influence behavior.

- analyze why behavior change plans aren't often effective.

▼Exercise 8.5 THE DISCRIMINATING DACHSHUND
ANALYZE: Infer

Mike and Laura's pet dachshund, Greta, loved to play fetch. While playing fetch one afternoon with a tennis ball, she accidently picked up the ball after it had, unfortunately, landed in a fire ant hill. Needless to say, Greta's mouth got many painful bites. From that point on, Greta avoided tennis balls and would only play with soccer balls. She also avoided any ball that was the same size as a tennis ball or smaller. How would Pavlov and Skinner each have explained this outcome?

Pavlov's explanation: _____

_____

Skinner's explanation: _____

_____

After completing this exercise, you should be able to:

- use learning theory terminology accurately.

- apply classical conditioning to explain avoidance behavior.

- use operant conditioning to explain avoidance behavior.

- discuss discriminating responses in both frameworks.

▼Exercise 8.6 LITTLE ALBERT REVISITED

EVALUATE: Take Perspective

Do you remember the story of poor Little Albert? Psychologist John B. Watson used the principles of classical conditioning to create Albert's fear response to a white rat (which later generalized to other white furry things). Watson's explanation of this outcome was that pairing the rat (the CS) with the loud noise (the UCS) resulted in a fear response to the rat (CR). However, Little Albert's experience with the rat was punishing so he wants to avoid encounters with the rat. Observational learning requires a bit of a stretch. For Little Albert to acquire a fear response to a rat through observation would require his observing others responding fearfully to a rat rather than being directly frightened by the loud noise. However, Little Albert could still be engaging in observational learning. In this case, he could learn through observation how to make little children cry.

All three have implications for treatment of the assorted problems that this scenario produces.

Fear of Rats

What would someone attempting to treat Little Albert's fear of rats do if she or he believed that classical conditioning provided the best explanation for the cause of the fear? How would it be different from the treatment used by someone who believed that the fear was the result of Little Albert's punishing experience with the rat? Can you use the appropriate terminology to explain what the treatment procedure might be?

_____

_____

_____

_____

_____

_____

Maltreatment of Children

Historians can make the case that the fear-generating protocol was abusive to Little Albert. Suppose that early exposure contributed to Little Albert growing up as someone who took pleasure in harming little children. What are the treatment implications for Little Albert as an adult?

_____

_____

No one knows what happened to Little Albert, although historians discuss the possibilities from time to time. What do you think might have happened to Little Albert's level of fear without intervention?

_____

_____

After completing this exercise, you should be able to:

- describe the original outcome of Watson's Little Albert conditioning study.
- suggest a treatment strategy that follows logically from a classical conditioning approach to fear.
- propose a treatment strategy that exemplifies operant conditioning logic.
- discuss observational learning and its impact in shaping abusive behavior.
- provide a plausible prediction about what happens to conditioned fear over time without intervention.

▼Exercise 8.7   REINFORCING RHYMES
CREATE: Invent

Learning principles can be serious business. Companies use them to determine effective pay schedules, parents use them to direct the behavior of children, and police officers use them to get you to obey the speed limit.

Learning about learning principles doesn't have to be so serious. These principles can be found (or inserted) in the most unexpected places. Common nursery rhymes can illustrate basic learning concepts. Rewrite a nursery rhyme so that it illustrates one or more of these principles. If no traditional nursery rhyme appeals, write your own. You might even feature your instructor or a classmate as the star of your rhyme.

Revised examples:

Mary Had a Little Lamb

Mary had a little lamb;
She wanted to teach it tricks.
Stay, come, and go
Were easy, you know,
When she gave it a peppermint stick.

There Was an Old Woman Who Lived in a Shoe

There was an old woman who lived in a shoe.
She had so many children she didn't know what to do.
Should she punish the bad or reinforce the good?
Reinforcement works best, if only she would.

Original examples:

Bountiful Bribery

Dr. Jones was a tough nut to crack.
His students felt put on the rack.
They finally agreed
That all would succeed
If they gave him his office key back!

Negative Reinforcement Rag

Tom was a bit of a heel.
His friends all knew he would squeal.
When the police got tough
And threatened rough stuff,
He spilled all he knew to appeal.

_____

_____

_____

_____

_____

After completing this exercise, you should be able to:

- recognize that examples of learning principles are widespread.

- create a plausible, but rhyming example of a learning mechanism.

- have others recognize your learning expertise.

▼Exercise 8.8   A WORKING HYPOTHESIS

CREATE: Design

Corporations often hire industrial-organizational (I/O) psychologists to help solve management and production problems. Learning principles are often part of the solution that I/O psychologists develop to help the employer.

The owner of ROYAS-R-US decides to employ you (as a budding I/O psychologist) to ensure that its workers make the most royas possible. The employer wants to know whether paying people for piecework or by weekly salary would be more effective in the production of royas. Design an experiment that will address this question and state the hypothesis in terms of reinforcement schedules.

Hypothesis: _____

Independent variable(s): _____

Dependent variables(s): _____

Extraneous variables for which you would control: _____

Basic experimental protocol: _____

Potential ethical concerns: _____

After completing this exercise, you should be able to:

- use experimental methodology to propose a solution for a corporation's production concerns.

- apply terminology regarding schedules of reinforcement to production.

- speculate about current ethical controls on research activities.

- explore possible job elements of I/O psychology.

THE PSYCHOLOGY ADVANTAGE

As you probably noticed, both as you studied the chapter and worked on these exercises, there is a lot of talk of parenting in the context of learning principles. And parenting *is* one of the most relevant "real life" places where understanding learning can make life easier. Knowing how to make undesirable behaviors decrease and how to encourage wanted behaviors can make parenting (and being a child!) less stressful and help encourage strong familial bonds of trust and respect. But parenting isn't the only place where this information is useful. Imagine how shaping behaviors in your workplace might be helpful. As a supervisor, you could effectively design reward systems to encourage positive productivity and cooperation, while as a team member or subordinate, you could behave in ways that would encourage sharing and cooperation among those with whom you work. Perhaps most important, however, understanding learning principles can give you the insight to change your own behavior. Want to quit smoking? Procrastinate less? Spend your money differently? With a good understanding of learning principles and the behaviors involved, the likelihood of successfully changing those behaviors significantly increases. Why not give it a try?

Chapter

◀ Memory ▶

Sometimes it feels like a precision instruction. Sometimes it feels like a dusty, locked file cabinet that has been undisturbed for years. Sometimes it yields up its contents only after we give up the pursuit. The human memory is a remarkable process whose secrets we have yet to understand in its entirety.

▼ Exercise 9.1 THANKS FOR THE MEMORY

PART 1: UNDERSTAND: Observe

Your psychology instructor probably will use objective testing (multiple-choice or true-false questions) as one way to determine whether you are learning effectively. At this point, we hope you have realized that this chapter on memory has information and suggests techniques you could apply to yourself to become a more efficient learner.

Read through the following strategies and compare them with your own practices for preparing for examinations in this class. For each strategy, circle the number that most closely corresponds to your present learning pattern. This inventory is uniquely your own; there won't be an answer in the back of the book for this exercise, but it may lead to improving your study habits.

Overlearning: Multiple Study Sessions

1 ———————— 2 ———————— 3 ———————— 4 ———————— 5

not at all characteristic
of my learning

very characteristic of
my learning

Active Practicing with the Material

1 ———————— 2 ———————— 3 ———————— 4 ———————— 5

not at all characteristic
of my learning

very characteristic of
my learning

Personal Elaboration of Meaning of the Material

1 ———————————— 2 ———————————— 3 ———————————— 4 ———————————— 5
not at all characteristic   very characteristic of
of my learning   my learning

Mnemonic Devices

1 ———————————— 2 ———————————— 3 ———————————— 4 ———————————— 5
not at all characteristic   very characteristic of
of my learning   my learning

Re-creating Learning Contexts

1 ———————————— 2 ———————————— 3 ———————————— 4 ———————————— 5
not at all characteristic   very characteristic of
of my learning   my learning

Anticipating Test Questions

1 ———————————— 2 ———————————— 3 ———————————— 4 ———————————— 5
not at all characteristic   very characteristic of
of my learning   my learning

Reducing Interference

1 ———————————— 2 ———————————— 3 ———————————— 4 ———————————— 5
not at all characteristic   very characteristic of
of my learning   my learning

PART 2: APPLY: Solve

Assuming that the principles of improving memory are accurate, which skills have you already developed reasonably well to support more effective long-term memory performance? _____

_____

_____

Which would be the most appropriate for you to develop in order to enhance your performance on objective tests? _____

_____

_____

Which skills would be more likely to result in a deeper understanding of the ideas you are trying to memorize? _____

_____

_____

What obstacles would you need to overcome to implement a more efficient system of study? _____

_____

_____

How motivated are you to make the changes that would be required to become a more efficient and effective memorizer? _____

_____

_____

After completing this exercise, you should be able to:

- identify the factors that account for effective long-term memory performance.

- evaluate your own strengths and weaknesses in long-term memory challenges.

- determine which memory improvement strategies are likely to produce more effective recall and learning.

- decide whether this issue is serious enough to prompt further problem-solving effort and personal change.

▼Exercise 9.2   STORY TIME

APPLY: Illustrate

Although there is no magic formula, there are techniques that can help people effectively remember important events and information. One of the most fun-filled of these techniques involves creating vivid stories that help organize words and ideas that need to be remembered. Vivid examples represent just one of many *mnemonics* that individuals can use as memory-enhancement aids.

Imagine that you are at a party that your significant other's parents are hosting to introduce you to the family. Needless to say, it is important to remember everyone's name. Once you are all seated at the restaurant, your friend introduces you to everyone. Going around the table, clockwise, you meet: Sally and Mike (the parents); Samantha (an aunt); Elaine, Vanessa, and Laura (sisters); Chris (an uncle); Melissa and John (grandparents); Larry (another uncle); and Tisha and Devon (Larry's children). Create a story that you can use to remember this horde of relatives' names. Test yourself two hours, one day, and five days after you create your story to see how many of the names and relationships you remember. If you didn't remember them all, what factors seemed to contribute to remembering the ones that you did remember?

_____

_____

_____

_____

_____

_____

_____

_____

After completing this exercise, you should be able to:

- describe organizing strategies to improve memory.

- exemplify creative storytelling as a mnemonic device.

- prepare effectively for your next social gathering.

▼Exercise 9.3   THE MAGNIFICENT SEVEN

PART 1: ANALYZE: Infer

Quickly! Name as many of the Seven Dwarfs as you can in the next minute. Be sure you provide seven names. Guess even if you aren't sure you're right.

_____   _____   _____   _____

_____   _____   _____

This may not be a fair question. The question assumes that you know a particular fairy tale, "Snow White and the Seven Dwarfs," which is popularly recounted in book and movie form in this culture. Yet, a surprising number of people cannot dredge up accurate names of the key figures from their long-term memories. Snow White used to hang out with Dopey, Happy, Sleepy, Grumpy, Sneezy, Bashful, and Doc. If you succeeded in retrieving all of them from storage in long-term memory, congratulations! That's an unusual accomplishment. For you to achieve that result, every element of memory processes had to work efficiently.

If you didn't succeed in retrieving all seven, you are in good company. Most people can't do this task easily. And that's very helpful to know, because we can use the results to demonstrate some important features of forgetting.

A simplified model of remembering involves a three-stage process: encoding, storage, and retrieval.

- *Encoding:* To become a memory, information must first be registered in sensory memory—it must stand out among the variety of stimuli and be selected for further processing. When stimuli are novel or important, they can be encoded as material available for later short-term memory processing.

- *Storage:* When we rehearse short-term memories sufficiently, we encode them for placement in long-term memory. We make a conscious decision to rehearse information when we think we will need it again for some future challenge.

- *Retrieval:* We seek information from long-term memory storage to assist in some adaptive problem; however, long-term memory storage is huge. Many kinds of processes can hinder effective retrieval, including
  —*Interference:* when other items in long-term memory clutter the retrieval of the specific items we are seeking.
  —*Insufficient cueing:* when we cannot retrieve specific items because we don't have quite enough information to facilitate finding the items we are seeking.
  —*Repression:* when the emotional consequences of recalling specific items might be too painful, we may unconsciously lose access to the potentially harmful memories.

The first part of this exercise demonstrates some problems that can crop up in long-term memory when we consciously try hard to dredge up semantic information to solve a problem, similar to the challenge we might experience when taking a multiple-choice test or playing a board game that relies on the quality of our long-term memory processes.

(Trivial Pursuit is one such game.) Describe the quality of long-term memory performance on the Seven Dwarfs task for someone who suffers from the following problems:

An encoding problem: _____

_____

_____

A storage problem: _____

_____

_____

An interference problem: _____

_____

_____

A repression problem: _____

_____

_____

PART 2: EVALUATE: Decide

Now, think about the answers you provided to the original recall problem. If you had trouble recalling all seven names, what explanation seems to apply to your pattern of forgetting? Why do you think so?

_____

_____

_____

_____

After completing this exercise, you should be able to:

- identify some common patterns in forgetting.

- deduce some explanations for error patterns that are consistent with memory processes.

- identify the explanation that best addresses your own errors.

- recognize the challenges of recalling stories accurately from childhood.

- remember the names of the "Magnificent Seven" (Dwarfs, that is) now because of your additional rehearsal.

▼Exercise 9.4   ROSEANNE'S DILEMMA

ANALYZE: Compare & Contrast

During the 1990s and early 2000s, there was a noted increase in the number of court cases involving recovered memories of childhood abuse. Some famous individuals reporting recovered memory experiences received considerable media attention. For example, comedian Roseanne Barr reported that she recovered memories of parental sexual abuse that involved episodes she claimed had occurred when she was less than two years old. Roseanne's family was outraged and vehemently denied her public charges. This case was well known at the time because it involved a celebrity; many families in private life experienced trauma when sons and daughters began to recall memories of abuse in therapy. Anecdotal reports suggest that some recovered memories of abuse are real, whereas others have not been independently verified.

When previously forgotten episodes are suddenly remembered many years after the event has occurred, we can raise many questions about whether these memories are valid. Because dealing with these memories is often devastating to the individuals involved, psychologists can contribute to an understanding of how real memories can suddenly resurface, as well as how events that never happened can be remembered as if they had actually occurred. Develop your understanding of these issues using the following questions as prompts.

- Formulate one hypothesis that might explain how a real, traumatic, and previously forgotten event could suddenly be remembered: _____

_____

_____

- Formulate one hypothesis to explain how people could remember something that never really happened: _____

_____

_____

- Describe one strategy that might help distinguish between real and false memories: _____

_____

_____

- Share your conclusions with a discussion group. How many different hypotheses and strategies can your group develop?

After completing this exercise, you should be able to:

- discuss the current controversy of recovered traumatic memories.

- explain how distant memories can be triggered by retrieval cues.

- speculate about how memory fragments might trigger inaccurate recall.

- discuss problem-solving strategies that distinguish between real and false memories.

▼Exercise 9.5   MAKING MEMORIES

EVALUATE: Take Perspective

Amnesia is a concept that is portrayed rather melodramatically in the media, particularly on dramatic television and in romantic literature. A person, usually a young woman, is injured in an accident or in an attempt on her life, and loses her memory. After undergoing some great trials and tribulations she suddenly recovers her memory and either finds the love of her life or is able to testify against the person who attempted to kill her. This scenario bears little resemblance to real life. Not only is amnesia quite rare, there is also nothing romantic about it.

Imagine the real-life case of Patsy, a young woman who received a head injury in a car accident. When her seat belt came loose in an automobile accident, her head hit the side window and the windshield. The front and side of the skull protect two areas of the brain that store long-term memories—the frontal and temporal lobes. When Patsy awoke several hours after the accident, she remembered nothing—not her name, the date, her 9-year-old daughter, any friends, or even how to walk or talk clearly. After spending much time in recovery, she was sent home, still not possessing any memory of the time before the accident. Although Patsy eventually developed a new and satisfying life, she never remembered anything about the "old" Patsy and is, according to the reports of friends and family, a different person.

Suppose you have been hired as a psychological consultant to help Patsy and her family adjust and adapt to Patsy's condition. Outline some of the physical, emotional, and social challenges they would face. What do you think they could do to help overcome these problems and to survive together as a family?

_____

_____

_____

_____

_____

_____

After completing this exercise, you should be able to:

- describe amnesia accurately and discuss why typical daytime soap opera treatments of the disorder are inaccurate.

- explain what happens to the brain to produce amnesia.

- imagine practical impacts on a family in which a member suffers memory loss.

- develop some opinions about whether a career in human services with clients who suffer memory problems would be satisfying.

▼Exercise 9.6 TOO MUCH OF A GOOD THING

EVALUATE: Assess

Most of the time we find ourselves in struggles related to memory. We forget an important phone number. We misplace our keys. We forget the deadline for an important assignment. Consequently, we curse our faulty memories as the villain in our own incompetence. Wouldn't it be great if our capacity to recall information could be dramatically improved?

Yes and no. Clearly, we would be in a much better position not to make typical memory blunders, but the quality of your life may not be improved. Individuals who by some fluke of nature have substantially greater recall capacity than most people suggest that there are serious challenges with having total recall. For example, the minutiae that you are likely to encode involuntarily represents a rather large investment of cognitive space for information that has no practical significance. If your observation and recall skills dramatically improved, would the balance of positive outweigh the negative consequences?

Suppose science makes sufficient progress so that someday in the near future you could take a pill that would allow you to exercise 100% recall. Would you take it?

_____

_____

After completing this exercise, you should be able to:

- describe the realistic capacity of human memory functions.

- appraise the degree to which your own memory functions serve you adequately.

- determine personal consequences for participating in scientific enhancement of memory.

▼Exercise 9.7   LOOKING AHEAD

CREATE: Plan

Think about areas of your life in which a more efficient and effective use of your memory would be helpful. Obviously, things that involve your education and schooling are easy to identify, but there are also bound to be others. Maybe you are not very good at remembering the names of people you meet, or you forget appointments you have made, or how to get to places you have been to before. Unless you are highly unusual, you should be able to think of several ways in which your memory could be improved. If you truly can't think of anything, ask those with whom you are close; they might have some suggestions that surprise you.

Once you have identified these areas, pick the one that is the most relevant or of the most importance to you right now. Try to determine the cause of the problem; for instance, is it a coding issue or a retrieval issue? How do you know? Once you have decided what the problem is, use the information in this chapter to create a personal plan for improvement. Articulate the plan, then implement it over the next several weeks, taking careful note of your progress. Did you improve? How do you know? Is this something you will continue to do in the future? Why or why not?

_____

_____

_____

_____

After completing this exercise, you should be able to:

- identify areas in your own life where it would be advantageous to improve some aspect of memory.

- articulate how such areas needing improvement impact your performance in essential ways.

- form clear and explicit hypotheses about the causes of inefficiencies in memory performance.

- develop strategies to improve memory performance.

- assess the effectiveness of a plan to improve memory and articulate its value to your own life.

▼Exercise 9.8   CREATING CONTEXT

CREATE: Design

Godden and Baddeley (1975) concluded that information was better remembered when it was recalled in the same context in which it was learned. You may remember their experiment. They had a group of people listen to a list of words. Half the group listened to the words as they sat on the beach, and the other half listened to the words while they were underwater. When later asked to remember the words in the list, the participants remembered more words correctly when they were in the same setting in which they heard the list. If a person originally heard the list while underwater, that person would remember more of the list if asked while underwater than if asked while sitting on the beach.

This finding has interesting implications for education. For example, a psychology professor interested in improving student performance on tests might choose to conduct her own experiment on the effects of context on recall. The basic hypothesis is that taking a test in a context similar to the learning context will improve performance. What are the specific variables and how might she conduct this experiment in "real life"?

Independent variable: _____

Dependent variable: _____

Extraneous variables for which she should control: _____

Outline of a basic experimental protocol: _____

After completing this exercise, you should be able to:

- recount the original findings of the Godden and Baddeley experiment.

- construct an experimental strategy to test a memory hypothesis.

- describe variables that need to be controlled to eliminate alternative hypotheses.

- speculate about how context-based learning could influence study habits.

THE PSYCHOLOGY ADVANTAGE

This is one area of psychology for which the advantages of learning about the subject matter are fairly obvious. Who wouldn't want to be able to find more effective ways to study and to remember important events and people? In addition to remembering things and improving performance in school, however, developing effective memory strategies and systems has other, less obvious and immediate benefits. With effective and well-practiced strategies, there can be a significant decrease in perceived stress. Knowing that you know how to remember things means that you just have to focus on executing the strategy, not developing one. That means more of your energy goes into focusing on the material, people, or events important to you, and less on worrying about them. Also, there is an increasing body of psychological research suggesting that rich and robust memory processes and strategies build more stable memory connections and provide some protection against the memory loss caused by aging and often found in the early stages of dementia.

Chapter

◀ Thinking and Language ▶

The topics discussed in this chapter examine how we adapt to our environments. We are born into cultures with established languages, belief systems for viewing the world, and methods for evaluating our experience. The following exercises give you an opportunity to explore challenging questions about how we learn and use language and specific cognitive abilities, as well as how these abilities are, or are not, unique to the human experience.

▼ Exercise 10.1 BASIC COMMUNICATION

UNDERSTAND: Explain

One of the joys of being around children is experiencing how they grow and change as communicators. Psychologists and linguists interested in language development have come up with some specific terminology that helps to capture the changes children demonstrate on their way to mature language management. Match the examples to the proper concepts.

> **Communication terms:**
> syntax, phonemes, morphemes, semantics, overregularization

1. **Example 1:** While she is eating her strained bananas, baby Rachel makes this sound: "muh…muh…muh…muh…"

   Term: _____

2. **Example 2:** At a family reunion, kindergartener Rachel struggles in sorting first cousins from second cousins.

   Term: _____

3. **Example 3:** Rachel's first word was "waggy," which her parents understood referred to her favorite possession, a rag doll.

   Term: _____

4. **Example 4:** Returning from a family outing, Rachel enthusiastically reported that all of them "goed to zoo."

   Term: _____

5. **Example 5:** Rachel yelled upstairs to her mother: "Throw me downstairs the broom," demonstrating her failure in managing conventional word order.

Term: _____

After completing this exercise, you should be able to:

- recognize how aspects of language control evolve over childhood.

- identify specific developmental milestones in language acquisition.

- predict when various language categories emerge.

▼Exercise 10.2   IF WE COULD TALK TO THE ANIMALS

PART 1: UNDERSTAND: Explain

Few controversies have so divided the scientific community as has the controversy about the apes' capacities for language. Although many scientists have made serious attempts at rearing apes in language-rich environments, the results have not overwhelmingly demonstrated that apes can use language as human beings use it.

At the heart of the argument are the criteria we use to determine true capacity for language. Generally, scientists specializing in the study of language impose the following criteria on the debate.

- Is the language *symbolic:* Can it be used to represent absent objects?

- Does the language have systematic *syntax,* or word order?

- Can the language be used in a creative or *productive* manner?

There are two opposing viewpoints on whether apes can truly learn human language. Some psychologists who believe apes are quite capable of acquiring language have gone to creative lengths to gather support for their position. Other psychologists dispute the idea that apes are capable of learning language.

Before attempting this exercise, review the evidence your psychology textbook presents for the topic of animal language. Find two examples that support the viewpoint of those who believe apes can learn language. Then find two examples that could be used by those who disagree with that position.

Two sources of evidence supporting the viewpoint that animals have the capacity for language.

1. _____

_____

2. _____

_____

Two sources of evidence challenging the viewpoint that animals have the capacity for language.

1. _____

2. _____

PART 2: EVALUATE: Justify

Identify the side you find more convincing and, if possible, explain how you have applied the appropriate language criteria to make your choice.

_____

_____

_____

After completing this exercise, you should be able to:

- identify why the scientific community is torn about the apes' potential to use language.

- report the criteria scientists use to make judgments about language capacity.

- support both perspectives with evidence from language research.

- evaluate the two perspectives and judge which is more strongly supported.

▼Exercise 10.3   HEURISTICALLY YOURS

APPLY: Examine

Heuristics are strategies we use to organize our world and to help us make decisions. Although this approach allows for rapid processing of information and decision making, it is not always accurate. In fact, a heuristic can make you quite prone to errors. Heuristics are especially tempting when time is of the essence—when you think you don't have the time to review all the available options extensively or exhaustively.

Your textbook discussed several different kinds of heuristics. Two heuristics—*the availability heuristic* and the *representativeness heuristic*—tend to have bottleneck features for learning because they feel a little abstract. In the former, you are likely to make mistakes in judgment because you inappropriately estimate the likelihood of an event based upon how easy it is to dredge up examples. The availability heuristic is to blame when people register more fear about flying than travel by car. Although air travel is statistically safer, the vivid treatment of plane crashes in the media technically make those accidents more available in shaping your judgment of risk. The representative heuristic relies on your tendency to build rich prototypes to help you make predictions about how "certain kinds" of people behave. Hence, we quickly generate stereotypical conclusions about others that may not capture their true nature. Sneaky car salesmen, subdued librarians, and crotchety oldsters all encourage us to think about those categories in ways that provide a foundation for how to interact with others who play that role. However, people often defy the predictions we make based on prototypical judgment.

For each of the two listed below, try to identify a time in your own life when you used that heuristic to make a decision. Describe the situation, how you used the heuristic, and whether the use of the heuristic resulted in an error.

Availability heuristic: _____

_____

Representativeness heuristic: _____

_____

After completing this exercise, you should be able to:

- describe how and why heuristics are used in decision making.

- identify instances of the availability and representativeness heuristics in your own experience.

- determine whether the use of these heuristics resulted in errors in your decision-making process.

- recognize situations in which the use of heuristics is likely and consider alternative strategies.

▼**Exercise 10.4 THERE'S GOOD NEWS AND THERE'S BAD NEWS**
APPLY: Illustrate

How we process our facts influences how we make our decisions, but "facts" can be "framed" in different ways, depending on our purpose and the context. For example, consumers are more likely to buy ground beef that is "80 percent lean" than to purchase the package labeled "20 percent fat." Both descriptions are accurate, and logically they are equivalent. But only one of them is likely to make us reach for our wallets to make a purchase. (The other may launch us on a fat-free self-improvement campaign.)

Framing comes into play in how we present information to others. A common practice when one North American needs to impart mixed news to another is to start with the statement, "There is good news and there is bad news. Which would you like to hear first?" By making this statement, we offer the news recipient an opportunity to influence how we will frame the good and bad details that will follow.

Examine the following situations and speculate about how you could frame the information to produce the intended outcomes.

Have I Got a Deal for You!

You sell used cars. The best car on your lot has 100,000 miles on it. How could you describe this car to a prospective buyer to make the purchase more attractive?

_____

_____

Making the Grade

You're carrying six full classes. You've had a hard semester, and you are about to talk with loved ones at a family gathering about how things have been going. You've excelled in five courses, but you know you won't pass the other course. How do you talk about your experience in this difficult semester?

_____

_____

IRS Blues

You've just started working for the Internal Revenue Service. Tax specialists have developed tax brackets to assist in equitable taxation. Will you work with taxpayers by describing how much tax they will pay or by explaining how much income they will keep?

_____

_____

Rain, Rain, Go Away

As a weather forecaster in an area that depends on the tourist industry, will you state your forecast as the likelihood of sunshine or as the likelihood of rain?

_____

_____

After completing this exercise, you should be able to:

- recognize how framing can influence decisions.

- identify two different versions of the "facts" of a situation.

- select the version of the "facts" that is more likely to produce a desirable outcome.

- offer a reasonable justification for your framing choices.

▼Exercise 10.5   MONEY IN THE BANK?

ANALYZE: Relate

The world of high finance demands the rapid processing of large amounts of information, and in this setting the use of heuristics to make decisions would be natural and almost automatic. Imagine that you are a consultant, hired to work with investors to help them make the wisest choices with their money. How could you use an understanding of the risk of using heuristics to help your investors make, rather than lose, money? How does the use of heuristics relate to confidence or overconfidence in decisions? If you need a suggestion to help you get started, focus on the availability heuristic. Identify what the availability heuristic is, how it might lead to errors that could cost the investors money, and what strategies the investors might use instead of relying on this heuristic.

What would you tell the investors about heuristics? _____

_____

_____

_____

What could you tell them about overconfidence and the way it might affect their investing decisions? _____

_____

_____

_____

What is the availability heuristic and how does it specifically affect investment decisions? _____

_____

_____

How have you seen these concepts reflected in your own money-handling experiences?

_____

_____

_____

_____

_____

After completing this exercise, you should be able to:

- describe how heuristics and overconfidence play a role in decision making.

- discuss the way in which these concepts affect decision making in the area of financial investing.

- discuss a specific example of the availability heuristic and its influence on investment reasoning.

- recognize how these concepts are reflected in your own money-managing experiences.

▼Exercise 10.6   SEEING IS BELIEVING

ANALYZE: Reason

You may have already experienced this phenomenon in the course of reading your textbook. Chances are that at some point in your reading, you have read, or will read, some research findings that directly contradict what you know to be true from your own experience. Most people tend to believe the validity of their personal experience over the findings of research, even when the scientific evidence is very compelling.

How would you use what you've learned about making decisions and forming judgments to explain this tendency? (A solid answer will discuss at least two different concepts from this chapter.) _____

_____

_____

_____

When might it be appropriate to rely on personal experience more than other sources of information when making decisions? _____

_____

_____

When would it not? _____

_____

_____

_____

After completing this exercise, you should be able to:

- describe how heuristics, overconfidence, belief bias, and belief perseverance can result in an overreliance on personal experience when making judgments and decisions.

- identify situations when it might be appropriate to weigh personal experience more heavily than other sources of information when making decisions.

- understand the complexity of the process of forming judgments and making decisions.

▼Exercise 10.7   POOR JOHN AND MARY

EVALUATE: Assess

John and Mary were found dead in a locked room. The following objects were found in the room with them: some water, a table, a dog, a chair, and a broken glass. How did John and Mary die?

This riddle illustrates many principles underlying the creative process. To solve the riddle, we must first *define the problem* by establishing the facts as we know them. John and Mary are dead. They have been found in a locked room with some objects. Our task is to determine how the deaths occurred. That seems straightforward enough.

As you begin to *analyze the problem*, pay careful attention to the components that you can *observe*. Do any solutions jump out? Probably not, which means we must approach the problem from another angle.

One important aspect of creative problem solving is careful scrutiny of inferences and assumptions. Have you drawn any *inferences* that will either help you solve the problem or—perhaps—just get in your way? Consider these assumptions:

- John and Mary died in the room.

- The objects—or some of the objects—are involved in their deaths.

- Because the room was locked, the possible causes of their deaths must be limited.

How can you find *relationships* among the facts of the case so that you will be able to *solve the problem?* You might ask whether all the objects are essential to their deaths. Are some objects more important than others? Did John and Mary die at the same time? Why was the glass broken? As you examine the relationships, you may reach a tentative *conclusion.*

All manner of hypotheses have been proposed to solve this problem, although there is really only one elegant solution. Perhaps John and Mary had a mutual suicide pact . . . but then how was the pact enacted? Perhaps the dog was rabid . . . but death by rabies takes a while, and how probable is it that both would die at the same time? Perhaps John and Mary drowned . . . but that would require a great deal of water. Maybe they starved to death… but why didn't the dog die, too?

The process we go through when solving riddles involves problem-solving processes and creativity in characteristic phases. Sometimes we have to think a long time before a solution comes to mind. This process is called *incubation.* When a solution arrives, we have *insight.*

What is *your* conclusion about John and Mary's deaths? If you haven't reached one yet, here is a hint: The water was once in the glass. Try asking yourself these questions: What kind of water? What kind of glass? Was the glass once a bottle? A dome? A pitcher? A vase? An aquarium? Did the hint help? Are you closer to solving the riddle?

_____

_____

_____

After completing this exercise, you should be able to:

- summarize the steps that are apparent in riddle problem solving.

- identify the roles that incubation, insight, and functional fixedness play in creative problem solving.

- describe how assumptions can limit our problem-solving abilities.

- recognize how practical problem-solving processes fit with everyday life.

- generate at least one proposal for John and Mary's deaths.

- drive your own friends and family crazy figuring out how John and Mary died.

▼Exercise 10.8   ALEX, THE ACCOUNTANT

CREATE: Design

The degree to which humans are the exclusive owners of language is one of the great questions of cognitive and comparative psychology. Researchers have worked with chimps, apes, dolphins, and even an African gray parrot to explore questions about animals' abilities to understand and express abstract concepts and to comprehend the semantic nuances of human language. One series of experiments involves Alex, an African gray parrot trained and tested by Irene Pepperberg and her associates.

When given an assortment of different objects, Alex can correctly answer questions of number and color. For example, if asked how many red blocks are on the table, Alex will answer correctly approximately 80 percent of the time. (One of the things that makes Alex such an interesting subject is that he has been trained to talk, so he gives his answers verbally.) Imagine for a moment that you are a researcher working with Alex. Given these findings, what other numerical concepts might Alex understand? How might you test them?

Generate at least one hypothesis about Alex's understanding of abstract numerical concepts and design an experiment to test it. For example, how would you go about establishing that Alex comprehends the terms "more" and "less"?

Hypothesis: _____

_____

_____

Briefly describe the experiment you would use to test this hypothesis, making sure to identify both the independent and dependent variables. _____

_____

_____

_____

_____

_____

_____

If your hypothesis is supported, how might this change our understanding of human language and thinking? _____

_____

_____

_____

After completing this exercise, you should be able to:

- describe experiments that explore the capacity of animals to use language.

- use the findings of one animal language experiment to generate a hypothesis about the ability of Alex, Irene Pepperberg's gray parrot, to understand abstract numerical concepts.

- identify the variables and basic experimental strategies needed to test your hypothesis about Alex's numerical conceptual abilities.

- discuss the ways in which the findings of such experiments affect our fundamental understanding of the uniqueness of human thought and language.

THE PSYCHOLOGY ADVANTAGE

Complex worlds require complex kinds of decisions. With a steady stream of information and the ability to move quickly and easily from one place to another, we are faced with environments that are fluid and very different from the relatively contained and stable environments in which we evolved, or even those of just a few generations ago. As we navigate this rich and ever-changing world, we need to recognize that those cognitive strategies and capacities constrained by the physical limits of our bodies and brains have not changed, that we are faced with increasingly more information than we can take in at any given time. Knowing all the ways humans make decisions, and understanding the automatic and intuitive ways in which we attempt to limit the amount of information to which we must attend is vital. Confirmation bias, overconfidence, the use of heuristics, and the reliance on personal experience are all very effective ways to minimize processing time and to maximize the number of things to which we can attend cognitively, but they are not always the most accurate. Understanding when these strategies are most prone to error can help make us aware of when we need to take the time for more comprehensive information-processing strategies, even if it takes longer and requires more effort. Think of how things might have been different in the recent Wall Street scandals if more people on all sides of the industry had been aware that people are often less skilled or accurate than they think they are, more aware of the times they were only looking for what they had seen in the past, or if they had taken the time to understand more than what was easily available in their own experiences and in the public memory.

Chapter

◀Intelligence▶

What, exactly, is intelligence? This question is at the core of a long-standing discussion in psychology. Although there is no one simple answer, most psychologists agree that it is not a specific or concrete entity of which individuals have some easily specified proportion; rather, intelligence is a set of abilities used to adapt to the environment. The potential to reason logically, to solve problems, and to learn from experience are only some of the diverse abilities that are typically included under the general heading of "intelligence." The activities in this chapter will help you understand and appreciate the diversity that is inextricably a part of any discussion about intelligence. We also address the challenge of measuring intelligence and the consequences of making judgments based on those tests.

▼Exercise 11.1 EINSTEIN'S THEORY OF INTELLIGENCE

UNDERSTAND: Translate

A famous quote often attributed to Albert Einstein is "You do not really understand something until you can explain it to your grandmother." Assuming that this is true, write a letter to your grandmother in which you explain one of the more complex key ideas from this chapter. Your letter should explain both the concept and its value. In other words, don't just tell Grandma what it is, tell her why it is important to you and why she should be interested.

After completing this exercise, you should be able to:

- identify complex concepts about intelligence that are relevant to you and of interest to your family.

- explain at least one aspect of intelligence to an interested, sympathetic, and older audience in lay terms that they will understand.

- practice writing about psychological concepts.

▼Exercise 11.2 "CHARACTER"ISTICS OF INTELLIGENCE

APPLY: Illustrate

Historically, intelligence was defined as a specific set of cognitive abilities used primarily in academic settings. Contemporary theories of intelligence, however, tend to stress "multiple intelligences," suggesting that mental abilities are too diverse to fall under one label. Although there is some disagreement over the exact nature of these different intelligences, Robert J. Sternberg, Richard Wagner, and some of their colleagues have described three different intelligences: academic, practical, and creative. Academic problem-solving skills are those measured by more traditional intelligence tests and focus on an individual's ability to answer well-defined problems with objectively correct answers. Practical intelligence is often termed "common sense"—the ability to successfully complete the often ambiguous and complex tasks that are a part of everyday life. Creative intelligence involves seeing unexpected patterns and solutions when presented with novel situations.

Below are some classic literary and cinematic figures. Using the triarchic classification of the Sternberg and Wagner framework of intelligence, analyze each character's intellectual profile. Provide a rationale for each answer. Then, pick some of your own favorite characters and identify their intelligences (and lack thereof).

Character	Academic	Practical	Creative
Scrooge	Strong: His career as an accountant dictates good analytic skills.	Strong: His money-making abilities attest to his street smarts.	Weak: He conforms to conventions to an extreme degree.
Mary Poppins			
Sherlock Holmes			
Winnie the Pooh			
Don Quixote			
Your example			
Your example			

After completing this exercise, you should be able to:

- explain the components of Sternberg and Wagner's theory of multiple intelligences.

- identify the intellectual strengths and weaknesses of fictional literary figures.

- apply the theory of multiple intelligences to new examples.

▼Exercise 11.3   BRAVE NEW WORLD

PART 1: APPLY: Classify

In *Brave New World*, Aldous Huxley described a society in which everyone was sorted into groups based on engineered characteristics that were then enhanced through specific experiences and educational practices. Although most people would agree that seeking ways to sort individuals for the purpose of limiting opportunities is not appropriate, we often do so unintentionally when we value certain characteristics more than others. (If you have trouble envisioning this, consider why aptitude, achievement, and intelligence tests are used, and what the result of their use often is.) Our society places great importance on analytic and academic skills but may be less interested in other dimensions of intelligence.

Imagine a world in which creativity was valued above all else. Using the five components of creativity—expertise, imaginative thinking skills, a venturesome personality, high intrinsic motivation, and a creative environment—identify the creative components that seem to be more genetically determined than environmentally influenced. In other words, which of the five seem to be more environmentally influenced? (Consequently, the right environment could enhance an individual's creative expression.) For each component, put an X in the column that best explains whether nature or nurture more strongly influences the creative dimension:

Creative Characteristics	Primarily Heritable	Primarily Environmental
Expertise		
Imaginative thinking skills		
Venturesome personality		
High intrinsic motivation		
Creative environment		

PART 2: ANALYZE: Relate

Describe how knowing the heritability of certain factors related to creativity might influence how creativity would be produced in the population, as well as how a home or educational environment could be designed based on understanding the role of environmental components in the expression of creativity: _____

_____

_____

_____

_____

_____

How appropriate do you think such actions would be? Why? Is it ever appropriate to sort people based on their expression of specific traits? _____

_____

_____

_____

_____

_____

After completing this exercise, you should be able to:

- reflect upon the ways in which we use intelligence and related characteristics to place people in different categories.
- identify the five components of creativity.

- articulate genetic and environmental contributions to the development of creative expression.
- speculate about how information about genes and the environment could be used to sort people and enhance creativity in a culture that valued creative expression above all else.
- make some judgments about if and when it is appropriate to sort people based on the expression of specific characteristics.

▼Exercise 11.4   CHALLENGING QUESTIONS

ANALYZE: Reason

Since the early 1900s, intelligence tests have been used in a variety of educational settings. Beginning with Alfred Binet and Théodore Simon's work in France in 1904, and continuing with Lewis Terman's later adaptation of their work in California, intelligence tests have become a popular way to predict the probable academic performance of children and to identify those children who might benefit from special attention. You have probably undergone significant experiences with testing that can be traced back to these early pioneers.

Today, psychologists use testing predictions to make decisions about the ways specific children should be educated. For example, a child who scores below 85 might be offered special support services while remaining in a traditional classroom. A child scoring below 70 might be placed in a special classroom, program, or school.

How might such an approach be advantageous for a child? _____

_____

_____

_____

_____

_____

_____

How might it be detrimental? _____

_____

_____

_____

_____

_____

What are the underlying values inherent in this approach and what impact does it have on society? _____

_____

_____

_____

_____

_____

Are there any corresponding differences in the way the academically gifted are treated?

_____

_____

_____

_____

_____

After completing this exercise, you should be able to:

- discuss the history of the development of intelligence tests.

- recognize that intelligence tests were designed to measure the potential for academic success rather than some inborn trait.

- speculate about the effects that separating children based on academic ability has on the children involved and on society.

- identify some of the underlying values related to intelligence testing and the resulting educational practices.

▼Exercise 11.5   IT'S ALL GOOD

ANALYZE: Categorize

Psychologists who focus on developing tests and inventories to measure constructs in psychology concentrate on whether or not their constructions are defensible. They must meet acceptable levels of *reliability* and *validity*. These terms aren't always easy to sort out.

Reliability has to do with the likelihood that a test will produce a consistent outcome. Test designers worry about different kinds of reliability. For example, will the same test produce the same results on future examinations (for example, test-retest reliability)? Will different judges administering the same test to the same person generate the same conclusions about performance (inter-rater reliability)? A third form of reliability involves making sure that all the parts of a specific test produce similar levels of achievement (split-half reliability). By alternating test questions into two halves, we should be able to compare the halves, and both should produce similar estimates of ability.

In contrast, validity refers to whether or not a test actually measures what the test designer originally intended (construct validity). Other forms of validity involve whether or not a test can be used to make accurate predictions about current performance (concurrent validity) or make predictions about future performance (predictive validity).

The following test cases demonstrate poor examples of test quality. See if you can identify the violated principle of test goodness in each case.

CASE 1: Ronnie's Bad Grade

Ronnie slaved on her writing assignment and was shocked to discover that the instructor marked her work with a D. She was so disturbed by the poor grade that she took it to an English graduate student she knew and asked for a fresh reading. The graduate student praised her work and said it was at least worth an A−.

What category of test quality is represented by two such dramatically different outcomes?

_____

CASE 2: Bruce's Dream Vocation

Bruce was interested in becoming a certified public accountant. The career counseling inventory he took suggested that he had limited mathematical aptitude. Despite the result, Bruce was able to complete graduate school, pass certification, and make a fine living as a CPA.

Which category of test quality is represented by this mismatch? _____

_____

CASE 3: Joshua's Wobbly IQ

Joshua took a newly developed intelligence scale for children when he was 9 and again when he was 12. On the first testing, his results suggested he was functioning below normal intelligence. However, on the second testing, his result changed dramatically. He was assessed in the bright normal range of intelligence.

Assuming nothing was problematic about the test conditions under which he took the

exam, in what way does the result suggest problematic test quality? _____

_____

CASE 4: Darla's Test-Taking Terror

Darla dreaded taking tests. She didn't mind essay questions because she could usually muster proper answers and do fairly well in that format. However, multiple-choice formats made her freeze up. Although her knowledge of the course remained the same, how well she did in grading seemed to be entirely a matter of the format the professor selected to test her knowledge.

What aspect of test quality comes closest to capturing this challenge in measuring course

expertise? _____

_____

CASE 5: Angelina's Honors Dilemma

About halfway through her college career, Angelina decided that her grades were strong enough to facilitate admission to her campus honors program. However, when she took a college aptitude test, the results suggested that her intellectual capacity wouldn't support enrollment in such a high demand program. That outcome was puzzling since her current grade point average was 3.8.

What challenge might be issued to the nature of the test quality? _____

_____

CASE 6: Dr. Swenson's Misfire

Dr. Swenson worked long and hard on developing an inventory that would measure potential for success as a real estate professional. Unfortunately, he discovered that the inventory didn't work well to capture the skills needed to do well in selling houses. It did appear to identify talent for computer coding instead.

Dr. Swenson's test suffered from what test quality problem? _____

_____

After completing this exercise, you should be able to:

- differentiate reliability and validity as measures of test quality.
- describe different potential testing malfunctions.
- recognize specific violations of criteria for test goodness.

▼Exercise 11.6   WHEN TO TEST

EVALUATE: Justify

Testing is an entrenched part of contemporary life. You have been tested at various stages of your educational experience. Chances are good that as you seek employment, you will have other opportunities to be tested. However, as a well-informed consumer of psychological services, you should also be equipped to spot faulty uses of testing. This ability should prepare you to challenge inappropriate uses of tests or to build solid rationales to obtain the testing services that you need.

Examine the problem situations below and construct your best argument about the course of action that you think would be most satisfying. Keep in mind that the strongest arguments will rely on the principles of test design and fair use. The best practical strategies should address standardization, reliability, or validity of testing. What strategies can you develop for the following situations?

Your prospective employer is interested in asking you to take a polygraph test to ensure that you won't steal office supplies. _____

_____

_____

Your little brother had a serious cold on the day that achievement tests were administered. His results suggest that he needs placement in a classroom for mildly retarded children. _____

_____

_____

A graduate program offers admission only to students who score in the top 10 percent on the GRE. They do not factor in other academic performance indicators. _____

_____

_____

Although you worked very hard on your English literature essay, you got back a "D" with no explanatory feedback. Your friend, who partied heavily the night before the paper was due, got back an "A" with no explanatory feedback. _____

_____

_____

An employer is deciding between the use of two tests for selecting sales representatives. The content of each test is complex but she's leaning in the direction of selecting the one that is less expensive and has a prettier cover. _____

_____

_____

After completing this exercise, you should be able to:

- describe typical situations in which testing is used to categorize ability.

- differentiate among standardization, reliability, and validity as measures of test goodness.

- determine how to create defensible arguments that challenge improper test applications.

▼Exercise 11.7 JUST TOO COOL

CREATE: Invent

One dimension that often becomes the basis on which we judge others is how "cool" they are. Of course, the problem with that concept is that it is not entirely clear whether what "cool" is for one person would be the same as it is for another. Being cool may be a particular dimension of social intelligence, but it probably varies a great deal by context. For example, a cool young adult probably differs in characteristics and behavior from a cool senior citizen.

Join with a group of students who are your age peers. See if you can construct a strategy for the measurement of "cool." First, you must operationally define what it means to be cool for the target group. Then try to develop a measurement strategy that would allow you to sort people on the basis of their relative cool. Finally, reflect as a group on the ease or difficulty of the assignment.

Operationally define what it means to be cool. _____

_____

_____

What strategies could you use to sort people according to levels of being cool? _____

_____

_____

Why was this assignment particularly challenging? _____

_____

_____

After completing this exercise, you should be able to:

- describe the process of developing an operational definition and explain its importance in testing.

- generate some viable strategies for measuring and comparing a dimension of behavior.

- reflect on the difficulties connected with test construction and use.

- articulate ethical concerns related to the comparing and labeling of people.

▼Exercise 11.8 TO RETEST OR NOT TO RETEST?

CREATE: Design

Taking achievement and aptitude tests has become a standard practice in American culture. Performance on achievement tests often determines whether you will gain access to the next level of training in a variety of fields. For example, at the end of high school, you probably took a Scholastic Assessment Test (SAT) or the American College Test (ACT) to determine whether colleges would admit you.

Sometimes performance on achievement and aptitude tests is disappointing. Test-takers who are strongly motivated to move to the next level of training then face the unsettling decision of whether to repeat the test. In principle, retesting should not influence a test-taker's score on an aptitude test. Nevertheless, we occasionally hear anecdotes about individuals who retested and scored startling gains on the second try. Sometimes these anecdotes are accompanied by compelling testimony in praise of some course in a particular aptitude or achievement area. The stories cause the power of additional training and the advantage of additional testing to seem very appealing. However, these stories rely on testimony, not on objective evidence derived through well-designed experimentation.

Your task in this exercise is to design an experiment. You are to imagine yourself as a psychology major nearing the end of your undergraduate education. You have decided that you want to attend graduate school in psychology to become an experimental researcher. Unfortunately, your scores on the Graduate Record Examination (GRE) were disappointing. They weren't dreadful, but they were low enough to disqualify you from some of the best programs, which were your first choices. Should you take the exam again? Or should you spend time enhancing other areas that might make up for low scores?

The experiment you will design will help you and others determine whether test-takers would be wise to retake an achievement exam if they were dissatisfied with their original results. You have been able to round up 100 volunteers who are willing to retest or retrain, regardless of their original scores. To begin setting up your experiment, answer the following questions. (See Answer Key.)

What is your hypothesis? _____

_____

_____

What is the independent variable? _____

What is the dependent variable? _____

How will you assign volunteers to test conditions? _____

_____

What elements of the experience will you need to control? _____

_____

After completing this exercise, you should be able to:

- generate a hypothesis consistent with the goal of evaluating the effects of retesting.

- identify an appropriate, simple dependent variable.

- recognize the complexity of extra variables that need to be controlled if alternative hypotheses are to be ruled out.

- understand that well-designed research processes are complicated and time consuming.

THE PSYCHOLOGY ADVANTAGE

As you were reading this chapter and working on these exercises, you were most likely very sensitive to the many ways that the construct of intelligence has had an impact on your life. From very personal things like the opportunities you were given and your family's expectations for your education, to the more subtle influences of the underlying structures inherent in the design of our national public educational system, the way we understand and explain intelligence shapes how and what we expect people to be able to learn. When you understand what intelligence is and is not, and when you are familiar with appropriate and ineffective ways to test it, you can make better choices for yourself and the people important to you when it comes to testing and making choices about those educational opportunities that might be most appropriate. This information and understanding could also inform how you vote and help shape public policy that relates to education and the educational system. The allocation of resources within school systems, the choice of programming, and, perhaps most important, who has access to the programming is all guided by implicit and explicit understandings of intelligence.

Chapter

◀ Motivation ▶

Why do we get up in the morning? Why do we study hard to be successful in a college course? Why do we shrink with horror from the sight of a grisly car accident? Why do we pursue specific dreams? All of these questions represent the terrain psychologists describe as motivation. Research in motivation explains how we meet our needs, select our goals, adopt our beliefs, and make our decisions.

▼ Exercise 12.1 THEORIES OF MOTIVATION

UNDERSTAND: Compare

In the history of psychology's exploration of the motivating factors behind behavior, three theoretical perspectives have proven the most influential: instinct theory, drive reduction theory, and arousal theory. Instinct theory came out of the growing evolutionary understanding of the origins of behaviors. It assumes that some complex behaviors are not learned and can be explained by a genetic predisposition to the behavior. This approach is most often applied to explain species-typical behaviors. Drive reduction theory states that a physiological need creates a psychological state that pushes the organism to behave in ways that reduce the need. Arousal theory suggests that some behaviors are motivating because they increase arousal; that is, that they stimulate the organism or individual in some needed fashion.

In the following list of motivated behaviors, identify which theories could be used to explain why each behavior occurs and describe how that theory would explain the behavior.

Behavior	Theories	Explanations
A human infant rooting to find the mother's nipple		
Getting a glass of water when you are thirsty		
Going for a walk when you are worried or restless		
Working on a difficult jigsaw puzzle		
Studying hard to pass an exam		
Crying when hurt or upset		
Developing a lasting, intimate relationship		

After completing this exercise, you should be able to:

- identify the three main theoretical perspectives used to explain motivated behaviors.

- use instinct theory, drive reduction theory, and arousal theory to explain why certain behaviors occur.

- recognize that motivated behaviors can be interpreted through more than one theoretical perspective.

▼Exercise 12.2   NOW HIRING

APPLY: Illustrate

Suppose you are a human resources specialist in charge of hiring just the right person to fill a new position on the management team. Your corporation is particularly focused on procuring individuals who have a strong intrinsic motivation to succeed. Consequently, the working environment tends to be high pressure, competitive, and results-oriented.

Which of the following standard interview questions would help you differentiate the candidate's need for achievement? Please circle your response.

How long did you work at your last job?	Yes	Maybe	No
What awards have you won based on your performance?	Yes	Maybe	No
What do you like to do in your spare time?	Yes	Maybe	No
What kind of co-workers appeal to you?	Yes	Maybe	No
What was the last book you read for pleasure?	Yes	Maybe	No
Why do you want to work here?	Yes	Maybe	No
How closely do you like to be supervised?	Yes	Maybe	No
Would you prefer short-term assignments that are relatively manageable or a longer-term assignment that is more exacting?	Yes	Maybe	No
What kind of vacations do you like to take?	Yes	Maybe	No
Have you ever been described as a workaholic?	Yes	Maybe	No
Where do you hope to be in five years?	Yes	Maybe	No
What do you typically do when you receive constructive criticism?	Yes	Maybe	No

After completing this exercise, you should be able to:

- describe the concept of need for achievement.

- recognize the kinds of questions prospective employers tend to ask to find appropriate hires.

- reflect on how you would demonstrate intrinsic motivation.

▼Exercise 12.3   THE WEIGHT-LOSS COUNSELOR

ANALYSIS: Reason

Jim has been attempting to lose weight for many months. No matter what weight-reduction method he attempts, he seems unable to lose and sustain his loss. Although some methods are initially effective, the weight returns, and within weeks the excess ounces become the "ten pounds from hell" that simply won't go away.

This exercise asks you to imagine that you have found employment after college as a weight-loss counselor. (Some students who graduate with a psychology major find this a suitable entry into a helping career.) In your new role, you will attempt to isolate as many variables as possible in trying to help Jim reach his objective.

Begin by considering all the behavioral, physical, and social influences that could undermine Jim's weight-loss efforts. From these influences, identify six variables that may prevent Jim from reaching his goal. For each of the six variables, formulate a question you could ask Jim to evaluate the impact of the variable. (See Answer Key.)

Variable 1: _____

Question: _____

Variable 2: _____

Question: _____

Variable 3: _____

Question: _____

Variable 4: _____

Question: _____

Variable 5: _____

Question: _____

Variable 6: _____

Question: _____

The number of factors you address in the problem-solving process is likely to influence your success as a weight-loss expert. Interpreting these variables as questions will add significantly to the available raw material you can draw on as you counsel your clients.

After completing this exercise, you should be able to:

- recognize that weight management is a complex behavior.

- isolate variables that influence weight control.

- transform variables into questions that shape problem-solving processes.

▼Exercise 12.4 YOU DON'T HAVE TO BE LONELY

ANALYSIS: Compare

Evolutionary explanations of mate selection compete with romantic notions about how and why couples get together. Romantic conceptions tend to invoke images of lovestruck couples who are magically drawn to each other, make a commitment, and then live happily ever after. Evolutionary explanations not only seem rather harsh by comparison, but suggest dramatically different strategies for dating for males and females.

This exercise prompts you to compare the fundamental gender differences at work in mate selection for men versus women, assuming a heterosexual norm. Parental investment theory suggests that males maximize their reproductive success by spreading their seed among the greatest number of partners. Consequently, their goals from an evolutionary standpoint lead to uncomplicated and uncommitted sexual activity. Since reproduction requires little from males after fertilization, they can move on to their next conquests. In contrast, evolutionary forces drive women to find partners who are willing to invest materially in any offspring that will emerge from conception.

Instead of focusing on the sexual process in potential partners, females are drawn to good providers. They engage in sex with fewer partners, seeking those who show some potential for commitment and protection.

How would an honest personal ad appear for a female versus a male demonstrating parental investment theory? _____

_____

_____

_____

After completing this exercise, you should be able to:

- describe the basic tenets of parental investment theory.

- recognize differences between gender in mate selection strategies.

- describe personal comfort with an evolutionary viewpoint.

▼Exercise 12.5   HUMANISTIC HISTORY

EVALUATE: Take Perspective

During the turbulent 1960s, Abraham Maslow suggested that some human needs must take precedence over others: the more immediate the need, the stronger the motivation to meet that need. For example, you might have a need to be successful and so would work very hard to accomplish this goal, but if you did not have enough food to eat, you would probably divert most of your energy to finding food to eliminate your hunger. Hunger, on the other hand, might lose its significance if you were deprived of air. Maslow speculated that physiological needs were the most essential; once these needs are met, needs for safety, belongingness, love, esteem, and the need to live up to one's fullest potential become motivating factors. Maslow's hierarchical framework was intuitively very appealing and became one of the most popular explanations of human motivation.

As the century came to a close, psychologists began to question the validity and usefulness of Maslow's approach. Critics have begun to generate examples of situations in which Maslow's hierarchy does not provide a solid explanation. Can you think of an example from contemporary life that would challenge the validity of Maslow's hierarchy?

_____

_____

_____

_____

_____

_____

_____

_____

_____

_____

After completing this exercise, you should be able to:

- describe Maslow's hierarchy of needs.

- recognize that there are differences in the way that individuals prioritize needs and are motivated to achieve them.

- generate a disconfirming example to weaken Maslow's theory.

- speculate about factors that contribute to an individual's prioritization of motivations and needs.

▼Exercise 12.6   CHICKEN OR EGG?

EVALUATE: Justify

In 1991, researcher Simon LeVay reported evidence from autopsies that suggested the brains of homosexual men were different from the brains of heterosexual men. Specifically, he identified a region of the hypothalamus in which a cell cluster was larger in heterosexual men than in women or homosexual men. Other researchers have used brain imaging techniques to identify potential differences in the brains of homosexual and heterosexual individuals (Gladue, 1994). For example, the corpus callosum in homosexual men was reported to be up to one-third larger than the comparable structures of heterosexual men (Allen & Gorski, 1992).

It is currently unclear whether the scientific community finds this evidence persuasive, particularly because the topic is fraught with political sensitivity concerns. However, even if these differences turn out to be reliable and significant, many questions still need to be answered. One of the most critical questions is related to the causal link between the behavior (hetero- or homosexuality) and neuroanatomy. Which came first? Can one be the cause of the other? For example, we already have evidence from a wide variety of developmental studies demonstrating how one's experiences mediate the development of visual neural pathways. Given the difficulty of establishing the direction of causality (which comes first—sexual behavior or neurological structure?), this research sets the stage for serious ethical dilemmas.

Assume that you are serving on an institutional review board which has been given the charge of determining whether additional funding should be devoted to research of this type. Formulate your position about whether such research should continue. If you believe funding is justified, what additional ethical safeguards should be put in place and why?

After completing this exercise, you should be able to:

- identify some potential links between brain anatomy and sexual orientation.

- recognize the role of an institutional review board in providing ethical oversight of research.

- formulate and defend an ethical position regarding politically and personally sensitive research.

▼Exercise 12.7   THE CREATIVE CONSULTANT
CREATE: Invent

Advertising professionals are specialists in human motivation. They usually start with a product, create a campaign to stir our impulse to buy, and wait to see if their expertise on human motivation will pay off in larger sales for their clients.

In this exercise, pretend you have been hired as an advertising consultant to develop an ad campaign to promote a new toothpaste. The toothpaste inventor believes his particular toothpaste will effectively reduce cavities. If you have ever studied the toothpaste section of a well-stocked grocery store, you will recognize how hard it might be to interest consumers in a new choice. How would you design your client's campaign to make his toothpaste more attractive than its competitors?

Your task is to identify four motives that you could exploit in developing the campaign. For each motive, select a name and an advertising image that will link the product and the motive. Then describe an approach based on that link. After you have described four approaches, select the one you believe would have the greatest success in generating customers for your client. Justify your choice by explaining why it could be more effective. (See Answer Key.)

Motive 1: _____

Product name: _____

Advertising approach: _____

Motive 2: _____

Product name: _____

Advertising approach: _____

Motive 3: _____

Product name: _____

Advertising approach: _____

Motive 4: _____

Product name: _____

Advertising approach: _____

Which of these four approaches would, in your judgment, be the most successful in

generating new business for your client? _____

Why would this approach be more effective than the others? _____

_____

After completing this exercise, you should be able to:

- identify four motives relevant to the challenge of selling a product.

- articulate any assumptions that might influence how you begin problem solving.

- generate some preliminary plans for advertising campaigns.

- show greater awareness of the way existing advertising campaigns link motives, product names, and advertising approaches in their attempts to influence consumers' purchasing habits.

▼Exercise 12.8 THE DIET RIOT

CREATE: Design

Dieting is an American obsession. Although there is growing evidence that changes in American diet and lifestyle have led to an increase in the percentage of people who are significantly overweight, some of the dieting craze is a result of a societal trend toward an ideal body type that projects "thin is in."

Using what you have learned about hunger, design an educational program that would help people make good decisions about weight loss. What would you teach about the physiology of hunger that might help your program members understand the purpose food serves for their bodies? _____

_____

_____

_____

_____

_____

_____

_____

Given what you have read about the psychological component of hunger, what practical suggestions for maintaining healthy eating habits and a healthy weight might you suggest? _____

_____

_____

_____

_____

_____

_____

_____

What information might you share with your program members about eating disorders? Why? _____

_____

_____

_____

_____

_____

_____

_____

After completing this exercise, you should be able to:

- describe the physiology of hunger, relying on terms such as metabolism, body chemistry, and set point.

- identify the variety of cultural and individual factors related to the development of eating disorders.

- provide realistic and practical suggestions about developing and maintaining healthy attitudes and behaviors related to food.

THE PSYCHOLOGY ADVANTAGE

Humans are endowed with powerful motives. Motives help maintain us in a steady state of homeostasis, such as the activities that moderate sleep, fluid intake, and eating. Sometimes motives encourage personal enrichment, such as the fueling of dedication that helps individuals stay the course in the pursuit of extremely difficult goals. With just one short life to live, motives organize and direct our behaviors to help us achieve the most satisfying decisions along the way.

Connections to family and friends can be enhanced by our knowledge of how motives affect behavior, particularly if we understand how powerful the appeal of short-term goals may be compared to long-term goals. For example, human relationships almost inevitably contain moments of disappointment when people tend to fall short of an idealized standard we maintain about how people should behave. We can more easily relate to why people fall away from commitments to living healthy lives. The short-term immediacy of a handful of M&M's tends to exert great power over the long-term commitment required to reach for vegetables and other healthy food substances.

Doing the right thing over the long haul has implications for the workplace as well. Taking short-cuts, minimizing what is really needed to achieve, or opting for reduced challenges may be satisfying in the short-term. However, true workplace success is more likely when we can muster the inner resolve to take in feedback, reformulate our goals, and continue to plug away on goals that require persistence to resolve. Greater workplace success will be more likely if you carefully consider what kinds of work will allow your intrinsic motivation to flourish.

Chapter

◀Emotion▶

In its common usage, the word *emotion* is synonymous with *feeling*. For psychologists, however, studying emotion involves more than examining feelings—it also includes exploring and explaining the physiological states, cognitive experiences, and measurable behaviors that are components of those feelings. The challenge of research in this area is synthesizing the uniqueness of the individual emotional experience to create a common ground of definitions and classifications that are amenable to study; one of this area's many rewards is the opportunity to explore and understand some of the most intriguing and mysterious areas of human experience. We designed these exercises in this chapter to help you practice the skills of defining and observing emotions and behaviors and to consider the significant role emotion plays in our interactions with others and with our environment.

▼Exercise 13.1 TOURIST TRAP

UNDERSTAND: Translate

Over your lifetime you will develop a remarkable ability to interpret the communications of others. You will be able not only to understand the spoken language addressed to you but also to decode the body language other members of your culture use to add visual emphasis to their communication. With practice, your interpretive processes will become so automatic that you will hardly pay conscious attention to what is communicated verbally versus what is communicated nonverbally.

This exercise offers you several examples of nonverbal behavior. Your task is to describe the behavior and then interpret it by stating the meaning our culture typically assigns to the behavior.

This task isn't as simple as it looks. Because these examples are familiar, your interpretation of them may be so automatic that you will find it hard to restrict yourself to simple behavioral descriptions. There is an interesting way to test whether your description is free from interpretation. Once you have derived your answers to the following set of questions, ask yourself, "If others had not grown up in my culture, would they describe this behavior in the same way?" Think about how a tourist to America might describe the sample behavior. Good *descriptions* of behavior should be similar across cultures; *interpretations* of behaviors may differ across cultures. (See Answer Key.)

Description of behavior: _____

_____

What meaning do North Americans assign to this nonverbal gesture? _____

_____

_____

Would tourists from other countries describe the behavior similarly?

Yes _____   No _____

Description of behavior: _____

_____

What meaning do North Americans assign to this nonverbal gesture? _____

_____

_____

Would tourists from other countries describe the behavior similarly?

Yes _____   No _____

Description of behavior: _____

_____

What meaning do North Americans assign to this nonverbal gesture? _____

_____

_____

Would tourists from other countries describe the behavior similarly?

Yes _____   No _____

Description of behavior: _____

_____

What meaning do North Americans assign to this nonverbal gesture? _____

_____

_____

Would tourists from other countries describe the behavior similarly?

Yes _____   No _____

Description of behavior: _____

_____

What meaning do North Americans assign to this nonverbal gesture? _____

_____

_____

Would tourists from other countries describe the behavior similarly?

Yes _____   No _____

Description of behavior: _____

_____

What meaning do North Americans assign to this nonverbal gesture? _____

_____

_____

Would tourists from other countries describe the behavior similarly?

Yes _____   No _____

You may be surprised to learn that these nonverbal gestures were selected for a specific purpose. Each gesture has a very distinctive meaning in the culture shared by most people who live in North America. You probably interpreted that meaning quite accurately. However, each gesture also has a decidedly different interpretation in other cultures. Turn to the Answer Key to see the kind of trouble that might result if you casually used these gestures in other lands. The idea for this exercise was based on material in Roger Axtell's *Gestures: Do's and Taboos of Body Language Around the World* (New York: John Wiley, 1991).

After completing this exercise, you should be able to:

- restrict your descriptions of behavior to a level that would be described similarly by individuals from any culture.

- describe how difficult it is to observe behavior without interpreting it.

- recognize how easily two individuals from different cultures could misinterpret each other.

- prepare more cautiously for foreign travel.

▼Exercise 13.2 PINOCCHIO'S LEGACY

UNDERSTAND: Predict

One of the great mysteries of childhood is how your parents could always tell when you were not telling the truth about something. If you think back on those moments, you probably can recognize that your parents were not practicing extrasensory perception. They were merely watching you carefully for telltale signs of discomfort (for example, averted gaze, scuffing the ground with one foot, pausing). Although your nose didn't lengthen like Pinocchio's when you told a lie, your nonverbal behavior broadcast that you were trying to get away with something.

Speculate about what would happen if there were some observable physical or behavioral changes when you told a lie. Let's assume your nose might really swell noticeably every time you told an untruth. Try to generate three creative ideas about what might happen to social behavior if such an outrageous outcome were possible.

Outcome 1: _____

_____

Outcome 2: _____

_____

Outcome 3: _____

_____

After completing this exercise, you should be able to:

- make simple predictions that result from a behavior change.

- practice making accurate behavioral descriptions.

▼Exercise 13.3   FORGET YOUR TROUBLES

APPLY: Illustrate

Happiness is an elusive feeling, according to psychologists who conduct research in emotion. Yet most of us harbor secret wishes about the things, events, or conditions that we believe would make us happier. In the mythical story of "Aladdin and His Magical Lamp" a genie grants the holder of the lamp three wishes. In this exercise, assume you've captured the genie. First, identify three wishes that you think would increase your happiness. Justify your wishes by explaining why you would be happier if each wish were granted. Finally, speculate about the impact of your good fortune—how long will your happiness endure?

Wish 1: _____

Justification: _____

_____

Speculated impact: _____

_____

Wish 2: _____

Justification: _____

_____

Speculated impact: _____

_____

Wish 3: _____

Justification: _____

_____

Speculated impact: _____

_____

Although fantasies about generous genies are fun, they don't provide much serious help in promoting happiness. The *adaptation-level principle* suggests that happiness is fleeting, no matter what wonderful things happen to us. When we make significant strides in being happy, we tend to adapt, adjusting our expectations by setting new goals that continue to make happiness somewhat elusive.

The *relative deprivation principle* offers more hope about putting our wishes in perspective. This principle suggests that we may feel better about our circumstances if we purposefully review situations that are far worse than the ones we are currently experiencing. This review can help us feel better or happier as we think of how much worse things could be.

Select just one of your three wishes and review the wish. What kind of scenario or comparison might help you feel better about your circumstances and let you capture elusive happiness for a little while? _____

_____

_____

_____

After completing this exercise, you should be able to:

- reflect appropriately on personal experience with positive affect.

- recognize the differences between the adaptation-level principle and the relative deprivation principle as regards views of happiness.

▼Exercise 13.4 EXPRESS YOURSELF!

ANALYZE: Reason

Self-help books and therapists alike regularly promote the conviction that expressing your emotions is nearly always preferable to keeping your feelings in check. Expressing emotion is a vehicle for solving problems as well as staying connected to others. However, there are situations in which expressing the fundamental emotions of fear, anger, sadness, and happiness might not be in one's best interest. Identify at least one situation for each of the emotions listed below in which the expression of the emotion might not be such a wise course.

Fear: _____

Anger: _____

Sadness: _____

Happiness: _____

After completing this exercise, you should be able to:

- distinguish whether you believe that the expression of emotion can be dictated by situation.

- describe appropriate risky consequences for the expression of emotion.

▼Exercise 13.5   'CAUSE I'M HAPPY

ANALYZE: Categorize

Singer Pharell Williams caused a worldwide sensation with his hit song, "Happy." He compared being happy to being "in a room without a roof." That exhilarating sensation of things going well with all kinds of possibilities represents what humanists would describe as "self-actualization" and what positive psychologists might describe as "flow."

Research on what makes people happy has generated some surprising findings. Perhaps you can anticipate whether certain variables appear to be correlated with happiness? See if you can categorize each of the following variables in the direction supported by psychological literature. Is the variable strongly related to happiness? Moderately related to happiness? Or has no relationship to happiness?

Happiness Variable	Strong Relationship	Moderate Relationship	No Relationship
Being a parent			
Love & marriage			
Social activity			
Personality			
Money			
Age			
Health			
Attractiveness			
Work			
Genetics			
Social activity			
Intelligence			

After completing this exercise, you should be able to:

- discuss how behavioral variables can influence happiness.

- distinguish variables that have a counterintuitive impact on happiness.

- identify which variables seem to apply to one's own level of happiness.

▼Exercise 13.6   A ROUSING WALK IN THE WOODS
EVALUATION: Choose

One of the more challenging ideas to comprehend regarding our understanding of emotions is that, to date, our understanding is pretty limited. Currently, four scientific perspectives offer alternative explanations regarding how we experience emotions.

1. **James-Lange Theory.** The first psychological theory to proffer an explanation of emotion appeared around 1885 when two theorists (James and Lange) derived similar conclusions about emotional origins. The theory suggests that we experience emotion as the result of specific autonomic patterns of arousal. I notice that I feel aroused and the specific form of arousal dictates what kind of emotion I am likely to feel. In the James-Lange theory arousal produces emotion.

2. **Cannon-Bard Theory.** In 1927, the Cannon-Bard theory countered James-Lange's approach by suggesting that arousal was more generalized rather than specific. Cannon-Bard said arousing stimuli will be processed below the cortex, probably in the thalamus. At that site, the signal splits with one pathway to conscious awareness while another pathway ramps up arousal. Arousal and conscious recognition of the emotional state happen simultaneously.

3. **Schachter Two-Factor Theory.** In the early 1960s, Schachter proposed the Two-Factor Theory to take into account human capacity for cognition in interpreting emotion. An arousing stimulus initiates autonomic nervous activity, but we consciously decide or label a specific feeling after the cerebrum conducts an appraisal to put the arousal in context. Arousal is mediated by cognitive appraisal before an emotional state transpires.

4. **Evolutionary Theories.** Although Darwin speculated about the origins of emotions as early as 1872, contemporary evolutionary theory suggests that humans are hard-wired for a specific set of emotional responses that don't really require cognitive mediation to work. The most powerful emotions confer a survival advantage.

Each theory provides some value although no theory has succeeded in displacing another. Each offers an interesting perspective on how emotion unfolds in human experience. Let's put that to the test with the following scenario.

Tasha decided to go for a walk in the woods. It was a glorious, warm day and she was in a terrific mood, having just learned that she passed her math midterm. As she turned a corner in the path, a large black snake slithered into her path. Before she could take action, a park ranger ran up the path and herded the snake into the brush. When the ranger turned around, Tasha was taken with how handsome the ranger looked.

The short story lends itself to an exploration and comparison of theory of emotion. See if you can choose the most relevant theories in connection with the following questions.

	Evolutionary	James-Lange	Cannon-Bard	Schachter Two-Factor
Which theory explains being in a good mood due to math performance?				
Which theory requires arousal as the first step in the sequence?				
Which theory fits best with fight-or-flight reactions?				
Which theory helps explain that the park ranger might be perceived as more appealing following his rescue activities?				
Which theory invokes subcortical activity as an essential step?				

After completing this exercise, you should be able to:

- distinguish among the four theories of emotion.
- identify commonalities that exist across the four theories.
- decide which emotion you like the best.

▼Exercise 13.7   HONESTY IS THE BEST POLICY

EVALUATION: Take Perspective

We don't always need polygraph machines to detect liars. Both business and government rely on honesty for their success, and both would welcome a magic machine that would be able to differentiate honest from dishonest employees. This quest for a magic box has led to an unfortunate and unjustifiable reliance on polygraph tests.

Although the American Psychological Association has advised the public about the limits of polygraph testing, professional lie detection in America is big business. The polygraph machine, which monitors physiological arousal, cannot distinguish "little white lies" from whoppers, but it can indicate that the person being tested is decidedly uncomfortable. We must assume that lying causes this discomfort. The examiner begins the test by establishing a resting level or base rate of arousal. To do this, he or she asks several questions that are assumed to provoke an honest response, such as "Is your name _____?" "Do you live at _____?" "Have you worked for the company for more than two years?" After establishing the baseline, the examiner asks a question designed to catch a liar. A significant increase in arousal is presumed to be caused by the strain of the moment and the fear of getting caught.

The use of lie detection as part of normal business practice is controversial and has been legally challenged. Your task in this exercise is to develop arguments for and against using lie detection in business settings and to identify the values that might underlie each of these positions. (See Answer Key.)

An Owner's Pro-Use Position

Assume that you are the owner of a shoe store and that for the last two weeks your cash register hasn't been balancing at the end of the day. You are certain that someone is shorting the cash drawer, but you have no evidence to suggest which of your employees is guilty. You propose a broad screening using a polygraph machine to try to narrow the field to a few probable culprits. What arguments could you use to persuade your employees to submit to the screening? What values are at the core of your plan of action?

Value(s): _____

_____

Arguments: _____

_____

An Employee's Anti-Use Position

Now assume you are an innocent employee working at the same store. You have not seen anyone shorting the cash drawer, although you recognize that someone could easily do so because business practices are quite loose in the store. You are being asked to submit to a broad screening, but you find the idea offensive. What key points would you propose in your opposition to the plan? What value(s) might reinforce your position?

Value(s): _____

_____

Arguments: _____

_____

After completing this exercise, you should be able to:

- develop two opposite positions about polygraph use in business settings.
- identify possible value systems supporting each position.
- recognize the connection between values and arguments.
- understand how two positions could be effectively justified and still be diametrically opposed.
- predict what you might do if asked to submit to a polygraph test.

▼ Exercise 13.8   WHAT IS THIS THING CALLED LOVE?

CREATE: Investigate

Songwriter Cole Porter once asked musically, "What Is This Thing Called Love?" That question has plagued psychologists interested in emotions and intimate relationships. How can one research a phenomenon that seems to be as unique as love? Psychologists can't exactly conduct experimental research on how people fall in love. (Imagine trying to set up a controlled observation in which you randomly assign individuals to "heartbreak" and "no heartbreak" conditions!) However, psychologists can try to study aspects of the phenomenon, although that too is a challenge.

Your task in this exercise is to figure out just what would be measured if you tried to quantify falling in love. Join with a group of students who are about your age. How many different indicators can you generate that might be evidence of falling in love? Why is there so little uniformity across individuals in such an important emotional experience? Of those indicators, do any particularly reveal the measure that is most relevant to your own experience?

Indicators: _____

_____

_____

Why is there so much variability across people? _____

_____

_____

Which indicators are most relevant to your own experience? _____

_____

_____

After you complete this exercise, you should be able to:

- describe a variety of measures that could be used to study love.
- provide a rationale for why variability exists in the outcome measures.

THE PSYCHOLOGY ADVANTAGE

Plato once said, "Human emotion flows from three main sources: desire, emotion, and knowledge." Remarkably, emotions have proven to be a particularly challenging arena for psychologists to make headway in understanding. However, even with what little we do know, psychology students have an advantage over those who haven't studied psychology in recognizing some implications that flow from emotion research.

First, emotions vary in intensity. Emotions range from very mild to exquisitely intense. We don't always communicate that full range of emotions when we talk with others. Recount how often you might report being "depressed" when actually you are just a little sad. That tendency to inflate reports can be an obstacle in helping others understand our true emotional states.

Second, emotions vary in impact. Emotions can enhance experience, taking an opportunity with positive potential into the realm of self-actualization. On the other hand, emotions can magnify negative outcomes. Adding negative feeling to negative events is the source of real human suffering.

Finally, emotions—good or bad—are fleeting. Human design doesn't allow for emotions to be sustained easily. In the case of bad things happening and their attendant unpleasant emotions, that's a good thing. Researchers tell us that most of us don't hang on to bad feelings for very long. The ugly breakup, the loss of promotion, the bad grade—all of them produce a funk that is temporary. Particularly when negative emotions prompt consideration of dire action (for example, suicidal impulses, revenge), you should stave off the impulse because the bad feeling driving the undesirable action will inevitably fade. On the other hand, that design that helps us rebound also means that positive emotions don't hang on either. The lesson is that one should wallow in powerful positive feelings when they do occur. Take advantage of good feeling while it is in full bloom.

Chapter

◀ **Social Psychology** ▶

Human beings are uniquely social organisms. Social psychologists study the systematic patterns that emerge as human beings interact with one another. Examples include the factors that increase obedience to authority figures, the influence of social roles and contexts on behavior, and even the variables that make people love each other. The exercises in this chapter highlight different specialized areas in social psychology and address critical thinking attitudes as well as critical thinking skills.

▼ Exercise 14.1 PRIDE AND PREJUDICES

PART 1: UNDERSTAND: Compare

Prejudice represents an enduring attitude that predisposes a favorable or unfavorable response toward a group. It is remarkably easy to acquire prejudice. Because our brains detect patterns in what we experience, we may be able to generate prejudicial conclusions based on very little evidence. Negative experiences with even one representative of a group can engender lifelong beliefs, emotions, and behaviors toward members of that group.

Many college students (and professors, too) deny that they have prejudices. Chances are that such broad claims are simply not true. For example, based on your life experiences to date, how would you rate your degree of prejudice toward the following categories of people?

Target	Very Negative	Negative	Neutral	Positive	Very Positive
Police Officers					
Cheerleaders					
Preachers					
Psychologists					
High School Vice Principals					

Continued

Target	Very Negative	Negative	Neutral	Positive	Very Positive
Redheads					
Bald Men Who Do the "Comb-Over"					
Hunters					
AIDS Patients					
Convicted Child Molesters					
Welfare Moms					

You can see the trend here. It is hard, if not impossible, to live a bias-free life.

PART 2: ANALYZE: Categorize

How does prejudice develop? We can acquire prejudice (either positive or negative) by generalizing from direct experience with one person to a group and through observation and imitation of the attitudes of others. Both social and cognitive factors encourage and sustain prejudice.

Social Factors

Social factors that promote prejudice include the following:

- *In-group bias* causes us to favor arbitrarily those we perceive to be like us.

- *Scapegoating* suggests that our frustrations are reduced when we can blame someone else for our problems.

- *Social inequalities* encourage perceptions that justify discriminatory beliefs and treatment.

Cognitive Factors

Cognitive processes can also sustain patterns of prejudice.

- *Categorization* encourages us to simplify the world by making people and events as predictable as possible. Categorizing sometimes produces stereotypes that offer the illusion of predictability.

- *Vivid cases* determine those instances in which we are likely to overgeneralize from a few exceptional cases to a group expectation.

- The *just-world phenomenon* allows us to blame the victim, thereby offering reassurance that good people will triumph and bad people will meet appropriately wretched ends.

Now revisit your prejudice ratings and determine which explanations may have influenced your ratings on the target groups for which you registered either a positive or negative bias. See if you can identify the likely sources of prejudice by checking those that may have contributed to your ratings. The manner in which the prejudice develops probably has some bearing on whether the prejudice can be modified.

	In-Group Bias	Scape-goating	Social Inequality	Categorizing	Vivid Case	Just World
Police Officers						
Cheerleaders						
Preachers						
Psychologists						
High School Vice Principals						
Redheads						
Bald Men Who Do the "Comb-Over"						
Hunters						
AIDS Patients						
Convicted Child Molesters						
Welfare Moms						

An honest assessment of the possible sources of your own prejudices can determine how open you might be to changing your point of view. William James, the father of American psychology, argued that the function of a good education is the "rearrangement of prejudice."

After completing this exercise, you should be able to:

- identify at least some target groups for which you had either a positive or negative predisposition.

- designate your individual profile of preferences and the sources from which these may have developed.

- speculate about the way in which a type of source may give rise to the prejudice as well as how modifiable the prejudice might be.

- discriminate between prejudices that might have negative, positive, or neutral impacts.

▼Exercise 14.2   DEAR ABBY

APPLY: Illustrate

Dear Abby,

I have been dating a young woman for about eight months. I fear she is losing interest in me. We attend different universities, so I can't spend as much time with her as I would like. I'm afraid she may have fallen for some other guy. Can you give me some advice about how to win her back?

Signed,
Worried and Weary

Advice columnist Abby has gone on vacation. The column editor, who knows you've been studying principles of physical attraction and love at school, has asked you to pinch-hit. He thinks you'd be just the right person to advise Worried and Weary. How could you use the following concepts from social psychology to make some recommendations that will help Worried and Weary with his romantic dilemma? (See Answer Key.)

How would *proximity* principles influence your advice? _____

_____

What could you recommend regarding *physical attractiveness*? _____

_____

How would *similarity* principles influence your advice? _____

_____

How would you incorporate *arousal* in your recommendations? _____

_____

How would you address the importance of establishing *equity* in enduring relationships?

_____

What role should *self-disclosure* play in securing the relationship? _____

_____

From these principles, draft your response to Worried and Weary:

Dear Worried,

_____

_____

_____

_____

_____

_____

_____

_____

Signed,
Glad When Abby Gets Back!

People vary in the ease with which they offer advice about managing the behavior of others. Evaluate your comfort level in serving as Abby's substitute by applying principles associated with interpersonal attraction:

_____

_____

_____

_____

After completing this exercise, you should be able to:

- apply principles of liking and attraction to create some meaningful advice.

- distinguish the relative effectiveness of these principles for developing a romantic strategy.

- question the use of psychology in influencing or manipulating the lives of others.

- determine whether knowledge of liking and attraction principles will influence how you proceed in your own relationships.

▼Exercise 14.3   THE SOUR GRAPES PRINCIPLE

ANALYZE: Reason

One life lesson you may have learned growing up is from one of Aesop's Fables called "The Fox and the Grapes." In the fable, a fox wants to eat some grapes but they are inaccessible. After much effort, the fox walks away but comments that the grapes were probably sour. Frustrated in his goal, the fox generated a rationale—or rationalization—that made the loss easier to manage. Many scholars have observed that Aesop's fable actually illustrated cognitive dissonance.

One of the hardest concepts to understand in Social Psychology is Leon Festinger's (1957) concept of cognitive dissonance. The reason is that his findings were counter-intuitive, meaning common sense predicts just the opposite outcome of what Festinger discovered. Asking research participants to engage in a mind-numbing, peg-turning experience followed by a review of how enjoyable the experience was typically leads to the conclusion that people who were paid $20 to engage in the experience would automatically say they liked it more. However, the findings didn't support that conclusion. Those who participated with minimal incentives ($1) on average reported that they "enjoyed" the experience more. Did they really "enjoy" the experience? Probably not. But the key to this unexpected outcome comparison is that the minimally compensated participants enjoyed it "more" than those who reaped more reward. Their enjoyment ratings were significantly different as determined by statistical analysis, but neither group probably loved the experience.

Once students get past the counterintuitive nature of Festinger's findings, the value of the principle Festinger established can easily be seen in multiple practical examples. Festinger claimed that humans could not sustain the condition of cognitive dissonance, the turmoil that transpires when you simultaneously entertain two incompatible ideas. Something's gotta give! Festinger predicted that people will either modify their original perception/attitude or change the behavior that produced the dissonance as a means of restoring order. Resolving the dissonance may involve distorting reality, as shown when people rationalize their behavior by offering explanations that don't quite fit with the facts of the matter. Applied to Festinger's original study, cognitive dissonance was resolved when the participants who were not well compensated justified their participation by reporting it to be more enjoyable. Their positive attitude reduced their cognitive strain by rationalizing that the experience wasn't really so bad.

In the following examples of college life, explain which path would be most likely—a change in attitude or a change in behavior? Justify your answer.

Dissonance Example #1: The Charming Math Teacher

You absolutely love your math teacher. She is vibrant, engaging, and approachable. You want to turn in a good performance on your first exam and you study hard. Unfortunately, your grade is barely passing. You are not only disappointed, but you worry about the negative impression your performance has cast.

Which is more likely? Will you change your attitude (for example, modify your favorable feelings about the teacher and stop worrying about her opinion) or will you strengthen your study habits in the hopes of a strong impression recovery?

_____

_____

_____

Dissonance Example #2: Paying Off Student Loans

You are very pleased with the education you are getting in college. The teachers are talented, the college administrators seem to care, and the setting is awe-inspiring. However, you learn that the college president has just proposed a 10 percent increase in tuition and a hefty increase in student fees to increase funding of the football team. Although you love the education, you are decidedly unhappy with the addition this will mean to your student debt load on graduation.

Which is more likely? Would you change your attitude (maybe the place isn't as great as you thought) or would you change your behavior (show less motivation to succeed or talk less favorably about your program)?

_____

_____

_____

Dissonance Example #3: Lonelyhearts

Your studies are going very well but after several months in college you recognize that you are lonely. Your college offers great academic life but leaves something to be desired on the social front.

Which is more likely? How do you resolve this dissonance? Do you change your attitude or behavior?

_____

_____

_____

Dissonance Example #4: Cram Regrets

How many times have you been told cramming is a bad idea? Yet test time rolls around and despite the good advice, you still find yourself up long after you should be in bed, trying to extract every bit of study time you can before your midterm. Using a cognitive dissonance explanation, how do you resolve the dissonance problem in knowing cramming is less effective but doing it anyway?

_____

_____

_____

After completing this exercise, you should be able to:

- describe how Leon Festinger originally demonstrated cognitive dissonance.

- explain how cognitive dissonance works to motivate changes in attitude or behavior.

- deduce a more likely pathway for the resolution of cognitive dissonance situations in college.

- justify why people engage in self-destructive behaviors when they know their behavior is damaging.

▼Exercise 14.4   FOR THE SAKE OF THE CHILDREN

EVALUATE: Assess

Many social critics are arguing about the best way to deal with violence in our children's schools. Many people, including psychologists, have offered suggestions to school systems to prevent future violence. Below we list several suggestions that have been proposed to help with the problem. Use psychological concepts from the social psychology chapter of your book to explain each suggestion's potential for effectiveness. Then offer some criticisms (both positive and negative) about the likelihood that the suggestion would be effective.

1. Metal detectors at the school entrances:
   a. Related psychological concepts: _____
   b. Positive criticism: _____
   c. Negative criticism: _____
   d. Predicted success: _____

2. The requirement to wear school uniforms:
   a. Related psychological concepts: _____
   b. Positive criticism: _____
   c. Negative criticism: _____
   d. Predicted success: _____

3. Sensitivity training built into the curriculum:
   a. Related psychological concepts: _____
   b. Positive criticism: _____
   c. Negative criticism: _____
   d. Predicted success: _____

4. Holding parents accountable for the violent actions of their children:
   a. Related psychological concepts: _____
   b. Positive criticism: _____
   c. Negative criticism: _____
   d. Predicted success: _____

After completing this exercise, you should be able to:

- discuss the relationship between basic principles of social psychology and the phenomenon of violence in the schools.

- evaluate the feasibility of a proposed solution to a social problem by weighing both its positive and negative features.

- predict likely success of a social intervention through reasoning.

- feel some empathy for the challenge that children may be facing today due to the threat of violence as a part of the expected school experience.

▼ Exercise 14.5   PEOPLE WERE STUPID BACK THEN

PART 1: EVALUATE: Take Perspective

In the early 1960s, Stanley Milgram conducted a unique demonstration of the perils of obedience to authority. His ingenuity in design captured the attention of the scientific and lay communities alike. By thrusting unwitting volunteers into the position of "teacher" in a seemingly random selection process, Milgram was able to demonstrate that a majority of normal individuals would go to extraordinary lengths to harm another person when they were encouraged to do so by an authority figure.

Despite the power of the demonstration, the impact of the original work can be hard to grasp. Students often exempt themselves from the obedience patterns that Milgram described. Some even claim that "people were stupid back then."

The purpose of Part 1 of this exercise is to put yourself in the shoes of the "teacher." Read the following description and try to imagine the thoughts and emotions of the teacher (the real subject in the Milgram research) so that you can develop an appreciation for the impact of conforming to the social expectations and demands of authority figures. (See Answer Key.)

You are ushered into a room with another volunteer who is a middle-aged man. Another man is already in the room; he is wearing a white coat, and he introduces himself as "the doctor" in charge of the experiment. He seems kindly enough. He begins to explain the procedure to you and the other volunteer. He suggests that the procedure that will follow may involve some pain from electric shocks.

What do you think and feel? _____

_____

The explanation continues. By a toss of a coin, you become the teacher. Your job will be to help the other volunteer to learn pairs of words. You will do this by punishing each of his mistakes, using an electric shock.

What do you think and feel? _____

_____

The researcher takes both of you to a small area away from the main room, and he begins to attach some electrodes to the other volunteer. The volunteer explains that he has a heart problem and wonders if that will be a problem in the procedure. The researcher says, "Not really."

What do you think and feel? _____

_____

The researcher demonstrates the shock by administering it to you at mild levels, telling you that this will give you an idea of the potential discomfort you will be administering. The level of shock you feel is fairly low, as demonstrated on the control box, but it is uncomfortable.

What do you think and feel? _____

_____

You return with the researcher to the main room where he explains your job as the teacher. You will punish incorrect word associations, which you will recognize by consulting a list you hold in your hand. You will be required to increase the voltage every time the learner makes an error.

What do you think and feel? _____

_____

You begin your role as the teacher. The learner's first few answers are accurate, but then he begins making mistakes. You hit the appropriate shock levers, and the learner protests mildly.

What do you think and feel? _____

_____

You turn to the authority figure with a questioning look. He calmly reassures you that it is important for you to continue for the sake of the experiment.

What do you think and feel? _____

_____

As you increase the shock levels, the learner's protests become louder. Eventually, the learner's protests stop altogether. When you turn to the researcher, he nods to affirm that this is the proper procedure and encourages you to continue. He states that he will assume full responsibility.

What do you think and feel? _____

_____

Just how far might you have taken the process? _____

_____

PART 2: EVALUATE: Justify

Psychological testing on the Milgram participants indicated that they were neither unusually mean-spirited nor abnormal in their relationships with others. Yet a large number (66 percent) increased the shock levels all the way to the end of the available range—despite clear warnings on the shock control mechanism that such an action could be dangerous. Can you generate some explanations of why this result—which no psychiatrists anticipated prior to the experiment—would occur? (See Answer Key.)

How did the setting contribute? _____

_____

How did the behavior of the learner contribute? _____

_____

How did the emotional state of the true subject (the "teacher") contribute? _____

_____

How did the teacher's experience of being shocked during the demonstration contribute?

_____

How did "luck" contribute? _____

_____

How did the demeanor of the researcher contribute? _____

_____

Were people more stupid back then? _____

_____

Most of the teachers were so engrossed in the situation that they didn't think critically about the situation. If they had, they might have been less vulnerable to the pressures of authority. For example, why would the researcher even need the teacher? If the goal was to find out the impact of punishment on learning, the researcher could have administered the shock himself. The critical thinking that did occur, as you may have demonstrated in your explanation, may have been much more focused on worry and fear about the impact of the actions than on the right of the researcher to require another person to perform harmful actions on others.

After completing this exercise, you should be able to:

- describe the process used in the Milgram "obedience to authority" study.

- infer the kinds of thoughts, feelings, and actions the teacher probably experienced in the Milgram demonstration.

- state how many features in the demonstration converged to form a powerful incentive to obey the authority figure.

- justify why normal human beings took the course of action they did in Milgram's study.

- speculate about the impact that your knowledge of this demonstration may have on your own obedience to authority figures.

▼Exercise 14.6   BUT MY TEACHER *MADE* ME DO IT!

CREATE: Invent

A standard assignment in social psychology is to ask you to violate a norm that governs social behavior and report the responses of people who observe you during the violation. This exercise asks you to perform a norm violation but adds four simple requirements:

1. Do the exercise in pairs. One individual should be the norm violator and the other the helper who can watch the reaction of observers. Then switch roles to see if the responses of the observers are the same.

2. The norm violation should not put you at risk for arrest.

3. Explain how this exercise demonstrates *attribution theory.* Contrast how you and your partner would explain the violation of the norm with how the observers would interpret it.

4. Your norm violation should be more creative than facing the rear wall in the elevator. Challenge yourself to come up with something that might be worthy of *Candid Camera.*

Your report: _____

Norm violation attempted: _____

Observations: _____

_____

Using attribution theory, how would you explain your motives for norm violation?

_____

How would an onlooker explain your norm violation? _____

_____

After completing this exercise, you should be able to:

- define norms and the roles they play in social interaction.

- describe behavior without adding interpretation.

- apply attribution theory terminology to distinguish how actors and observers explain their own motivations.

- explain why extremes in norm violation often involve the police.

▼Exercise 14.7   HOW CAN I HELP?

CREATE: Design

Social psychologists have long been intrigued by the conditions that give rise to helping behavior. For example, the horrifying case study of Kitty Genovese, in which a New York apartment dweller was killed while several people in the neighborhood heard screams yet took no action, suggests that people will deny help if they can assume that someone else will come to the rescue. On the other hand, people are more likely to spring into action if they have the impression that no one else is around to take action. There are gender differences in forms of helping, too. For example, men may be more likely to take personal risks than women when it seems that it would be physically unsafe to help another.

Suppose we want to find out about helping factors among college students in loaning notes from a missed class. Design an experiment that will help you test a hypothesis about a factor that is most likely to elicit a helpful response from a college student. Describe your experimental design by following these steps:

First, brainstorm some variables that might influence the decision to loan class notes:

_____

_____

Select one variable and work with the following questions to develop an experimental design on altruistic behavior:

What is your hypothesis regarding "class note-loaning behavior?" _____

_____

Who should be the participants in the study? _____

What would be the dependent variable and how would you measure it? _____

_____

Describe your procedure, including any elements that you would attempt to control:

_____

_____

What independent variable would you be testing, and why does that variable appeal to you? _____

_____

Do you think the experiment would confirm your hypothesis? _____

_____

After completing this exercise, you should be able to:

- speculate about variables that influence altruistic behavior.

- design a simple experiment that can explore a hypothesis about loaning class notes as a form of altruism.

- correctly distinguish between independent and dependent variables in social psychology experiments.

- reflect on your own sensitivity about being helpful to peers who make this request of you in the future.

THE PSYCHOLOGY ADVANTAGE

Knowing social psychology can produce far-reaching personal consequences. Recognizing the reach of bystander apathy may facilitate a faster and more helpful response during an emergency. You may be able to exercise greater self-protection by resisting emotional appeals to persuasion and actively rejecting inappropriate requests for you to conform or become obedient to authority figures. You may be able to overcome group pressures following a sports victory to act up and act out.

In dealing with friends and loved ones, the lessons associated with perspective taking can make a huge difference in how you resolve conflict, particularly with regard to putting the brakes on some automatic processes we use to draw conclusions. For example, understanding attribution processes will make you more vigilant about the degree to which you engage in excusing yourself regarding misbehavior but exercise hypercritical judgment about the misbehavior of others. If you recognize that you can't know all the variables that are involved in explaining any behavior, it can make you less hesitant to jump into the fray with the "truth." Truth is relative and personal. If anything, that insight slows you down before blaming, criticizing, or other behaviors produce regret and real damage to a relationship.

Chapter

◀ Personality ▶

Personality is a puzzle. On any given day, we can be alternately crabby or charming, aloof or appealing, abrasive or ingratiating. We can even pull off those extremes within one hour. Although we may experience many variations in the social self that we present to others, psychologists prefer to study our enduring traits or characteristics in order to describe, explain, and predict how we will behave. Psychologists, of course, are not the only ones interested in describing personality. Astrologers, handwriting analysts, and fortune tellers also specialize in developing portraits of personality that, although they may be appealing, fall far short of the scientific standards that psychologists observe.

▼ Exercise 15.1 FREUD MEETS MOTHER GOOSE

UNDERSTAND: Translate and Predict

Sigmund Freud was a man of singular accomplishments. His speculations about the structure and motives of human behavior have always generated significant controversy. His ideas were initially unpopular because they suggested that sexual motives were much more responsible for human behavior than his own Victorian culture would easily tolerate. Despite Freud's controversial beginnings, many of his contributions to understanding human behavior have endured.

Part of Freud's work was a stage theory of human development that organized significant stages around pleasurable activities. First is the *oral stage.* Freud suggested that infants derive pleasure through oral exploration. Further, he indicated that disturbances in the weaning experience will contribute to distinctive personality structures as the children mature into adults. Oral challenges to personality involve management of eating patterns and overall activity levels, whether impulsive (excessive) or restrictive (deficient).

Next is the *anal stage,* in which the child's attention shifts to the pleasures of elimination. Strain in the anal stage usually results in characteristic styles of handling possessions and orderliness, whether uncontrolled and sloppy or overcontrolled and precise.

In the third or *phallic stage,* children are attentive to the pleasures derived from sexual and gender identification. Fixations in this stage tend to produce exaggerated adult sexual responses, whether overactive or underactive.

In the *latency stage,* according to Freud, children's sexual motives go underground, waiting only for adult maturity for complete sexual expression.

The final stage is the *genital stage*. People who escape fixations at earlier stages are able to experience mature sexuality. Freud was quite pessimistic about the number of people who could realize this stage of development without scars from early developmental trauma.

Another of Freud's most interesting contributions is the concept of the defense mechanism. Freud suggested that we cope with our anxieties by converting them into more socially responsible activities that symbolize the original conflict. He called this conversion process *sublimation,* and he believed sublimations were responsible for many socially acceptable achievements. In this exercise, we are going to assume that sublimation has been at work in the creation of the nursery rhymes that you probably learned as a child. For example, what psychoanalytic insights could you propose about the author of the following nursery rhyme?

> *Jack Sprat could eat no fat.*
> *His wife could eat no lean.*
> *And so between them both,*
> *They licked the platter clean.*

One might propose that oral fixation dominates this nursery rhyme about eating. Jack is probably thin. His wife is probably fat. However, they appear to spend all their time fretting about food, a characteristic of those who are orally deprived. The theme of this nursery rhyme may present some frustrations the author experienced in the oral stage. Freud would suggest that the author might be inclined in adulthood to show other problems related to oral fixation. Orally fixated adults show one of two patterns. They may be focused on oral stimulation—taking in food or performing other behaviors—such as sucking on pens, chewing ice cubes, and kissing—that will stimulate the pleasure center of the mouth. Or they may avoid oral stimulation and lose conscious interest in eating or other pleasurable mouth activities.

Assuming that each of the following nursery rhymes represents sublimation, analyze how Freud might interpret the real motives that lie behind the author's creation of the story. Identify the stage in which you think the creator of the nursery rhyme was fixated; then speculate about the kind of personality the creator might have had. (See Answer Key.)

Jack and Jill

> *Jack and Jill went up the hill*
> *To fetch a pail of water.*
> *Jack fell down and broke his crown,*
> *And Jill came tumbling after.*

Likely developmental stage at fixation: _____

Justify your answer: _____

Predict the character of the creator's adult personality structure: _____

Three Blind Mice

> *Three blind mice. Three blind mice.*
> *See how they run. See how they run.*
> *They all ran after the farmer's wife.*
> *She cut off their tails with a carving knife.*
> *Did you ever see such a sight in your life,*
> *As three blind mice?*

Likely developmental stage at fixation: _____

Justify your answer: _____

Predict the character of the creator's adult personality structure: _____

Mary, Mary, Quite Contrary

Mary, Mary, quite contrary,
How does your garden grow?
With silver bells and cockle shells
and pretty maids all in a row.

Likely developmental stage at fixation: _____

Justify your answer: _____

Predict the character of the creator's adult personality structure: _____

After completing this exercise, you should be able to:

- speculate how a significant Freudian theme could be translated into a literary work.

- support speculations of Freudian interpretation, using appropriate examples.

- recognize that fixations can produce different patterns of adult behavior.

- predict adult personality patterns based on your speculations about the fixations.

▼Exercise 15.2   MATCHMAKER, MATCHMAKER

APPLY: Classify

One of the more compelling and popular approaches to explaining personality patterns is the framework referred to as the Big 5. This approach suggests that there are five fairly stable dimensions on which we can make judgments about personality. Not only are the dimensions stable, but they appear to have some cross-cultural applicability as well. According to this theory, we can evaluate personality along the following five dimensions:

Conscientiousness _____ Irresponsibility
Stability _____ Neurosis
Extraversion _____ Introversion
Open to experience _____ Closed to experience
Agreeableness _____ Hostility

Suppose that you decide to set up a dating service based on the Big 5 principles. What kind of connection could occur when you match extremes on each of the dimensions? How would you classify the likely outcome of the following matches? On the surface, would such matches be workable, unworkable, or hard to determine? Justify your answer.

a. Conscientious + Conscientious: _____

  Conscientious + Irresponsible: _____

  Irresponsible + Irresponsible: _____

b. Stable + Stable: _____

  Stable + Neurotic: _____

  Neurotic + Neurotic: _____

c. Extravert + Extravert: _____

  Extravert + Introvert: _____

  Introvert + Introvert: _____

    d. Open + Open: _____

       Open + Closed: _____

       Closed + Closed: _____

    e. Agreeable + Agreeable: _____

       Agreeable + Hostile: _____

       Hostile + Hostile:_____

After completing this exercise, you should be able to:

- describe the Big 5 theory of personality.

- discuss how the Big 5 characteristics might differ in other cultures.

- classify the interaction potential of mixed styles according to the Big 5.

- recognize what a foolish business enterprise this would be!

▼Exercise 15.3   MASLOW'S DECLINE

ANALYZE: Solve

For decades, Abraham Maslow's hierarchy of needs has been one of the most popular frameworks to emerge in the formal study of psychology. His original conception proposed that lower-order needs, such as safety and satisfying biological urges, take precedence over higher-order needs, such as love and self-esteem. Poised at the top of Maslow's pyramid is the noble concept of self-actualization, which Maslow proposed is an optimal, satisfying life experience. Although the hierarchy seems to be intuitively obvious, research support for the fundamental principles expressed in the hierarchy has cast some doubt on the validity and the utility of the framework. The mounting criticisms suggest that Maslow's hierarchy is definitely losing ground as one of the revered frameworks in psychology.

How would you solve the following problems that have surfaced about the quality of Maslow's hierarchy of needs?

Criticism 1: The sequence in the hierarchy is too rigid.

_____

Criticism 2: Self-actualization promotes selfishness.

_____

Criticism 3: The hierarchy doesn't apply well outside western cultures.

_____

Criticism 4: The hierarchy may not apply well to subcultures within western culture.

_____

After completing this exercise, you should be able to:

- describe the elements of Maslow's hierarchy.

- identify contemporary criticisms of the framework that appear to be reducing its power.

- suggest modifications to Maslow's hierarchy to address current criticisms.

▼Exercise 15.4   ME ON THE RISE

ANALYZE: Explain

In Greek mythology, Narcissus was a young man so enamored with his own image that he stared at himself relentlessly in a pool of water, fell in, and drowned. Narcissism is a concept that has emerged in personality theory to capture those who demonstrate excessive self-regard. Experts suggest that narcissism is a paradox. Individuals who are narcissistic crave approval and admiration, yet may suffer from fairly fragile self-esteem. They may engage in all kinds of activity to defend against any hint of disrespect or disapproval. Over time, the initially charming, charismatic character may turn into an attention-hogging, entitled braggart.

Psychologists have reported concerns that the incidence of narcissism may be on the rise. In fact, narcissistic personality is so prevalent in American culture that many question whether it is a diagnostically sound concept. In other words, idea may not help us differentiate one person from another.

Why would narcissism be on the rise? See if you can articulate at least five reasons why Americans might be demonstrating substantially more entitlement concerns in contemporary life.

_____

_____

_____

_____

_____

After completing this exercise, you should be able to:

- discuss the origin of the concept of narcissism.

- describe the essential characteristics of someone who is narcissistic.

- formulate some hypotheses to help explain how a personality characteristic's prevalence can be linked to sociohistorical features.

▼Exercise 15.5   YOU CAN'T CHEAT AN HONEST MAN

ANALYZE: Identify

One of the most challenging problems that trait personality theorists face is that human beings may not always produce consistent behavior patterns across situations. For example, you probably consider yourself an honest person, but are you *always* honest? What are the factors that affect how honest (or not) you are in your interactions with others? Identify four variables that could influence honest dealings with others that you might need to address in research designed to examine the trait of honesty. What would be the complications in trying to conduct research in this area?

_____

_____

_____

_____

After completing this exercise, you should be able to:

- isolate how context factors can make a difference in how individuals behave.
- describe person-situation interaction.
- discuss why personality research is challenging.
- recognize the potential for ethics conflicts in conducting the research.

▼ Exercise 15.6   RORSCHACH'S FATE

EVALUATE: Justify

Projective testing is one of the activities that distinguishes the clinical psychologist as a mental health professional. Only psychologists undergo the intensive training required to use tests such as the Rorschach inkblot test to make diagnostic judgments about personality. You have probably seen this practice parodied in movies and on television. The psychologist presents a nondescript symmetrical blob of ink on a card and instructs the client, "Tell me what you see." After taking copious notes on the client's responses, the psychologist will make some interpretations of those statements by comparing the responses to normative judgments. The patterns in the Rorschach blot can determine how the psychologist will judge the relative normality of the client.

The use of the Rorschach in making diagnostic decisions is controversial. Many research scientists believe that the Rorschach practices simply do not live up to the criteria of good science. That is, Rorschach results produce neither reliable nor valid findings. On the other hand, seasoned practitioners express enormous faith in the accumulated successful experiences that they have had in interpreting Rorschach findings. These practitioners point to the popularity of the instrument in making decisions that are sometimes critical to the outcome of court cases.

Would you agree to having a Rorschach conducted as part of a psychological evaluation? Are there some circumstances in which the questionable validity and reliability of the Rorschach would make you less inclined to rely on its findings?

_____

_____

_____

After completing this exercise, you should be able to:

- describe which mental health practitioners can and cannot use projective test techniques.
- explain the basic procedure involved in Rorschach protocol and interpretation.
- describe why the Rorschach is controversial.
- speculate about circumstances in which the use of the Rorschach would be personally acceptable.

▼ Exercise 15.7   HOPELESS—OR NOT?

EVALUATE: Take Perspective

As we explore the various perspectives on personality development, you may notice that theorists differ about the degree to which change is possible. Psychologists refer to this as the principle of "determinism." Review the list of theorists on the next page and categorize each theorist's position as "deterministic" (personality is fixed) versus "nondeterministic" (personality is flexible).

Theorist	Deterministic or Nondeterministic?	Why?
Freud		
Skinner		
Rogers		
Maslow		

After completing this exercise, you should be able to:

- explain the principle of determinism.

- compare and contrast how four major personality theorists can be categorized based on the principle of determinism.

- justify how different theorists view the potential for personality change.

- develop your own views about the degree to which personality is determined.

▼Exercise 15.8   PSEUDOSCIENTIFIC PERSONALITY EXPLANATIONS
CREATE: Invent

Many people believe in pseudoscientific methods of describing personality or predicting the future. From fortune cookies to palm reading, many individuals seem especially vulnerable to simplistic approaches conveyed by clear and concrete descriptions of personality. Many believers can offer powerful testimonials about the incredible accuracy of the predictions of their favorite astrologer. Psychics now offer their services by phone, charging by the minute. The popularity of these false sciences truly attests to the famous appraisal "There's a sucker born every minute," often attributed to P. T. Barnum.

The purpose of this exercise is to use your creative processes to develop your own abilities to "read" people and to predict their behavior. (See Answer Key.)

The Stock Spiel

You will begin by generating a *stock spiel*, a trait description so general that few people could deny that it applies to them. Try to include at least five observations that anyone might find believable about himself or herself. Keep in mind that the more credible spiels are not entirely positive; some mild negative characteristics tend to enhance the realism of the statement.

_____

_____

_____

_____

Inferences from Physical Cues

To maximize the effectiveness of the ruse, you can personalize the stock spiel by adding other elements to the interpretation, based on inferences you make from physical cues offered by your "client." Can you think of five different inferences that could be justified by a person's physical traits, language, clothing, or behavioral cues, and that could enhance the credibility of your personality assessment?

Inference 1: _____

Derived from what kind of cue? _____

Inference 2: _____

Derived from what kind of cue? _____

Inference 3: _____

Derived from what kind of cue? _____

Inference 4: _____

Derived from what kind of cue? _____

Inference 5: _____

Derived from what kind of cue? _____

Now combine the inferences with the stock spiel to make a compelling personality descriptor. Does the combination of generic comments and inferred characteristics make the pseudoscientific interpretation more credible?

_____

_____

_____

_____

_____

After completing this exercise, you should be able to:

- identify five characteristics that would appeal to most people seeking pseudopsychological explanations.

- recognize the role of incorporating some negative characteristics to enhance the realism of the description.

- personalize the descriptions by generating some personal characteristics based on typical physical or behavioral cues.

- challenge pseudoscientific explanations of behavior.

THE PSYCHOLOGY ADVANTAGE

Human beings spend substantial spans of time enmeshed in the consequences of personality. In grade school, you may have gotten "citizenship" reports at grade time that actually reflected your teacher's expert opinion about how your personality was developing. Did you play by the rules or refuse to color within the lines? Did you get along well with others or prefer to hang solo? Were you cheerful and eager to take on challenges or reluctant, fearful, and rebellious?

Personality factors continue to play a big part in your success as a college student. Most professors will grudgingly acknowledge that students tend to develop a "social bank account" by their behavior in class. Students who are conscientious, approachable, and enthusiastic are likely to get the benefit of the doubt when it's time to determine grades. For example, it is easier to interpret a borderline grade as worthy of higher value if you have been a constructive contributor.

Similarly, success in the workplace can sometimes be more influenced by personality factors than professional competence. People who are hot-tempered, narcissistic, entitled, slow to learn, oblivious to the context, or disloyal can easily be on the fast track to unemployment, regardless of their accomplishments.

Learning about personality and exercising the critical thinking skills associated with personality renders significant advantages in both personal and professional contexts. These lessons reinforce the vast differences that exist across people. Yet, we all engage in protective strategies to defend against anxieties. The very act of using defense mechanisms virtually guarantees that we don't share the same reality. Two people in conflict—whether personal or professional—will be struggling not to be the one to blame. Being aware that you, too, distort reality without really realizing it should serve as a permanent reminder to be temperate in conflicts and patient with those who don't see the world as you see it.

16
Chapter

◀Psychological Disorders▶

Scholars in psychiatry and psychology collaborated in an unprecedented manner to produce the fifth version of the *Diagnostic and Statistical Manual (DSM-5),* which offers a comprehensive description of every significant variation in behavior that falls outside normal expectations. Although the diagnostic compendium remains somewhat controversial, the *DSM-5* offers an impressive range of disorders that remind us of how fragile normal experience can be. It may be impossible to cruise through life without experiencing at least a few of the disorders captured in the *DSM-5.* The following exercises address the problems psychologists encounter when they attempt to make diagnostic judgments about normal versus disordered behavior.

▼Exercise 16.1 HOW MUCH CRAZY?
UNDERSTAND: Explain

Everyone, not just psychologists, appears to be fascinated by the range of behavior of which humans are capable. Some behaviors definitely qualify as out of the ordinary. Psychologists apply some simple criteria before determining whether a behavior should technically be classified as "disordered" or abnormal. First, psychologists focus on whether the behavior is typical of most people. Behaviors that violate the "norm" of what most people would do technically constitute disordered behavior. Behaviors that produce maladaptive activity, meaning that the behavior makes the individual not function well in society, make up the second criterion for abnormality. Related to adaptation, sometimes the dysfunctional behavior can prove to be a danger to self or others, representing the third criterion. Finally, behavior that generates personal distress is the final criterion for making a judgment about whether or not a behavior is normal.

Use the following grid to explain whether or not an identified behavior can be considered disordered:

Type of Behavior	Is It Atypical?	Is It Maladaptive?	Is It Dangerous?	Is It Personally Distressing?	Does It Meet the Criteria for Abnormality?
Making obscene phone calls					
Shoplifting					
Flaming others on the internet					
Hearing voices when no one is around					
Avoiding picnics for fear of snake encounters					
Cheating on course examinations					
Hitchhiking					
Starring in a reality television show					
Serial killing					
Feeling too blue to get out of bed					

After completing this exercise, you should be able to:

- list the characteristics of disordered behavior.

- explain why some specific behaviors technically can be classified as abnormal.

- identify behaviors that could be targets of debate about abnormality.

- apply the abnormality framework to other behaviors of interest.

▼Exercise 16.2   AND THE WINNER IS...

APPLY: Illustrate

It is commonly said during Oscar season that the best way for an actor to win an Academy Award is to play a deeply disturbed person. A recent example of this strategy was Jennifer Lawrence, who played a wacky, but endearing, widow with aspirations to win a dance competition in the film *Silver Linings Playbook*.

See if you can develop a list of performances in movies by gifted actors and try to identify the disorders that they are skillfully portraying.

If you have time during this part of the semester, you might benefit from watching a film and studying the treatment of the disorder. But, watcher beware! Sometimes artistic portrayals of psychological disorders may not truly capture the complications caused by the problem or the heroic measures their sufferers take in coping with the disease.

The answer key describes some classic performances and offers a roster of good movie watching.

_____

_____

_____

After completing this exercise, you should be able to:

• discuss why actors might prefer to take roles of those with psychological disturbances over those with normal behavior.

• recognize how syndromes can be portrayed in a variety of contexts.

• speculate about the nature of research an actor might need to complete to be effective in a role portraying a psychological disorder.

• identify specific performances that capture psychological disorders.

▼Exercise 16.3   LOVE AND WORK

APPLY: Solve

Sigmund Freud once stated that good choices in work and love make all the difference in whether individuals will lead happy lives. In the case of individuals suffering from personality disorders, long-term structural problems make interaction with others problematic so that finding the right vocation and the right partner who will put up with some disordered behavior is definitely more of a challenge. However, this exercise assumes you have the capacity to match individuals with personality disorders to the right kind of partner as well as the right kind of occupation that might make their life course a bit more satisfying. In the grid below, identify the chief characteristics of each personality disorder, then speculate about a career choice that would work with their respective eccentricities. Then play matchmaker. What kind of individual might be willing to put up with the challenges that their partner's personality structure will entail?

Personality Disorder	Key Features	Possible Occupation	Possible Partner
Narcissistic			
Avoidant			
Schizoid			
Borderline			
Antisocial			
Paranoid			
Histrionic			
Dependent			
Obsessive-Compulsive			
Schizotypal			

▼Exercise 16.4   THE END

ANALYZE: Investigate (Part 1)
EVALUATE: Choose (Part 2)

You have been worried about your friend Mitchell for some time. He seems easily upset and filled with gloom. Few things make him smile. When he does talk, he makes vague references about his capacity to surprise people, and he often says that someday the people who have disappointed him will be "really sorry." The challenge Mitchell is offering is the possibility that he might be one of the 25,000 people in the United States who will end their lives by suicide this year.

The purpose of this problem-solving exercise is twofold. First, you will try to identify aspects of Mitchell's history that might help you evaluate how serious the threat of suicide is in his case. You'll generate a list of questions that would help you investigate whether he will try to kill himself as a way out of his depression. Second, you will apply a decision-making process to determine the risk involved in either of two courses of action to help you choose the preferred course of action: (1) Take action: confronting Mitchell with your concerns and following through with appropriate support to get him the help he needs; or (2) Take no action: rejecting your original suspicions about the significance of the depressive signs and hoping for the best.

Investigating with Questions

Begin by formulating five questions whose answers might enable you to make a wiser judgment about the course of action you should take. Designing your questions may be easier if you think about the possible variables or characteristics that could contribute to depression and suicide decisions. Some of these are health status, disappointment, crisis, relationship strain, discouragement, revenge, and employment challenges. Can you think of others?

1. _____

2. _____

3. _____

4. _____

5. _____

Choosing Based on Risk Analysis

When you must make a decision, you can sometimes structure the decision in a matrix, as follows. There are four possibilities, or conditions. In two of the four conditions, you have the potential to be right (a "hit," in decision-theory terminology). In the remaining two conditions you will be wrong (a "miss").

Decision Matrix	Mitchell Is Really Suicidal	Mitchell Is Really Not Suicidal
You predict suicide	Correct diagnosis HIT	Incorrect diagnosis MISS: False Positive
You predict safety	Incorrect diagnosis MISS: False Negative	Correct diagnosis HIT

As the matrix shows, Mitchell (as the potential suicide) and you (as the diagnostic problem solver) can each make one of two choices. He can either kill himself or stay among the living. You can either decide that he is suicidal or judge that he is depressed and upset but not suicidally so.

The next part of your task is to consider these four conditions and describe the advantages and risks involved in each of them. As you do so, consider the consequences for you and for Mitchell. (See Answer Key.)

A "hit": Mitchell is suicidal and you correctly identify his intentions.

Advantages: _____

Risks: _____

A "hit": Mitchell is not suicidal and you correctly identify his intentions.

Advantages: _____

Risks: _____

A "miss": Mitchell is suicidal and you don't correctly identify his intentions.

Advantages: _____

Risks: _____

A "miss": Mitchell is not suicidal and you don't correctly identify his intentions.

Advantages: _____

Risks: _____

After completing this exercise, you should be able to:

- identify variables that may influence suicidal intentions.

- formulate questions that might lead to more insight into the choices that prompt suicide as a solution.

- examine decisions in terms of "hits" and "misses."

- plan how you might intervene if you were confronted with this problem as a real challenge.

▼Exercise 16.5   I'M JUST NOT MYSELF TODAY

EVALUATE: Criticize

The psychological disturbance called dissociative identify disorder (DID), formerly known as multiple personality disorder (MPD), is one of the most fascinating patterns that confront scholars of abnormal psychology. How could it be that a seemingly normal-looking individual could shelter multiple entities with separate interests and talents? When MPD first emerged in diagnostic circles, the problem was thought to be quite rare. However, the frequency of MPD dramatically increased through the 1970s and 1980s. MPD even emerged as a defense in murder trials. Most curiously, one young woman brought charges against a sexual partner when she indicated that only one of her personalities was in agreement with the sexual proposition.

In the late 1980s and in the 1990s, the diagnostic validity of MPD was challenged and the concept of dissociative identity disorder replaced the diagnosis in the DSM. Practical problems with the diagnostic entity continued to proliferate. Some patients were challenged about using DID symptoms to try to escape legal consequences. Some patients accused their therapists of exploitation after having been convinced in therapy that they had DID. Even some of the classic cases of DID have been speculated to be fraudulent.

How can we use the benefits of experimental design to address this problem? Some enterprising researchers recruited patients who had been diagnosed as having

MPD and conducted positron emission tomography (PET) scans on those patients. PET reveals thermal activity in the brain based on degrees of glucose use. The researchers asked the patients to do similar kinds of activities when they were experiencing different personalities and noted significant differences in the blood flow to different parts of the brain depending on their personality status. The researchers' preliminary assumptions indicated that thermal activity on a given task should be reflected in the same areas in an intact brain but might show up in different areas if MPD produced a different physiological infrastructure for each personality. Preliminary results showed different thermal activity in the same brain of an individual reporting to be functioning out of different personalities.

Based on your knowledge of experimental design, is this evidence sufficient to conclude that MPD causes the brain to become differentiated? Justify your answer.

_____

_____

_____

After completing this exercise, you should be able to:

- describe the controversy surrounding the validity of Multiple Personality Disorder.

- formulate your own position on the validity of the disorder.

- discuss the rationale of positron emission tomography in capturing brain activity.

- apply experimental design principles in forming a judgment about scientific evidence.

▼ Exercise 16.6   THE LABELING CONTROVERSY

EVALUATE: Justify

Clinical psychologists confront a challenging task each time they sit across from a new client. Every individual has a unique story to tell—often filled with pain, confusion, and other symptoms that in most cases will be interpreted as a specific diagnosis.

Although the use of diagnostic labels is a widely accepted practice, it is still somewhat controversial. Fueling the controversy, David Rosenhan conducted a field study in which he and his friends became "pseudopatients" in various inpatient settings. By reporting some symptoms that were interpreted by hospital staff as auditory hallucinations, the researchers found that they could easily be admitted as hospital inpatients; however, when they continued to act normally, they couldn't get out.

In this exercise you will do a critical analysis of the Rosenhan study by arguing both sides of the controversy: *The Rosenhan study is or is not a valid (trustworthy) test of the problems associated with labeling.* First, establish two arguments to support each side of the controversy. Then decide which side of the controversy you find more convincing.

The Rosenhan study is a valid test of the problems associated with labeling.

Argument 1: _____

_____

_____

Argument 2: _____

_____

_____

The Rosenhan study is not *a valid test of the problems associated with labeling.*

Argument 1: _____

_____

_____

Argument 2: _____

_____

_____

Which side of the controversy most closely represents your own beliefs about labeling?

Why? _____

_____

_____

After completing this exercise, you should be able to:

- recognize the relationship between the Rosenhan study and the problem of labeling in mental health today.

- identify some elements of the Rosenhan study that can be challenged.

- develop an adequate defense of Rosenhan's approach to the labeling problem.

- speculate about the role of preconceptions in making sense of psychological disorders.

▼Exercise 16.7   THE END IS NEAR (AGAIN)

EVALUATE: Take Perspective

Humans have a remarkable capacity for worry. Sometimes the worry can take on catastrophic proportions as illustrated by cyclical predictions about the world coming to an end. For a noteworthy example, as the last century came to a close, we witnessed near frenzy as many individuals believed that predicted massive computer malfunctions would produce an apocalypse dubbed "The Y2K Problem." Consequently, believers stockpiled supplies, in case there was a significant disruption of services. They stocked up on canned food and bottled water. Some bought generators. Unfortunately, some stockpiled gasoline and propane, which created new risks because of the fire hazards.

More recent doom and gloom predictions have included a 2003 prediction that the earth would collide with a giant planet-sized object named Nibiru. Nibiru worries were resurrected again in 2013 in world-ending predictions referred to as the Mayan Apocalypse. Various religious figures have unsuccessfully predicted the "Rapture," or return of Jesus, accompanied by fire storms, floods, and nuclear war. We are not in short supply of those who don't hold out much hope for the future of humanity.

Apocalyptic predictions tend to generate an array of unusual behaviors, including stockpiling foods and supplies or increasing religious service participation. When predicted dates come and go with no sign of the disturbances that were predicted by the news media, the believers who stockpiled supplies and predicted doom and gloom seem in retrospect "abnormal" and perhaps even a bit silly. In fact, the *DSM-5* probably gives you some ideas about how extreme cases of doomsayers might be diagnosed.

a. What *DSM-5* diagnosis comes the closest to capturing the abnormal pattern of stockpiling goods in anticipation of doomsday?

_____

_____

b. How people respond to a doomsday threat gives us an opportunity to explore the notion of a continuum of disorder. How might behaviors of a people who are not vulnerable to the anxieties of doomsday prediction differ from those whose fears were incapacitating?

No difficulty: _____

Minor difficulty: _____

Moderate difficulty: _____

Serious difficulty: _____

Extreme difficulty: _____

c. Finally, what if the stockpilers had been right? It seems rather easy in hindsight to label the problems of doomsday fanatics as disordered. However, if predictions of gloom and doom had been right, those who had not prepared in dramatic ways for the apocalypse would have been at a distinct disadvantage. In fact, they might be perceived as the abnormal ones. Assuming that apocalyptic fears might be justified (and there would be anyone left to debate the question), what *DSM-5* labels would be useful in explaining how underprepared individuals ignored all the obvious signs of impending doom and failed to protect themselves and their families?

_____

_____

After completing this exercise, you should be able to:

- recognize personality dynamics surrounding catastrophic but unfounded predictions.

- describe variations in intensity of a similar underlying concern.

- apply the *DSM-5* to recurring doomsday phenomena.

- consider the role of context in making abnormal judgments.

▼Exercise 16.8 ALL I NEED IS AN AGENT!

CREATE: Invent

In a prior exercise you explored the ways that actors have portrayed various psychological disorders in film. In this exercise you become the writer. Review the chapter on psychological disorders and pick one of the problems described. Identify the psychological disorder and list its symptoms. Then draft a story line that would demonstrate the full range of difficulty someone with that disorder might experience.

DSM-5 diagnosis: _____

Characteristics: _____

Plot: _____

_____

_____

After completing this exercise, you should be able to:

- describe one psychological disorder thoroughly.

- speculate about the kinds of difficulties that disorder would cause the person who suffered from the disorder.

- develop reasonable empathy for persons afflicted with the specific psychological disorder you explored.

- evaluate your potential for screenwriting!

THE PSYCHOLOGY ADVANTAGE

You've heard it expressed in dozens of ways. Here is just a sample:

- Her elevator doesn't go all the way to the top floor.

- He is two beers short of a six pack.

- A few sandwiches shy of a picnic.

- A few fries short of a Happy Meal.

- Nuttier than a fruitcake.

- The lights are on but nobody's home.

- Bats in the belfry.

- Has a screw loose.

- Mad as a hatter.

- Not playing with a full deck.

- His Wikipedia is missing some entries.

New and colorful descriptions pop up all the time to capture the essence of someone who is not behaving according to the expectations of others. All of the metaphors imply something is wrong with the behavior in question. However, people with a psychology background have an advantage in understanding the nuances of abnormality. For example, a psychology background prompts questions about the severity, duration, and frequency of the problem as well as any contextual factors that might influence the demonstration of the behavior. Those trained in psychology know that generalized descriptors, such as "having a meltdown" or undergoing a "nervous breakdown," don't really capture the specifics that a psychologist would explore. We also know to look for anxiety, depression, or long-term personality challenges at the core of the difficulty. When stress becomes a challenge on the home front or in the workplace, those with psychological backgrounds anticipate that there may be complex issues that, once understood, make the problem easier to address, to adjust, or to work around.

Chapter

◀ Therapy ▶

The stereotyped image of therapy usually involves a patient lying on a couch unraveling personal stories about life's injustices to a concerned but well-trained listener. In contemporary therapies, reality is likely to be far different. Freud's "talking cure" has evolved into a remarkable array of therapy modes, most involving therapists in active collaboration with the client. Therapy is more than listening. Helping others professionally provides an opportunity for the exercise of refined critical thinking skills, from selecting the right therapeutic strategy through designing outcome studies that demonstrate therapeutic effectiveness. The exercises in this chapter offer a simulation of the processes researchers and practitioners employ in therapy.

▼ Exercise 17.1 HOW DOES THAT MAKE YOU FEEL?

UNDERSTAND: Translate

You may have been surprised to find that therapists practice clinical arts in so many different ways. Estimates of the distinguishable "schools" of therapeutic treatment vary, but there may be as many as 400 different psychotherapeutic approaches to solving human problems in therapy. The exercise below will give you an opportunity to match a major school of therapy to the statement most representative of a practitioner from that school. See if you can determine how specific phrases reveal the practitioner's preferred approach.

Letter	Statement
__ 1.	"Tell me about your earliest memories from childhood."
__ 2.	"What were the consequences that happened after you punched your boss?"
__ 3.	"Rank order the things that frighten you from 'least' to 'most'."
__ 4.	"Let's explore how your role as a daughter, mother, and wife might influence the problem."
__ 5.	"Have you been having recurring dreams?"
__ 6.	"In what ways do you think you have fallen short of your ideals?"
__ 7.	"Pretend that your grandmother is sitting in the chair over there and tell her how you feel."
__ 8.	"You have developed a very powerful mental set that you are a loser."
__ 9.	"If you can refrain from losing your temper, you'll get two red stars."
__ 10.	"Let's try to figure out how your feelings of inferiority might be linked to your family."

Major Schools of Treatment

a. Token economy

b. Cognitive therapy

c. Gestalt therapy

d. Freudian therapy

e. Feminist therapy

f. Behavior therapy

g. Adlerian therapy

h. Humanistic therapy

i. Jungian therapy

j. Systematic desensitization

After completing this exercise, you should be able to:

• identify key characteristics of schools of therapy.

• use appropriate terminology in connection with a specific school of therapy.

• describe the main schools of therapy that are currently popular.

• explain why there might be more than one way to address a psychological disorder.

▼Exercise 17.2   EVEN DOMESTIC ENGINEERS GET THE BLUES
APPLY: Solve

Ellen looked awful. She said she had spent three relatively sleepless nights and had eaten little, and it showed. She couldn't sleep because she felt tormented by feelings of shame, guilt, and loss. She thought that it had nothing to do with her family. She had been "happily married" for nine years. The family members were all healthy. The family was financially stable and seemed to have a strong network of support in the community. Nothing was really wrong with them. Oh, sure, the kids and her husband weren't home much. He worked overtime very often. The kids were always running to soccer or other commitments. But that was the way it was supposed to be. Ellen thought her "blues" had more to do with her brother. She hadn't been able to escape strong feelings of self-recrimination since her brother died. They had had a serious fight the night before his car accident, and she had never had a chance to apologize. The last few months had been a nightmare because of the impact her unrelenting sadness was having on Ellen and her family.

The purpose of this exercise is to experiment with matching a client with an appropriate therapy. You will do this by considering the characteristics Ellen is bringing into her first clinical session and by determining the advantages and disadvantages that each of seven schools of therapy might offer her. After considering the seven frameworks, select the one that might be most helpful for the symptoms Ellen is presenting. (See Answer Key.)

Psychoanalysis
What would you expect the therapist to focus on or to do? _____

_____

What would be the advantages of using this approach? _____

_____

_____

What would be the disadvantages of using this approach? _____

_____

_____

Person-Centered Therapy

What would you expect the therapist to focus on or to do? _____

_____

_____

What would be the advantages of using this approach? _____

_____

_____

What would be the disadvantages of using this approach? _____

_____

_____

Aversive Conditioning

What would you expect the therapist to focus on or to do? _____

_____

_____

What would be the advantages of using this approach? _____

_____

_____

What would be the disadvantages of using this approach? _____

_____

_____

Cognitive Behavior Therapy

What would you expect the therapist to focus on or to do? _____

_____

_____

What would be the advantages of using this approach? _____

_____

_____

What would be the disadvantages of using this approach? _____

_____

_____

Drug Therapy

What would you expect the therapist to focus on or to do? _____

_____

_____

What would be the advantages of using this approach? _____

_____

_____

What would be the disadvantages of using this approach? _____

_____

_____

Family Therapy

What would you expect the therapist to focus on or to do? _____

_____

_____

What would be the advantages of using this approach? _____

_____

_____

What would be the disadvantages of using this approach? _____

_____

_____

Electroconvulsive Therapy

What would you expect the therapist to focus on or to do? _____

_____

_____

What would be the advantages of using this approach? _____

_____

_____

What would be the disadvantages of using this approach? _____

_____

_____

Which framework would you select for Ellen? _____

_____

_____

Justify your answer: _____

_____

_____

After completing this exercise, you should be able to:

- identify general differences in the activities that would take place in different therapeutic approaches.

- for each of the seven possible therapeutic frameworks, specify one advantage.

- eliminate some choices of therapy for this client, based on their disadvantages.

- understand how therapists may select elements of various frameworks as they develop treatment strategies.

- clarify the characteristics of therapy schools that you might find personally helpful if you needed to seek treatment in the future.

▼Exercise 17.3   FLAG ON THE PLAY

APPLY: Predict

Psychologists who are trained as therapists abide by many ethical constraints to ensure that the caliber of therapy they deliver meets the highest standards possible. State licensing practices provide screening to ensure that individuals who don't have sufficient therapeutic knowledge or who don't fully grasp their ethical obligations are prevented from establishing a legitimate practice.

Examine the ethical principles below that constrain psychologists' behavior. Predict the consequences of violations of each of those standards.

Principle 1: Therapists must maintain confidentiality about client disclosure.
What would happen if the therapist violated this principle?

_____

Principle 2: Therapists must offer the least restrictive alternative for treatment planning.
What would happen if the therapist violated this principle?

_____

Principle 3: Therapists must warn individuals who have been targeted for violence by their clients.
What would happen if the therapist violated this principle?

_____

Principle 4: Therapists must allow their clients full access to their treatment records.
What would happen if the therapist violated this principle?

_____

Principle 5: Therapists should encourage clients to participate fully in treatment planning.
What would happen if the therapist violated this principle?

_____

After completing this exercise, you should be able to:

- explain why ethical standards are needed in clinical care.

- identify parameters of ethical treatment in clinical care.

- predict potential negative outcomes from ethical violations.

▼Exercise 17.4   NOT SO CLEVER HANS

ANALYZE: Reason

Hans Eysenck created a huge controversy early in the history of clinical psychology by publishing a study in which he concluded that therapy was no more effective than the passage of time in producing improvements in psychological disorder. He conducted what is now referred to as a meta-analysis. He synthesized the results of many treatment studies by comparing the improvement in symptoms of those who received treatment with those who were placed on a "waiting list," the equivalent of a control group. Eysenck said that psychological therapy was relatively ineffective. He thought it was just as effective to wait for time to heal psychological wounds.

The treatment community was up in arms. Eysenck's finding certainly didn't fit with their own experiences in treatment offices, and they appropriately began to question the procedure that Eysenck used to come to his conclusion. More recent meta-analytic studies have concluded that many therapy forms produce significant symptom reduction and contrast starkly with Eysenck's early observations.

What kinds of questions would you raise about the process Eysenck used to produce his controversial finding? Identify at least three variables that a good outcome design would need to address before it could allow making broad conclusions about the overall effectiveness of therapy.

_____

_____

_____

_____

_____

_____

After completing this exercise, you should be able to:

- describe Eysenck's early findings and indicate why they were so controversial.

- identify the function and complexity of a meta-analysis.

- consider why seeking therapy rather than waiting for time to improve conditions may be more adaptive.

- isolate variables that need to be controlled in well-designed outcome studies.

▼Exercise 17.5   WHO'S WHO AMONG THERAPEUTIC PROFESSIONALS

ANALYZE: Categorize

People in trouble can turn to a variety of individuals to get assistance. Professionals who provide therapy come from the fields of psychology, psychiatry, nursing, social work, and the specialized field of marriage and family therapy. Keeping track of the range of therapies available can be challenging. Use the matrix below to indicate the privileges and limitations of various treatment providers by placing an X in the box for each characteristic of that kind of provider.

	Clinical Psychologist	Counseling Psychologist	Psychiatrist	Social Worker	Counselor	Psychiatric Nurse	Marriage & Family Therapist
Who undergoes the longest training?							
Who is most likely to administer psychological tests?							
Who would you most likely find working in a school system?							
Who deserves to be called "Dr."?							
Whose treatment would be the most expensive?							
Who would be the most reluctant to work on an individual outside of the individual's system?							
Who would most likely pay attention to feelings as the dominant information to guide therapy?							
Who would provide care in hospital settings?							
Who works with children?							

After completing this exercise, you should be able to:

- discuss the variety of professions that provide mental health interventions.

- differentiate what psychologists do compared to other providers.

- compare and contrast types of providers.

- make reasonable decisions about how to identify potential care providers, should the need arise.

▼Exercise 17.6   THERE MUST BE 50 WAYS TO LEAVE YOUR SHRINK
EVALUATE: Choose

Psychotherapists endure a lot of criticism about keeping their clients or patients longer than they really need to as a way of sustaining their own practices. Although some less-than-ethical therapists might engage in keeping clients over time, the majority of practitioners take on new clients with the express intent of making themselves dispensable.

But how do you know when you are ready to go? What if the therapist doesn't pronounce your work completed? Try to generate five "indicators" that might help you determine that your therapy has been effective. (And it wouldn't hurt if you added some humor to your answers!)

_____

_____

_____

_____

_____

After completing this exercise, you should be able to:

- recognize the inevitability of completing psychological treatment.

- describe multiple strategies for ending a significant relationship.

- question the ethics of therapists who may engage in protracted treatments that cannot be justified by the symptoms.

- demonstrate flexibility in planning personal expression.

▼Exercise 17.7   WHO'S GOT THE CHECK?
EVALUATE: Take Perspective

Access to good quality mental health care is especially problematic for people without insurance resources. Psychologists are regularly criticized for electing to work with the "worried well," rather than people who are in greater need of the kind of assistance psychologists could provide.

Think about your own position in relation to mental health care and its funding. Should this treatment be a regular part of health insurance? Should it be part of a national health care plan? How committed are you to equal access to good mental health care? Come up with three justifications to support your point of view. Whatever your position, try to anticipate the critical elements of the opposite side. Try to think of three justifications to support the opposite side.

Justifications:

1. _____

   _____

2. _____

   _____

3. _____

   _____

Counter-Arguments:

1. _____
_____

2. _____
_____

3. _____
_____
_____

Finally, does a more thorough evaluation of both sides affect your original position?

_____
_____

After completing this exercise, you should be able to:

- describe the current national status of funding for mental health care coverage.

- articulate the arguments "pro" and "con" for increased funding and access to mental health care.

- justify your own position regarding improved access to mental health care.

▼Exercise 17.8   OUT, DAMNED SPOT

CREATE: Design

Suppose you had just developed a revolutionary new treatment for compulsive hand washing. Preliminary results with your own clients suggest that your approach is not only effective (it makes the chronic hand-washing rituals go away) but also efficient (it makes the rituals go away faster than does any other approach currently being tried).

To gain the attention of the mental health community, you will need to demonstrate that your method is effective. Assuming you could get 100 people who suffer from compulsive hand washing to volunteer for an experiment, how would you design an experiment that would demonstrate the superiority of your methods? (See Answer Key.)

What is your hypothesis? _____
_____

What is your independent variable? _____
_____

How will you assign subjects to treatment conditions? _____
_____

How will you measure your dependent variable? _____
_____

What other elements will you need to control in order to rule out alternative hypotheses?

_____

If all proceeded as planned and you obtained the results you intended, would your study offer proof of the superiority of your treatment? Justify your answer. _____

_____

_____

After completing this exercise, you should be able to:

- isolate the independent variable and create treatment conditions that reflect your emphasis.

- identify a strategy that will measure the dependent variable while accurately reflecting changes in the anxiety condition.

- specify important influences that need to be controlled to rule out alternative explanations.

- describe whether such a design would offer definitive evidence of the superiority of a new technique.

THE PSYCHOLOGY ADVANTAGE

Life can be pretty rugged at times. It is almost inevitable that at some point in your life, you and your family will need to avail yourselves of some mental health expertise to weather some specific challenges that lie ahead, whether it's a senior relative who is in serious cognitive decline, a nephew who is having adjustment problems in kindergarten, or you, simply trying to manage the wide range of stressors that college has to offer. You may already have been involved with a therapist who may have contributed to your decision to pursue a college degree.

When people are in the throes of crisis, it can be challenging to try to come up with a game plan that will resolve the crisis. Whom do you call? What kind of therapist would work the best for the identified problem? How do you identify a specific individual with a track record that would inspire confidence that your problem will be addressed efficiently and effectively? Although you can initiate a blind referral through the Yellow Pages, it probably makes more sense to track down individuals who know about local mental health care providers and who can refer you to someone with a solid reputation. Googling the prospective therapist may also provide you with some background to help you make a good decision about whom you will select for this most important relationship.

Getting some exposure to the complexities of treatment planning and delivery will facilitate your being a savvy consumer of mental health services. That advantage should be apparent as you enter a therapeutic relationship not just armed with assorted questions that will help you navigate the challenge but also bolstered by the knowledge that you should not behave passively in this situation. Among other things, an enlightened consumer will want to know the following from a prospective therapist:

1. What is your training background?

2. Are you currently licensed for therapeutic practice? Are you in good standing?

3. Do you have a particular therapeutic orientation?

4. Have you dealt with a challenge like this in your history as a licensed professional?

5. What might your expectations be for how long it might take for the challenge to recede?

Asking questions like these will signal to the therapist that you will be a major resource in your own care. You also will have the sophistication to know that if it isn't working, it is time to depart the therapeutic relationship and find someone with whom you can develop a stronger alliance.

18 Chapter

◀ Stress and Health ▶

Our ancestors in more primitive times probably experienced stress as they faced the challenges of survival—securing sufficient nutrition and avoiding danger. Although the goal of survival in contemporary life is the same, the array of sources of stress is much richer. We have a wider selection of possible goals as well as a broader range of stimulating and threatening experiences. As a result of our knowledge about the relationship of stress to the quality of life, many people conscientiously learn all they can about ways to reduce stress and promote healthy lifestyles.

▼ Exercise 18.1 BETWEEN A ROCK AND A HARD PLACE

UNDERSTAND: Translate

A very commonly used metaphor for being placed in the difficult position of choosing between two unattractive alternatives is "being caught between a rock and a hard place." Although you have two distinct choices, the negative impact will be virtually the same—unpleasantness—no matter which one you choose. Psychologists refer to this problem as an *avoidance-avoidance conflict*, since either selection produces frustration, conflict, and withdrawal.

Ironically, choices do not need to have a negative impact to promote stress. *Approach-approach conflicts* challenge the individual to choose between two *attractive* alternatives. However, selecting one often means eliminating the possibility of having the other.

A third variation, the *approach-avoidance conflict*, also generates feelings of stress and strain. In this case, the individual is confronted by only one attractive option, but that option has some distinct negative features attached to it. By pursuing this goal, you guarantee some unpleasantness embedded in the positive experience.

In this exercise, you will personalize your own response to stress by predicting the intensity of stress that various conflict situations might generate. For each situation, label the conflict pattern it represents (approach-approach, avoidance-avoidance, or approach-avoidance), and estimate how much stress each situation would generate for you personally. (See Answer Key.)

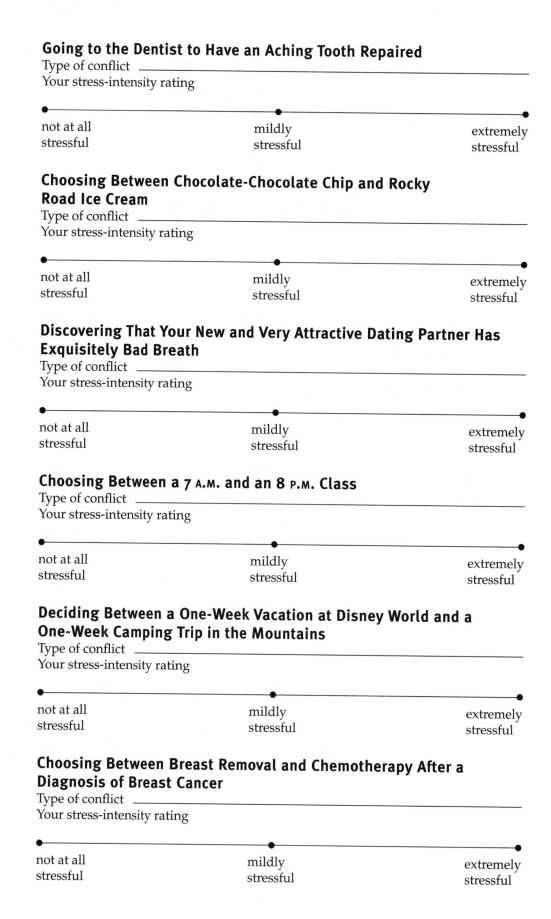

Going to the Dentist to Have an Aching Tooth Repaired
Type of conflict _____
Your stress-intensity rating

not at all
stressful

mildly
stressful

extremely
stressful

Choosing Between Chocolate-Chocolate Chip and Rocky Road Ice Cream
Type of conflict _____
Your stress-intensity rating

not at all
stressful

mildly
stressful

extremely
stressful

Discovering That Your New and Very Attractive Dating Partner Has Exquisitely Bad Breath
Type of conflict _____
Your stress-intensity rating

not at all
stressful

mildly
stressful

extremely
stressful

Choosing Between a 7 A.M. and an 8 P.M. Class
Type of conflict _____
Your stress-intensity rating

not at all
stressful

mildly
stressful

extremely
stressful

Deciding Between a One-Week Vacation at Disney World and a One-Week Camping Trip in the Mountains
Type of conflict _____
Your stress-intensity rating

not at all
stressful

mildly
stressful

extremely
stressful

Choosing Between Breast Removal and Chemotherapy After a Diagnosis of Breast Cancer
Type of conflict _____
Your stress-intensity rating

not at all
stressful

mildly
stressful

extremely
stressful

Selecting One of Two Highly Rated Colleges That Have Admitted You
Type of conflict _____
Your stress-intensity rating

not at all   mildly   extremely
stressful   stressful   stressful

As a Vegetarian, Being Asked Whether You Want Steak or Ribs
Type of conflict _____
Your stress-intensity rating

not at all   mildly   extremely
stressful   stressful   stressful

Deciding Whether to Buy a Low-Priced, Beautiful Used Car That Needs a Major Repair to Its Engine
Type of conflict _____
Your stress-intensity rating

not at all   mildly   extremely
stressful   stressful   stressful

Having Plastic Surgery to Correct a Bump on the Bridge of Your Nose
Type of conflict _____
Your stress-intensity rating

not at all   mildly   extremely
stressful   stressful   stressful

After completing this exercise, you should be able to:

- distinguish the three kinds of conflict that generate stress about making choices.
- recognize that stress can be generated even by positive choices.
- describe variations in stress intensity among individuals.
- speculate how stress ratings may change over time.

▼Exercise 18.2   MY SCREW-UP PROFILE

PART 1: APPLY: Illustrate

PART 2: EVALUATE: Prioritize

Humans screw up on a regular basis. It is part of our design. When you mix one imperfect human with another, the screw-up possibilities are compounded. When we encounter inevitable roadblocks and frustrations, we can sometimes gloriously rise to the occasion. We admit fault, shoulder responsibility, apologize for our shortcomings and then move on to the next opportunity that will allow us to triumph or to falter. Life's frustrations are so plentiful and creative that we are constantly bombarded with new and challenging decisions about how to cope.

This exercise examines your own history of how you resolve stressful situations. Each category below represents an unhealthy alternative to a healthy coping strategy. Try to identify an example from your own personal history that fits each maladaptive coping strategy. Also, as candidly as you can, describe either a short-term or long-term consequence for resolving a conflict in an unhealthy fashion. When your matrix is complete, look over the list and try to determine if you tend to show preferences for certain kinds of poor coping strategies. Identify which bad strategy you use most often and which you use least often.

Maladaptive Coping Strategy	Your Personal Example	Consequence
Giving Up/Learned Helplessness		
Blaming Yourself		
Aggression Against Others		
Self-Indulgence		
Use of Defense Mechanisms		
Avoidance		
Passive-Aggressive Revenge		

Most Regularly Used Bad Strategy: _____

Least Regularly Used Bad Strategy: _____

Hint 1: Depending on many variables, including personality style, you may not be able to come up with a good personal example. If your own history is bereft of bad behavior in any category, find an example to illustrate the category from among your friends and loved ones. There are bound to be plenty of examples from which to choose among those other imperfect beings.

Hint 2: Applying defense mechanisms to your own behavior is particularly tricky. Why? These strategies tend to operate at a subconscious level. You engage in self-deception so you won't have to feel so acutely the attendant anxiety associated with the screw-up. You may not recognize that you have distorted reality as a means of diminishing your anxiety. Consequently, you have employed many defense mechanisms and have probably not been aware of doing so. Once you learn about defense mechanisms, you may find yourself plagued with a bit more anxiety as you debate whether you have offered a sound justification or a less effective example of self-deception.

After completing this exercise, you should be able to:

- outline multiple types of strategies that represent poor coping skills.
- describe the consequences of using an unhealthy coping strategy.
- identify historic priorities or preferences for mishandling frustration.

▼Exercise 18.3   STEP ON THE GAS
ANALYZE: Classify

Despite the fact that there are many different types of stressors to which an organism can respond, the stress response itself follows a predictable pattern. Hans Selye

(1976) called this pattern the General Adaptation Syndrome (GAS). Selye said that there are three phases of stress response. The first is the alarm reaction, in which the sympathetic nervous system is suddenly activated by the detection of the stressor. During the resistance phase you cope with the stressor, and the sympathetic nervous system remains aroused to provide energy and protection against illness. The final stage, exhaustion, occurs when you deplete your body's energy. During this stage the organism's resistance to illness is diminished, and energy levels are low.

Using this framework, explain your own reaction to a significant stressor in your life. Make sure that you clearly identify each stage with your accompanying physical, emotional, and cognitive experiences. _____

_____

_____

_____

_____

_____

_____

Given your knowledge of this process, what might you do to minimize the negative effects of stress the next time you are in a stressful situation? _____

_____

_____

_____

_____

After completing this exercise, you should be able to:

- describe Selye's General Adaptation Syndrome.

- use the GAS to explain a significantly stressful event in your own life.

- speculate about how you might use your understanding of this process to minimize the negative effects of stress in future stressful situations.

▼ Exercise 18.4   CUSTOMIZED STRESS ASSESSMENT

EVALUATE: Assess

Holmes and Rahe (1967) created the Social Readjustment Rating Scale (SRRS) to apply some metrics to stressors and establish correlations between stress and bodily function. They identified a full range of potential stressors from the stressor with the highest impact (for example, death of a spouse rated at 100 points on the scale) to the lowest impact (minor violations of the law at 11 points). In addition, Holmes and Rahe included positive events as part of the mix (outstanding personal achievement at 28 points). Through weighting various challenges in day-to-day living, they were able to demonstrate a positive correlation between accumulated stress points and vulnerability to catching colds. A few high-impact stressors had a more adverse impact on physical health than several episodes of low-impact stressors.

College students who examine the SRRS don't always relate to the scope of what Holmes and Rahe decided stress would look like for adults in 1967. Your task in this exercise is to do a minimum-modification of the SRRS, adapting it for a specific purpose. Examine the 1967 version, taking note of what stressors still work and speculating about stressors that might not be as potent in contemporary life. Then select a particular population that would be interesting to adapt to the SRRS from the following suggestions. Identify ten stressors you think would best capture the strain associated with being in that role. Speculate about the level of impact of each of the ten stressors by assigning your best guess of the value if 100 is the highest stressor level and 1 is the lowest stressor level.

Potential Target Populations: New college students
New military recruits
Newly engaged couples
New parents
New retirees
New employees
Video gamers

Which target population will you choose? _____

Proposed Stressor	Proposed Rating	Rationale
1.		
2.		
3.		
4.		
5.		
6.		
7.		
8.		
9.		
10.		

After completing this exercise, you should be able to:

- describe the historic value of the Holmes and Rahe survey on stressors.

- evaluate which elements of the survey still apply to contemporary life.

- predict the elements of what constitutes stress for a targeted population.

- reflect on how personal stressors are linked with physical health concerns.

▼ Exercise 18.5   THE GAME OF LIFE

EVALUATE: Justify

At some point during your educational career, you have probably been presented with one of a variety of fictional dilemmas asking you to make choices based on your value system. They generally follow the format of "If you can only save 10 of the following 50 people from some disaster, who would you save and why?" In the following activity you must select a given number of items from the following lists of stressors, with the intention of maximizing your health and resiliency. In each list, which items would be the least discombobulating? From which would you be able to rebound the most quickly? Once you have made your selections, explain why you chose the items you did, and what impact you would expect them to have on your health and happiness. Compare your answers with those of your classmates and discuss the differences in personality, event appraisal, and personal habits that led to your decisions.

Category I (choose 1)	Category II (choose 3)	Category III (choose 5)
Living in a country experiencing war	Death of a close relative	Getting stuck in construction traffic and being three hours late getting home
Living through a major earthquake	Losing a job	Waiting in line at the post office for 1 hour to mail your tax returns
Losing your home and possessions because of a fire	Having triplets	Having two exams the day before your sister's wedding
Living near a nuclear disaster site	Living 2,000 miles from family	Locking your keys in the car
Having a close relative die in a plane crash	Moving to a new city	Forgetting your notes for a presentation
	Developing a serious illness	Getting a speeding ticket
	Buying an expensive house	Losing your keys on the morning of a big job interview
	Getting a promotion at work	Having a fight with your roommate
	Having a 2-hour heavy-traffic commute every day	Bouncing a check
	Getting divorced	Having to find a new apartment

Take a look at the items you selected. What effect would you expect them to have on your health and well-being? _____

_____

_____

_____

Would your health be affected differently if these things happened at different points in your life? How might you respond differently if the event you chose from Category I happened when you were 8 instead of when you were an adult? _____

_____

_____

_____

After completing this exercise, you should be able to:

- discuss the effects that various stressors might have on your health.

- identify the ways in which your own personality, event attributions, and personal habits affect the ways in which you respond to various stressors.

- justify your choices based on your priorities and values.

- speculate about how catastrophic stressors affect individuals differently based on their stage of development.

▼Exercise 18.6   HEALTHY LIVING

EVALUATE: Take Perspective

Stress is a word that has many uses in everyday conversation. In the technical vocabulary of psychology, however, it refers to the process an organism uses to evaluate and respond to the threats and challenges in the environment. As you learned in your study of perception, the stimuli in the environment are interpreted through the senses and expectations of the perceiver. This means that any two individuals, when experiencing the same event, may interpret and respond to it differently, depending on their personalities, personal habits, level of social support, and personal appraisal of the situation. Individuals who see most of life's events as a challenge, who are optimistic and easygoing, with plenty of social support and who get plenty of exercise, don't smoke, and eat nutritious foods are more likely to be healthy than individuals who see these same events as threats, who are depressed or pessimistic, without a strong social support network and who smoke, are sedentary, and follow a poor diet.

For the scenario given below, assume that your tendency is toward health, and describe how you might react to the situation. Be as specific as you can, identifying your appraisal of the event, your personality, personal habits, and relationships with other people. Once you have completed this part of the task, assume that your tendency is toward illness and show how your response would be different. Again, you should be as specific as possible, describing the same factors of appraisal, personality, personal habits, and social supports.

Scenario: You are a 42-year-old working woman with two teenage children and a husband. During your annual review at work, your boss tells you that you are up for promotion. The new job is one that you've always thought you'd like, and the salary is significantly higher than what you are making now. The job involves a tremendous amount of travel, however, and you would be on the road approximately two weeks out of every month. Your teenage children are involved in many different school and social activities, and your husband also has a full-time job. In particular, your daughter is one year away from college and is beginning to plan to visit the schools in which she is interested. You have two weeks to make your decision.

Describe how you spend your two weeks if your general tendency is toward health.

_____

_____

_____

_____

How do you spend these two weeks if your tendency is toward illness?

_____

_____

_____

_____

Which of the characteristics you have described above is similar to the way that you deal with life events? Can you identify ways in which you can approach decisions and activities in a healthier fashion? _____

_____

_____

_____

_____

_____

After completing this exercise, you should be able to:

- define stress, stressor, and stress response.

- recognize that the same event can have different effects on an individual's well-being based on that person's interpretation of the event.

- identify the factors that influence a person's perception of a stressful event.

- describe health-prone and illness-prone responses to a given event.

- consider ways in which you can respond in health-prone ways to your own life events.

▼Exercise 18.7   ENHANCING IMMUNE FUNCTION

CREATE: Design

In a series of experiments with rats, Ader and Cohen (1985) demonstrated that the immune system can be classically conditioned. After many pairings of sweet water with a drug that suppressed the immune system, the sweet water suppressed the immune system when presented by itself. With the immune system suppressed, the rat was much more likely to acquire a variety of illnesses. Many researchers think that if it is possible to condition immune suppression, it should also be possible to condition immune enhancement. This could help people fight off illness and lead healthier lives.

Because our understanding of the factors that enhance immune function is less well defined than our understanding of those that suppress immune function, operationalizing and selecting the variables for experiments testing immune enhancement is difficult. Assume that you are part of a team working on research in this area. Your team has decided that the placebo effect—improvement in a person's condition with treatments that have no physiologically significant effect—may be the result of conditioned immune enhancement. In other words, because medication administered in the past has resulted in improved immune function, similar administration of something an individual believed was medication also improved immune function. Working from this hypothesis, your team decides to modify the way in which the placebo is given in one set of medication trials to make it less like other experiences individuals have with medication. One of the placebo groups will be given the placebo in pill form (traditional group), while the other will receive it dissolved in a cup of coffee (novel group).

Given this basic design, what are some of the extraneous variables your team needs to consider? _____

_____

_____

_____

_____

_____

_____

If the results show a significant difference between the two groups, what conclusions might you reasonably draw? _____

_____

_____

_____

_____

_____

What are some ethical considerations in using placebos in experiments dealing with people's health? Do you think the benefits justify the methods? Explain your answer.

_____

_____

_____

_____

_____

_____

_____

_____

_____

After completing this exercise, you should be able to:

- describe experiments demonstrating classical conditioning of the immune system.

- identify extraneous variables that might influence classical conditioning of immune function.

- interpret the results of a hypothetical experiment of classically conditioned immune response.

- discuss the ethical considerations of placebo studies.

▼Exercise 18.8   HEALTHY EXECUTIVES

CREATE: Plan

You are a consultant being hired by a large investment firm to set up an on-site wellness program. The company has noticed that its health insurance rates are increasing because of the high utilization of the health insurance by their employees. Many of the health concerns of the employees are related to high blood pressure, coronary artery disease, obesity, and other illnesses that might be stress-related. They have asked you to help them create fitness and wellness programs designed to decrease the negative stress responses of their employees and to help them become more fit. This project is a particularly challenging project because of the fast-paced work atmosphere. Most of the employees work 10-hour days and only take 30 minutes or so for lunch or a break.

Based on your understanding of psychology and the specific needs of this type of organization, propose a stress-management program that takes into consideration the special needs of this group. You should have at least two different components to your program; very strong programs will have three or more. _____

_____

_____

_____

_____

_____

_____

_____

How might your program design have been different if you had been working with a group of teachers instead of investment executives? _____

_____

_____

_____

_____

_____

_____

After completing this exercise, you should be able to:

- identify the risks of a high-stress lifestyle.

- create a stress management program that includes exercise, relaxation, and social support components.

- recognize the ways in which a program must fit the needs of the individuals for whom it is designed.

THE PSYCHOLOGY ADVANTAGE

It would be nice if merely studying psychology made you less vulnerable to the effects of stress. The tuition you paid for the course would have some amazing and long-lasting benefits if you were able to implement many of the ideas presented in this chapter on stress and health.

In some ways, knowledge of health psychology can promote commitment to living a healthier lifestyle. For example, if you know the short- and long-term effects of binge drinking, chances are you will be much less inclined to join in social outings that have all the markers of an evening of excess. If you know sitting too long before a computer poses multiple health risks, you may be more inclined to adopt strategies that promote movement and stretching to improve your circulation and joint health. Of course, you won't continue smoking or eating to excess.

However, armed with the most compelling evidence about the deleterious effects of unhealthy or risky behaviors, humans still manage to conduct lives that appear to be oblivious to the risk. Why? It is because we have an extraordinary capacity for self-deception. It is probably adaptive at some level not to worry needlessly about the full range of possible threats to your existence, and a mindset of "it won't happen to me" helps to keep anxiety away from your door. Unfortunately, that mindset will also prevent you from taking proactive steps to conduct healthful practices in the short-term to facilitate a "longer" and healthier long-term.

Having a background in basic psychology should confer multiple advantages for managing stress. First, you get comfortable with the fact that stress is going to be part of your life's fabric no matter what path your life takes. Second, you won't be surprised by how hard it is to embrace and adhere to a healthy lifestyle. Third, you are likely to be more understanding when you can't influence your loved ones to embrace and adhere to a healthy lifestyle.

◀ Answer Key ▶

Chapter

◀Thinking Critically▶ with Psychological Science

▼Exercise 1.1 THE CASE FOR INTERFERENCE
UNDERSTAND: Explain

The Problem of Child Abuse: *Correlational*
When social scientists study existing records of foster care children, they are not interfering in the normal process. They are making careful observations of the reports that describe the children's lives. In effect, they are combining many individual case studies and trying to define their common characteristics. Therefore, this approach is correlational. Although it will not produce strong cause-effect conclusions, a correlational study may provide some direction about the most important factors in the development of foster care children. Also, child abuse is an area in which it is extremely difficult to do experimental research. Scientists would be ethically opposed to constructing controlled conditions in an experiment that might place any child at risk for physical abuse or not exercise sufficient protection of children.

Charlie's Weight Loss: *Experimental*
Charlie's ambitious weight loss plan represents a good experimental approach to understanding weight management, if he carefully imposes the limitations he describes from the outset of his plan. In effect, his approach simulates something called a single-subject design. In this case, Charlie's eating behavior is "interfered with" in a systematic fashion. He carefully records his progress and then is able to make a reasonably sound conclusion about the relative effectiveness of one method over another. This advantage assumes that Charlie is successful in abiding by the conditions he has established.

The Curious Teacher: *Experimental*
Ms. Tucker's strategy for evaluating teaching methods represents a good classroom experiment. There are some interesting problems with her design that threaten the validity of her conclusion. For example, she may be an advocate of active learning and may inadvertently construct her final exam to be easier than the midterm. Experimenter effects of this kind threaten the validity of conclusions. However, she does propose a controlled comparison, which would qualify as an experimental approach.

The Lucky Pen: *Neither Experimental nor Correlational*

Peter's observation that his pen is lucky is a good example of superstitious behavior. Human beings are inclined to reach unfounded conclusions of this nature because our brains are geared to find patterns even where patterns do not exist. Although this description sounds like it might be correlational because it does not show interference by a scientist, it does not qualify as correlational because it does not take a systematic approach to the problem. The observations are haphazard and there is no attempt to quantify the relationships.

The Best Neighborhood: *Correlational*

Because the researcher is working with existing records, a careful comparison of SAT performance with geographic location represents a good correlational approach. The researchers are not interfering with the process but merely reporting existing relationships. However, as often happens when nonscientists try to make sense of the data, the researchers go too far by pronouncing the superiority of one school district over another. There are simply too many variables (for example, parental income, access to computers) that might explain the superiority of one sector over another. This is the risk with correlational approaches: We cannot be confident in the cause-effect relationships that they suggest.

Copycat Crime: *Correlational*

It may be tempting to conclude that watching a violent film can induce violent behavior, but we do not have sufficient controlled evidence in this case to make that pronouncement. The reporter is not manipulating conditions in this situation (no interference), so the interpretation would be based on correlational methods. The relationship established would be that teens who see the violent example in the film would be more likely to commit a similar violent act than teens who had not seen the film. Obviously, we would be loathe to construct an experiment to narrow down the cause-effect relationship suggested by this finding.

Doctor's Choice: *Experimental*

This interesting physician appears to be embarking on an experimental approach to evaluate the effectiveness of a new expensive medication. He does many things right, including random assignment to conditions by using a coin toss. However, no matter how good his intentions are, the physician does violate ethical protocol for the protection of research participants. His patients have the right to know that they are being "experimented" upon and that there are other treatment options.

▼Exercise 1.2   STATS-R-US

UNDERSTAND: Translate

1. Correlation #1: HOURS OF PRACTICE VERSUS REGIONAL RANKING = +.45

There is a moderately strong, positive correlation between reported hours of piano practice versus ranking in the regional piano competition, which means that those who reported having practiced more than the average number of hours tended to report more success in the competitions.

2. Correlation #2: NUMBER OF PHONE CALLS VERSUS NUMBER OF PHONES OWNED = +.03

Although the correlation between the number of phone calls made last week versus number of phones owned is positive, the strength of the correlation (.03) indicates that there is not much of a relationship between the two variables.

3. Correlation #3: HOURS ON SOCIAL MEDIA VERSUS GRADE POINT AVERAGE = −.88

A very strong and negative correlation between reported hours per week spent on social media versus grade point average suggests there could be an important connection between the two. The intense negative correlation suggests that those who spend a lot of time on social media tend to underachieve at school, whereas those who limit their time on Facebook and the like are probably going to be more academically successful.

4. Correlation #4 NUMBER OF TRAFFIC TICKETS VERSUS GAS DOLLARS = +1.33

Uh, oh! This one can't be interpreted as anything but a computing error. When the data are properly entered in a correlation formula, the resulting correlation must fall within the range of −1.0 to +1.0. Therefore, Tyler needs to check his math and potentially start over on this correlation.

5. Correlation #5 NUMBER OF SIBLINGS VERSUS GRADE POINT AVERAGE = −.26

A negative correlation of .26 is very weak, suggesting that there is not much association between number of siblings and academic performance. The correlation is a puny one, suggesting only the slightest tendency for people with fewer brothers and sisters to do better in school.

6. Correlation #6: BLOOD ALCOHOL LEVEL VERSUS DRINKS CONSUMED = +.92

Tyler's correlation of .92 between blood alcohol level and number of drinks consumed works intuitively with what you already would have predicted. The more drinks one downs, the higher the blood alcohol level. Conversely, people who don't drink much won't have much impairment. Both patterns are embedded within the information communicated by +.92 as the correlation between blood alcohol level versus number of drinks consumed prior to the blood alcohol test.

▼Exercise 1.3 YOU NEED AN OPERATION
APPLY: Illustrate

The Sloppy Roommate
Jack could operationally define the problem as follows:
  Jack is unhappy because Ed

- leaves his clothes in inappropriate places.

- does not do the dishes on an equitable basis.

1. "It seems to me that you are not picking up your things. You have a lot of clothes in the living room that could be moved to your bedroom."

2. "I have done the dishes for the last five days straight. You need to take your turn doing the dishes if we are going to be able to share the apartment."

The Surly Boss: "Why Don't You Like Me?"
Joe could operationally define his problems with his boss as

- receiving no feedback.

- getting looks from his supervisor that he cannot interpret.

- observing his supervisor laugh and wondering if the laughter is about him.

1. "Although I think I've been doing a good job, I haven't received any formal feedback from you in the last six weeks. May we please set up a time when we could review my work?"

2. "I don't think you and I are making a good connection. I noticed this week on three occasions that you seemed to be staring at me, and it made me think that something was wrong."

Bonnie's Worry: "Emily Seems Slow"

Bonnie will be more helpful to Emily's parents if she can articulate her concerns about Emily more precisely:

- playing alone 80% of the time.

- taking toys from other children.

- talking to herself more than to other children.

- focusing on single objects and tasks longer than other children.

1. "Emily spends a greater proportion of her time talking to herself than she does talking to other children. Does that ever seem to be a problem at home?"

2. "Sometimes Emily spends long periods of time at a single task. This makes it difficult for her to participate in all of the activities the other children enjoy."

▼Exercise 1.4   CONSUMER SAFETY

ANALYZE: Reason

The Tanned Rock Queen

Principle 2: Don't settle for cause-effect statements without sufficient evidence.

Personal testimony is not effective evidence even when it is given by someone famous. How do you know the rock star isn't fresh from a cruise to the Caribbean?

The Moralizer

Principle 1: Don't expect simple cause-effect relationships.

Violence is a complicated behavior that has multiple causes.

Principle 4: Don't mistake correlation for causation.

Two alternative explanations are (1) that heavy metal music reflects a violent culture rather than causing violence within the culture, and (2) that both heavy metal music and violence are caused by other variables.

The Laundry

Principle 5: Do look for experimental comparisons that involve control conditions.

Although television moms do demonstrate questionable reality testing from time to time, this test included good controls in design; if all conditions were equal, the experiment should provide valid evidence that the new detergent is more effective.

The New Car

Principle 6: Do examine how behaviors are defined or operationalized.

Just what does "pizazz" mean? How does the company operationally define the goal? Will you have more dates? More intense contacts with loan officers? More challenges to drag race? More speeding tickets?

Halloween Wisdom

Principle 2: Don't settle for cause-effect statements without sufficient evidence.

What is the psychologist's evidence? Did a well-designed study lead to these conclusions? Even though a person's credentials seem impressive, we should not suspend appropriate criteria in evaluating a cause-effect claim.

One Bad Apple

Principle 2: Don't settle for cause-effect statements without sufficient evidence.

Subjective experience with one representative of a group is likely to be insufficient in making judgments about all the representatives of a group. Beware of making generalized conclusions about groups based on experience with one representative. This is sometimes referred to as the "*n* of 1" error, where *n* represents sample size.

The Blind Date

Principle 3: Don't confuse interpretations of behavior with behavior itself.

Recycling discarded cans on a date could represent a serious commitment to the environment, but it could also mean that your date is just broke (or cheap). Remember to distinguish actual behavior from the inferences or conclusions you draw about the behavior.

The Burglars

Principle 4: Don't mistake correlation for causation.

Even though a "full moon effect" may be an appealing explanation for unlawful or extraordinary behavior, there is a simpler and more plausible explanation than unexplained lunar forces. A full moon may provide more light, enabling burglars to see better and to break in more easily.

▼Exercise 1.5 PSYCHOLOGY'S PERSPECTIVE
EVALUATE: Take Perspective

Issue: Drug Abuse

Neuroscience: Psychologists in this area are interested in the physiological processes underlying emotions, memories, and sensory experiences. Questions from this framework would include:

- How do particular drugs affect the way that the brain sends and receives messages?

- How does long-term cocaine use damage the brain?

- How does LSD cause hallucinations?

Evolutionary: When using this framework, psychologists focus on how traits have enabled organisms to survive and pass along their genes to future generations. When studying drug abuse, this perspective might lead one to ask:

- How might addictive behavior patterns have enabled our distant ancestors to survive?

- Does the tendency to seek stimulation through drug use confer any survival advantage?

- What influence does widespread drug abuse have on the quality of the gene pool?

Behavior Genetics: This perspective asks to what degree our genes and our environment contribute to our individual differences. Psychologists in this area might ask questions such as:

- To what extent is the propensity toward addiction inherited?

- What are the environmental and genetic risk factors for drug abuse?

- Does gene therapy show promise for treating drug addiction?

Behavioral: Psychologists in this area are interested in how we learn our observable behaviors. In the area of drug abuse, the following questions could be posed:

- What reinforcing contingencies encourage teenagers to use heroin?

- How important are role models in developing addictive behavior?

- How can we design effective drug treatment programs to help people overcome addiction?

Cognitive: Because they are interested in how individuals process, store, and retrieve information, cognitive psychologists might ask the following:

- How do individuals assess the risk of drug use?

- What kind of problem-solving strategies do drug addicts use to obtain their drugs or hide their addictions from friends?

- What is the best way to educate people about the dangers of drug abuse?

Social-Cultural: Psychologists interested in how behaviors and thinking differ across cultures and situations might ask:

- Why is the rate of alcoholism higher in the United States than in Sweden?

- Why do groups from different cultures and ethnic backgrounds have differing rates of abuse for various drugs?

- How do different peer groups affect a teen's choice to use drugs?

Issue: Love

Neuroscience: Questions with a physiological focus could include:

- What neurotransmitters are involved in our experience of love?

- What roles do different brain areas play in falling in love?

- Are there drugs that could serve as a "love potion?"

Evolutionary: When exploring how organisms pass along their genes, evolutionary psychologists might ask:

- How does falling in love help perpetuate the species?

- Are people who experience love strongly more likely to reproduce successfully?

- What physical characteristics seem most important in mate selection?

Behavior Genetics: Psychologists working from this perspective explore behaviors that could be influenced by genes. Their questions could include the following:

- Can the tendency to easily fall in love be inherited?

- What genetic and environmental factors promote falling in love?

- Is there a genetic basis for how quickly an individual can rebound from a broken heart?

Behavioral: A behavioral psychologist, interested in how consequences shape behavior, could ask any of the following questions:

- How do we learn socially appropriate ways to express love?

- How are the actions of love different from the actions of kindness or friendship?

- How do behaviors differ with different love objects (family, friends, significant others)?

Cognitive: Some of the questions of interest to researchers who study thinking and problem solving include:

- How is thinking different when a person is in love?

- How might loving someone change the way we interpret that person's actions?

- Does being in love influence the capacity to empathize with others?

Social-Cultural: When investigating situational and cultural differences in love, psychologists might ask questions such as these:

- How are dating/courtship rituals different in different cultures?

- Do differences in family structure explain how young adults develop intimate relationships?

- What is the relationship between sex and love in different cultures?

Issue: Intelligence

Neuroscience: A neuroscientist would be interested in exploring questions such as the following:

- Do differences in brain structures account for differences in intellectual abilities?

- How do neurotransmitters assist in the accurate storage and rapid retrieval of information?

- What role does the frontal cortex play in making connections among novel concepts?

Evolutionary: Some examples of questions of interest to individuals working from this perspective include:

- What types of intelligence make survival more likely?

- How does intelligence affect survival rates?

- Under what circumstances might low intelligence be considered adaptive?

Behavior Genetics: The contribution of genes and the environment to intelligence would be of interest to psychologists in this area as illustrated by the following questions:

- Is intelligence inherited?

- How successful is providing a stimulating environment in raising IQ scores?

- What are the relative contributions of genetics and environment to various measures of IQ?

Behavioral: The behaviorist's questions would focus on observable behaviors and their consequences. Questions might include:

- How can we measure intelligence?

- How might an educational system be designed to encourage effective learning strategies?

- What rewards are most effective in promoting learning?

Cognitive: Cognitive psychologists would seek to answer questions such as:

- What is the relationship between intelligence and memory?
- Is there any difference in the way that highly intelligent individuals store and retrieve information?
- What are the cognitive processes involved in different types of intelligence?

Social-Cultural: Social-cultural psychologists would be interested in how different cultures define and measure intelligence. Their questions might include:

- Are there meaningful differences between the overall intelligence of men and women?
- How do some individuals from impoverished backgrounds overcome these conditions to have successful, productive lives?
- What factors account for stable performance differences across ethnic groups on IQ tests?

▼Exercise 1.6   CRITIQUING EXPERIMENTAL DESIGN
EVALUATE: Assess

The Colorful Boss

Focal behavior: Work production among clerical staff, operationally defined as projects completed.

Hypothesis: Environments painted blue cause workers to produce a greater volume of completed work than will environments painted yellow.

Independent variable: Color of paint used in the environment (blue versus yellow)

Measurement of dependent variable: Number of projects completed by clerical staff

Controlled variables:

- New paint applied to cubicle walls of two departments
- Productivity measured over the same time period

Uncontrolled variables:

- Absence of random assignment creates the possibility of alternative explanations for different volumes of work produced by the two groups.
- Knowledge of boss's hypothesis may have influenced worker performance so that workers in the preferred-color environment outperformed those in the non-preferred environment.
- Number of tasks may differ from department to department. Without better control procedures, the boss is comparing blueberries and bananas.

Valid results?: No. Perhaps this boss should find something more important to do than experimenting with the effect of color on work production.

The Bad Driver

Focal behavior: Frustration-induced aggression in drivers, operationally defined as speed in horn honking.

Hypothesis: People show their frustration more quickly with low-status drivers than with high-status drivers and do so by blowing their horn after a shorter delay if the driver blocking their path is a low-status driver.

Independent variable: Presumed status of driver (high versus low)

Dependent variable: Duration in seconds from onset of green light until driver honks the horn operationalizes the level of aggression demonstrated by the participant drivers.

Controlled variables:

- The driver

- The neighborhood

- The afternoon

- The length of time in car

Uncontrolled variables:

- Time of day (the 3:00 P.M. to 5:00 P.M. time slot may include rush hour traffic)

- Subject drivers (not randomly selected)

- Condition of experimenter's cars (undented versus very used)

Improvement:

1. Use two drivers following a similar course during the same time on the same day.

2. Have the same driver follow the same course during the same time on two days similar with regard to weather and time of year.

3. Use brand new cars that differ only in the socioeconomic status represented by the car, not the condition of the car.

Did you spot any other improvements?

Going for the Gold

Focal behavior: Preparation of Olympic athletes

Hypothesis: In developing award-winning athletes, self-esteem training during sleep is superior to diet and steroid use and to no preparation.

Independent variable: Type of training (self-esteem sleep training, versus diet and steroid preparation, versus control)

Dependent variable: Number of gold medals that three groups of athletes win in the Olympics

Controlled variables:

- Amount of time at camp

- The setting

- Random assignment to conditions, which minimizes the systematic influence of other variables

Uncontrolled variables: Condition 2 is poorly defined. Manipulating both diet and steroids reduces the comparative statements the researcher can draw. In addition, the use of steroids creates serious ethical problems.

Would you fund this experiment? No. The ethical and economic concerns present significant obstacles to adopting Rita's proposal. Design flaws limit the usefulness of the results. The study could be improved as follows:

1. Eliminate steroids from the experimental design.

2. Reconsider other dependent variables to measure training effectiveness.

3. Control for the order in which the experimental groups are treated.

4. Ensure that the group assigned to the self-esteem tape condition actually does play the tape while sleeping.

5. Ensure that the group assigned to the self-esteem tape condition gets the same amount of sleep the other groups get.

Can you think of other ways to improve the design?

▼Exercise 1.7 ANIMAL ADVOCACY

EVALUATE: Justify

Arguments in favor of the use of nonhuman animal species in research:

- We can learn about general laws of behavior that apply to both humans and the species being studied.

- We can learn specifics about the behavior of the species participating in research.

- We can use experimental treatments with nonhuman animal species that wouldn't be appropriate for use with the human species.

- Research on nonhuman animals represents a fairly small percentage of all the work that is accomplished.

- The American Psychological Association provides regulation for oversight of animal care that reduces the likelihood of either trivial or inappropriately painful research involvement.

- We have made advances in important areas of human function that wouldn't have been possible without animal research.

Arguments against the use of nonhuman animal species:

- Nonhuman animal species are entitled to the same treatment as humans.

- Nonhuman animal species tend to be subjected to unnecessary and painful treatments.

- A great deal of psychological research with nonhuman animal species is trivial.

- The results of nonhuman animal research may have no relevance for human animals.

- The APA is too remote from actual research processes to provide realistic oversight.

- The trade-off for human progress is not worth the cost to nonhuman animal participants.

▼Exercise 1.8 WHAT MAY COME

CREATE: Imagine

The limits here are only those of your creativity. How do you anticipate the future professional opportunities associated with understanding, predicting, and controlling behavior might translate into jobs in the future?

Chapter

◀ Neuroscience and Behavior ▶

▼Exercise 2.1   HOW DO YOU DO THAT?

UNDERSTAND: Describe

Here are some examples of how brain components could contribute to the leisure activity of playing bridge.

Brain Site	Function?	Involvement?
Hypothalamus	Maintains autonomic nervous system (popcorn and soda intake)	Regulates body temperature and appetite
Occipital lobe	Processes visual information	Registers cards dealt and body language of opposing players
Reticular formation	Controls arousal and attention	Maintains vigilance, even during boring plays
Cerebellum	Coordinates voluntary movement and balance	Holds you upright in the chair and supports appropriate card selection
Parietal lobe	Processes sensory input through sensory cortex	Prompts subtle shifts in movement when body parts "go to sleep"
Corpus callosum	Connects two hemispheres	Keeps unified eyes on players on both sides of the table
Medulla	Controls heartbeat and breathing	Increases heart rate during exciting play and promotes breathing even through challenging play
Temporal lobe	Processes auditory information	Monitors the bidding voices of other players
Frontal lobe	Manages speaking and muscle movement. Makes plans and judgments	Determines proper bidding, announces bid, and judges when to be pleased or irritated with partner's performance
Thalamus	Directs messages to the sensory areas in cortex and transmits replies to motor areas	Coordinates images of cards played with motor movements involved in own selection

Continued

Brain Site	Function?	Involvement?
Amygdala	Involved in governing emotion	Yes. Many bridge players work hard to manage their emotions for more controlled play.
Hippocampus	Processes explicit memories for storage	Yes. Monitors thoughts of "what beats what"

▼Exercise 2.2   CALL 911!
UNDERSTAND: Compare

Sympathetic Effect	System	Parasympathetic Effect
Speeds up	Heart Rate	Slows down
Increases	Respiration Rate	Decreases
Relaxation	Bladder Integrity	Constriction
Increases	Sweat Gland Activity	Decreases
Dilation	Pupillary Action	Constriction
Inhibition	Salivation	Stimulation

▼Exercise 2.3   THE SPLIT-BRAIN PROBLEM
APPLY: Classify

Studying concepts from psychology is primarily a left-hemisphere activity (L) because most concepts presented in your book are presented verbally. However, textbook illustrations and graphics also involve the right hemisphere (R), though to a lesser extent.

Drawing a map of your campus engages both hemispheres (L and R). The left hemisphere interprets the labels and the right hemisphere interprets the images.

Daydreaming about your next holiday trip is primarily a right-hemisphere (R) function. Our fantasies generally take the form of images, which are processed on the right side of the brain.

Listening to a piano concerto is essentially a right-hemisphere activity (R). The absence of lyrics leaves the left hemisphere less involved.

Listening to rap music engages both hemispheres (L and R); the right hemisphere attends to the powerful tempo and musical elements of the music while the left interprets the lyrics.

Thinking about your next "night out" draws on the right hemisphere (R) because the activity involves fantasy, which is processed primarily on the right.

Reading junk mail usually engages the left (L) hemisphere, unless the junk mail contains fancy attention-getting graphics to capture your attention.

$6 \times 4 - 2 + 5 =$ This sequence, like other mathematical expressions, is processed and evaluated by the left hemisphere (L).

Redecorating your room engages the right hemisphere (R), as this is a highly spatial activity.

Doodling engages the right hemisphere (R) in processing spatial stimuli; however, a right-hander's motor control in executing fine motor movements of the right hand will be governed by the left hemisphere (L).

Completing this exercise probably starts out as a left hemisphere (L) event, activated by processing the words on the page. However, when you have to picture in your mind the image created in the words, this shifts some thinking to the right hemisphere (R). Writing down your answer again involves both hemispheres, through language processing and fine motor movement.

▼Exercise 2.4   THE NEUROTRANSMISSION DOCTOR
ANALYZE: Solve

Normal Regulation Functions	Neurotransmitter	Disorders Implicated in Dysregulation
Skeletal muscle control Attention Arousal Memory	ACETYLCHOLINE (ACH)	Alzheimer's disease
Voluntary movement Reward pathway	DOPAMINE (DA)	Parkinson's disease Schizophrenic spectrum disorders Addiction problems
Pain relief Stress recovery Eating regulation	ENDORPHINS	PTSD Eating disorders
Anxiety Sleep/arousal	GAMMA-AMINOBUTYRIC ACID (GABA)	Anxiety disorders
Mood Arousal	NOREPINEPHRINE (NE)	Depression
Sleep/wakefulness Eating regulation Aggression	SEROTONIN	Depression Eating disorders Obsessive-compulsive disorders

▼Exercise 2.5   PHANTOM PAIN
ANALYZE: Reason

This young man's pain is probably phantom pain and is the result of the neural reorganization underway in his somatosensory cortex. As the neurons in the motor cortex that would have received the signals from the arm die from lack of stimulation, other motor neurons take advantage of this new space to extend their neural branches. However, because there are still neural connections between the motor cortex and sensory cortex, the area of the sensory cortex responsible for the missing arm receives information from these new connections. Other areas of the brain interpret these signals as pain.

The most likely sources of the new neural signals are the areas adjacent to those that were connected to his arm: the neck, forehead, or eyebrow.

▼Exercise 2.6   CARING FOR PHINEAS
EVALUATE: Take Perspective

Whatever your answer, you should recognize that the sudden change would have been difficult for everyone. His friends would have been faced with the shock of his injury, his likely frightening physical appearance (at least initially), and his bizarre behavior. They would have had to get to know the "new" Phineas; a task made more difficult by the fact that this new person may have been less likeable. They may have even disliked him and then felt guilty because the change was not his fault. If they thought Phineas *did* have some control over his behavior, and that he was simply acting inappropriately, then they might have been angry and ostracized him.

Phineas may or may not have been aware of the changes in his personality and behavior. Given that there was nothing wrong with his memory, however, he probably was aware of them. Because he had been a well-liked and respected young man, the change in how people felt about him probably was disturbing. He might well have felt frightened and angry over his lack of control. He might even have been angry at himself, wondering *why* he couldn't control his behavior. It would have been very easy for him to want to be by himself, especially when others were probably not anxious to be with him.

If you were a social worker assigned to Phineas and his support network now, what types of services might you offer them?

The services could include counseling for both Phineas and his supporters to help them develop new strategies for relating to each other and dealing with feelings of anger and guilt. You might refer him to a physician who might be able to offer medical options to help him manage his behavior through the use of drugs or surgery. Phineas would probably function best in a structured environment, so you could help the family explore educational and supervised living arrangements that would allow him to be as independent as possible. Phineas would always need care, so assisting supporters in arranging for Medicare and SSI and coordinating resources with Workers' Compensation would be an important part of your job.

What would be your expectations for the rest of Phineas's life? Why?

You should recognize that Phineas would always need some form of care and assistance. Because the areas of his brain that are responsible for judgment and planning were permanently damaged, he would need supervision to function safely at work and home. Because his behavior would now be impulsive and often socially inappropriate, he would need continual guidance and reinforcement in order to maintain and develop healthy relationships. His life would be very different from the one he formerly led, but it might be possible for him to eventually establish a new life with dignity and some degree of independence.

Speculate about what other kinds of changes might have occurred in Phineas's recovery if the tamping rod had pierced the brain at a different location.

If the rod had gone through the back of his skull and damaged the occipital lobe, Phineas would have probably lost his vision, and his recovery would have been focused on learning how to function without this sense. If the rod had injured the hindbrain, particularly in the area of the medulla, he would not have survived because the areas responsible for controlling vital functions such as breathing and heart rate would have been damaged. Injury to the side of his head, in the area of the temporal lobe (Broca's area), could have interfered with Phineas's hearing or speech. Injury to the top of his head in the area of the motor cortex or somatosensory cortex would have interfered with motor function or sensation. Memory impairment would have been the result if the hippocampus and other structures in the limbic system had been damaged. Damage to the limbic system could also result in excessive aggression, fear, or significant changes in sexual behavior.

▼Exercise 2.7   THE NEW SUPERHEROES

CREATE: Invent

Here are some possible examples of creative new superheroes:

Thermostatman: This superhero is capable of voluntarily shifting his temperature to adapt to his surroundings. The augmented brain structure is the hypothalamus. Thermostatman would be especially helpful in tolerating extreme temperatures, rescuing volcano or arctic research teams whose missions have gone awry.

Scribewoman: This superhero is able to retain every detail spoken to her. The augmented brain structure is the hippocampus. She is the perfect team member to have on complicated projects, particularly a spy mission when obvious note taking might endanger the group.

Vigilboy: This superhero could stay awake for extended periods of time. The augmented brain structure is the reticular formation. Vigilboy would excel at surveillance sessions.

These three examples demonstrate how you can use your imagination to come up with new arrangements. Once your superhero emerges from your creative process, you apply appropriate criteria to determine whether your creation is satisfying. How original and playful are the examples provided in this text? How original and playful are your examples?

▼Exercise 2.8   THE ADDICTED BRAIN

CREATE: Design

There are many brain areas that could be responsible for contributing to the addict's behavior and experiences. Some of these include:

- The medulla—responsible for heartbeat and breathing

- The reticular formation—responsible for arousal

- The amygdala—responsible for aggression and fear

- The frontal lobe of the cerebral cortex—responsible for forming judgments and making plans (especially the prefrontal lobe area or association areas)

Your hypothesis statement will depend on the brain area and behavior you chose. It should include a specific prediction and be written so that the independent and dependent variables are clear. In the same way, your experimental design should describe your variables operationally and briefly outline how you might conduct your test.

Animal studies are an important part of psychology. Although many psychologists study animals simply out of an interest in animal behavior, many more use them to explore questions in which it is difficult or impossible to study humans directly. This is a good example of such a question. Although a rat's brain and bodily processes are not identical to those of a human, they are similar enough in structure and function so that scientists are able to use rats to learn about basic metabolic, physiologic, and behavioral responses to drugs. Nevertheless, such studies give only a limited understanding of the role that higher cognitive functions play in mediating basic responses. For example, although studies with rats can tell us that a drug has an excitatory effect on a particular brain structure, they cannot tell us how a human being's perception of, and cognition about, the experience could minimize or magnify that effect. In this exercise, it probably would be unethical to conduct an experiment on human beings. Psychology's code of ethics would prohibit a psychologist from administering a drug that would cause permanent harm or from damaging brain areas as part of an experimental control. What we must also remember is that many of these guidelines apply to animal research. In all cases in which animals are used, it is important that the experimenter not use them recklessly and that care be taken to provide the animals with humane conditions and procedures that are as pain-free as possible. Experimenters must always balance the knowledge that they can gain with the potential harm to the animal.

Chapter

◀ States of Consciousness ▶

▼Exercise 3.1 CONSCIOUS CONTROL

PART 1: UNDERSTAND: Observe

Obviously, there is no way to predict what activities and experiences you might have selected. A good answer would include at least 12 items, selected over the course of the day, and involving different levels of awareness and consciousness. One example might include: a) turning off your alarm in the morning, b) making breakfast, c) listening to music on the way to class, d) taking notes in your chemistry class, e) giving a presentation in your psychology class, f) having lunch with a group of friends, g) daydreaming, h) finding your way to a new café to meet your significant other for coffee, i) talking with your mom on the phone, j) eating popcorn while watching a movie, k) studying for an exam tomorrow, l) brushing your teeth and getting ready for bed, and m) bolting awake when you realize you forgot to do something for class tomorrow.

PART 2: APPLY: Classify

Again, there is no way to evaluate what you have written, and you might not agree with our own specific rankings, but we offer below a general set of categories that might help as you think about your own experiences.

The *least conscious control* category would include:

a. turning off your alarm in the morning
b. eating popcorn while watching a movie
c. listening to music on the way to class

Actions demonstrating *a little more conscious control* would include:

a. making breakfast
b. brushing your teeth and getting ready for bed
c. having lunch with a group of friends
d. daydreaming

The category demonstrating *the most intense conscious control* would include:

a. talking with your mom on the phone
b. finding your way to a new café to meet your significant other for coffee

c. taking notes in your chemistry class

d. giving a presentation in your psychology class

e. studying for an exam tomorrow

f. bolting awake when you realize you forgot to do something for class tomorrow

You may have noticed as you talked over your rank order with others that individuals may differ in the way they experience the degrees of conscious control associated with similar activities and experiences. Why might that be so?

▼Exercise 3.2 TO SLEEP, PERCHANCE TO DREAM

APPLY: Classify

Freud's Wish Fulfillment Interpretation

Freud would have a field day with Maria's dream. Since dreams represent "the royal road to the unconscious," Maria's libidinal urges have been translated into images of well-built, but unsatisfied male customers. The restaurant is also decorated with representations of the Eiffel Tower and Leaning Tower of Pisa, which Freud would point out are phallic symbols, further reinforcing the sexualized latent content of Maria's dream.

Rosalind Cartwright's Problem-Solving Interpretation

Maria had a particularly tough day at work as a waitress before she fell asleep. The demands of the day created residue from her work that probably involved responding to endless demands of impatient customers. Her inability to satisfy the intensity and frequency of customer demands resulted in a cognitive meltdown, symbolized by her inability to take any action due to her melted feet. She clearly had a bad day in which she failed to meet the expectations of her customers and her boss.

J. Allan Hobson's Activation Synthesis Model

Because Hobson proposes random signals from lower brain centers as the basis for his theory, it is a bit more challenging to determine what elements of Maria's dream might fit the bill. However, the emergence of church bells in the dream could represent her lower brain centers responding to the racket of her alarm clock. The external stimulus ended up being integrated into the dream, although the presence of the alarm was translated into church bells in processes we can't quite understand.

▼Exercise 3.3 A MIDSUMMER NIGHT'S DREAM

ANALYZE: Reason

Peter will begin to feel sleepy and generally lethargic. Over the course of the four days, he will experience a decreased ability to concentrate and will notice impaired creativity, irritability, slowed performance, slight hand tremors, and altered perceptions when performing monotonous tasks. Eventually, he will experience hallucinations and speech and movement problems. He probably will *not* notice a difference in his performance on short, highly motivating tasks (for example, outrunning rabid seals), however. His immune system will not fight off viral infections with the same efficiency, and his body will have increased levels of a variety of pathogens.

When he returns to the land of sleep, Peter will probably experience one or two nights of lengthened sleep and increased REM activity during sleep, but he will then return to his normal sleeping patterns.

▼Exercise 3.4   THE LIGHT AT THE END OF THE TUNNEL
PART 1: ANALYZE: Infer

Summary: *The Spiritual Hypothesis.* This position assumes that humans are endowed with a soul that exists apart from the corporeal body at the time of death. This position is supported by religious traditions in which the promise of an afterlife is prominent. Given this support, the spiritual hypothesis is characterized by a sense of optimism and a belief in the continuity and perhaps even indestructibility of the human spirit.

Summary: *The Physiological Hypothesis.* This point of view stresses that physiological principles govern brain function, regardless of the specific experience reported. Cognitive science proposes oxygen-deprivation hallucination as an alternative hypothesis to explain the reported qualities of the near-death experience. Those who hold this position do not need to posit a special spiritual existence to explain the near-death phenomenon. They are more inclined to see the event as the brain functioning under stress rather than the triumph of the human spirit. They are skeptical that human beings can transcend the physiological limitations of the brain.

PART 2: EVALUATE: Justify

Which has greater personal appeal? This answer, of course, depends on your own values and beliefs. Do they more closely match the spiritual hypothesis or the physiological hypothesis?

▼Exercise 3.5   JOBS AND DRUGS DON'T MIX: PROFESSIONAL PROJECT HOPE
EVALUATE: Assess

Profession or Preferred Activity	Riskiest Drug Substance	Performance Impairment
Bicycle messenger	LSD	LSD would make navigating busy city streets almost certainly lethal, as fantastic pictures, kaleidoscopic displays, and a sense of panic interfere with weaving between buses and darting across busy intersections.
Marathon runner	Any depressant (for example, barbiturates or opiates)	Depressants slow down neural activity and can depress physiological functions such as respiration and heart rate through their impact on the brainstem. At the least, such drug use would make it hard to keep up with competitors; at worst, it would be fatal. Depressants are tempting for athletes to use because they can decrease the pain and anxiety that are often a part of this profession.

Continued

Profession or Preferred Activity	Riskiest Drug Substance	Performance Impairment
Artist	Cocaine; crack	Cocaine or crack are risky for the artist for a variety of reasons. Not only do such drugs speed up neural activity so that fine motor control may be difficult to maintain, but the crash that inevitably follows results in headaches, depression, and exhaustion—a difficult state in which to work. Also, these drugs are expensive and could quickly push someone into the "starving artist" category.
Stay-at-home mom	Alcohol	Alcohol is dangerous for the stay-at-home mom because it impairs judgment and slows reaction time, both potentially disastrous effects when small children are present.
Sword swallower	Marijuana	Marijuana has the potential to end a sword swallower's career fairly quickly. Not only does it impair motor coordination, perceptual skills, and reaction time—all of which are critical when putting long pointy objects down your throat—it increases sensitivity to taste and touch stimuli, making gagging a real possibility.
Teacher	Barbiturates	Barbiturates are one of the many classes of drugs that would be lethal to a teacher's career (and potentially his or her life, as well). They slow reaction time, impair memory and judgment, and can induce sleep. In large doses, the depressive effects can sometimes cause death.
Tightrope walker	LSD	The hallucinations caused by LSD would not be an enjoyable experience for someone walking on a narrow rope far above the ground. The sense of being separated from one's body, combined with altered visual perception, would make it impossible for a tightrope walker to make it safely to the other side.
Accountant	Cocaine; crack	Cocaine would be particularly dangerous for the accountant, especially during tax time. Although the rush of energy might seem beneficial, increased aggression would make fistfights with tense clients a real possibility, and the crash following the high would make it impossible to concentrate on the level of detail necessary in this type of work.

▼Exercise 3.6 ROCK-A-BYE BABY
CREATE: Invent

> Was the theory of sleep or dreaming apparent in your adaptation? Do you think your new version or original composition would catch on?

▼Exercise 3.7 REMEDIES FOR JET LAG
CREATE: Design

> *Your hypothesis.* You would attempt to demonstrate the superiority of one jet-lag intervention strategy. For example, the use of meditation may be superior to preventive vitamin B and aerobic exercise. You would design the experiment to demonstrate this difference.
>
> *The independent variable.* Your experimental design would need at least three, preferably four, groups. Three groups would have an intervention: vitamin use, aerobic exercise, or meditation. The fourth group could serve as the no-treatment control group; this group will illustrate the normal course of jet lag without intervention.
>
> *Measuring the dependent variable.* Measuring jet lag is a problem. One approach may be to ask individuals how many hours of sleep they would need to feel caught up. Or you could measure how many days elapse until each participant reports feeling "back to normal." Assuming your experimental design includes some treatments that are effective for jet lag, participants in these conditions will need fewer hours of sleep to feel caught up or will report that fewer days are needed to get back to normal. If no treatment is effective and the study has been well designed, the dependent-variable measurements will not differ among the groups.
>
> *Controlling other variables.* Ideally, the subjects should be matched for age, gender, and travel experience. This process helps to rule out alternative interpretations of any changes reported within the experiment. In addition, all subjects should travel the same distance at the same time of day in a direction that will exaggerate the reaction. All subjects should be randomly assigned to treatment conditions, again to control for alternative explanations. Once the plane has landed, you should take precautions to ensure that all subjects performed their assigned treatment. You should measure their jet lag at the same time. You should also prevent other activities that would artificially add to the lag (for example, no dancing!).

4

Chapter

◀ The Nature and Nurture ▶ of Behavior

▼Exercise 4.1 IT'S ALL ACADEMIC

UNDERSTAND: Explain

Assuming that the premise of the program would still be to facilitate the success of low-income children in school, children would probably be given an IQ test to determine who had the innate (genetic) ability to succeed academically. Administrators of the program might also examine the school records of the parents of the children; in this framework, children with academically successful parents would be more likely to be successful themselves. Little or no consideration would be given to the way that the children's environment, health, or general well-being might affect their performance. The children's success would be seen as a product of their innate ability and not much affected by outside influences. It also would be unlikely that the program would solicit the involvement of the community or the parents.

If this philosophy were continued in the public school system, funds would not be available for those special services designed to facilitate the performance of children who do not easily succeed in traditional academic settings. For example, there might not be any special education programs or programs for students with learning disabilities. Taken to its extreme, there would not be any meal programs; after all, environment doesn't affect academic performance.

The idea that schools and teachers are accountable for the performance of their students is a clear reflection of the opposite belief—that student performance is strongly, if not completely, dependent upon environmental factors. Although it is unlikely that legislators believe there is no genetic component to intelligence, the creation of a law that says most children must reach a certain standard of academic performance, and that schools and teachers are responsible for making this happen, indicates the belief that support services, teaching techniques, and curricular and extra-curricular resources influence the level of performance a student reaches. If those things are adequate, then all (or most) students will perform well; if they are not, then students will not perform well. This places the responsibility for the possibility of student success on the educational system.

You may hold any one of a number of different views about the role genetics plays in intelligence. Maybe you think that intelligence is primarily inherited. If so, many of the ideas in the first two paragraphs of this answer will make sense to you. You might think that intelligence is strictly a product of the environment and that, if the environment were equal for everyone, everyone would perform equally well. Most likely, your views fall somewhere in between. Regardless, you will have the opportunity to explore this issue more when you work with Chapter 11, later in the term.

▼Exercise 4.2   NATURE OR NURTURE?

APPLY: Classify

The key to successfully completing this exercise is recognizing the assumptions about how we become who we are that underlie each statement. For example, the assumption upon which "Handsome is as handsome does" is based is that behavior, not a particular configuration of features, is attractive. In other words, genetics is not what determines beauty, learned patterns are. This, then, is a nurture argument. Can you identify the assumptions for each of the following?

"Sugar and spice and everything nice, that's what little girls are made of . . ."	NATURE
"Handsome is as handsome does."	NURTURE
"The apple doesn't fall far from the tree."	NATURE
"You can't teach an old dog new tricks."	NURTURE
"Early to bed and early to rise, makes a man healthy, wealthy, and wise."	NURTURE
"Boys will be boys."	NATURE
"You are what you eat."	NURTURE
"Blood will tell."	NATURE
"All men are created equal."	NURTURE

What examples did you come up with?

▼Exercise 4.3   WHO'S TO BLAME

ANALYZE: Infer

When this shocking episode occurred, the public was quick to find culprits who contributed to the actions of the 6-year-old killer. Many critics suggested that lax controls in the school were somehow to blame *(nurture argument)*. Many more individuals pointed to the more compelling explanation of the absence of a significant care provider *(nurture argument)*. At age 6, this child had already learned to fend for himself and to make judgments without adult supervision. Even if he had received attention, he was raised in the home of a drug dealer so he might have had questionable moral instruction *(nurture argument)*. Given that his mother's life had gone badly off course, there is also the possibility that the child could have some genetic predisposition for poor judgment *(nature argument)*.

▼Exercise 4.4   KEEP ON TRUCKIN'

PART 1: ANALYZE: Compare and Contrast

Social learning theory: This theory states that children learn gender-linked behaviors based on the consequences of their imitation of the behaviors they have observed in adults. A young girl giving a doll a pretend bottle may be told, "You are such a good mommy," whereas a boy doing the same thing might be asked, "Why don't you go play with your trucks?" Similarly, a boy crying might be told that "boys don't cry," but a girl might be comforted or consoled. Such patterns lead children to adopt the behaviors that are "appropriate" in the eyes of the authority figures in their lives.

Example: Boys are given trucks and cars as gifts and are encouraged to learn how engines work. Men who are good with cars or trucks are seen as desirable and "manly." Girls are often discouraged from getting dirty or being loud, activities that are a natural part of playing with cars and trucks or learning about engines. All of these factors combine to make it less likely that a girl or woman would adopt the activities and skills around cars and trucks that boys and men might.

Gender schema theory: Gender schema theory suggests that individuals develop a gender "lens" through which they view the world. There are concepts of maleness and femaleness in every culture, and children learn the appropriate gender-typed way to act by comparing their own behavior with these concepts. Individuals also compare the behaviors of others with these concepts and can judge the "appropriateness" of others' behaviors by the standards set by the culture. Cultural ideals are presented through the media, use of language, and the actions of adults.

Example: Truckers are portrayed as big, tough, and often a little grubby. In our culture, this image is more compatible with the image of masculinity. The image of femininity is a little softer, more sensitive, cleaner, and neater. We tend to judge women truckers as not very feminine and perhaps conclude that they have something wrong with them. We might also judge them as less competent at their work, even if that is not the case.

PART 2: EVALUATE: Justify

Which Theory Did You Select and Why?

A good answer to this question would identify both a theory and at least one reason for selecting it that recognize both the mechanism of action (the consequences of behaviors for social learning theory and the comparison of behaviors with cultural images for gender schema theory) and the context for the question (male truckers hassling female truckers). For example, you might decide social learning theory is the best choice, because it is easier to talk about behaviors and consequences objectively than positive and negative gender ideals. On the other hand, you could decide that because the issue appears to be related to ideals of masculinity and femininity, explaining where those ideals arise and how they are portrayed makes the most sense. This option would mean your choice would be gender schema theory. These are simply examples; you might have other reasons.

Example: An example that promotes social learning theory might involve getting authority figures for male truckers to endorse the benefits of having women in the occupation. Similarly, male truckers might get some incentives for agreeing to train or mentor new female truckers. Social learning theory requires that reinforcers for desirable behavior must change. Gender schema themes require changing the lens through which one filters experience. You might place posters that show men and women who otherwise fit the cultural gender schema performing tasks that are not gender typical. Perhaps they could show a big, burly man holding a baby or taking care of an elderly woman; other posters might depict an attractive woman firefighter or trucker. These images could help expand the employees' perception of gender-appropriate roles, both for themselves and the people they work with. Did you come up with a different strategy?

▼Exercise 4.5   BROTHER, CAN YOU SPARE A DIME?

EVALUATE: Decide

The researchers explained their findings by suggesting that the high socioeconomic status environments were also highly enriching, that children reared in these environments had enough exposure and opportunity to access intellectually stimulating experiences to reach more of their potential. In other words, these children were more likely to show their maximum potential on the tests used to determine intelligence, and that this maximum is likely to be genetically determined. On the other hand, twins reared in low socioeconomic status environments were more likely to live in intellectually impoverished circumstances and lack the necessary stimuli to fully reach their genetic potential. In these situations, the twins are more likely to show the environmental effects, and intelligence measures are more likely to vary. It is a complicated argument, but it essentially says that the environment influences how much of an effect genes have on the expression of intelligence. Rich intellectual environments allowed for more of the genetic influence to be expressed, while this genetic influence was masked in the more disadvantaged environments.

▼Exercise 4.6   YOUR PERSONAL HONOR CODE

EVALUATE: Choose

Kohlberg's stage theory of moral development would suggest the following classifications.

	Preconventional	Conventional	Postconventional
Rationales for those who maintain integrity			
I'm afraid of what would happen if I got caught.	X		
I believe my personal integrity would be damaged if I don't do my own work.			X
I want to follow the rules that have been laid out by the instructor.		X	
Raltionales for those who cheat			
Everybody else does it.		X	
I don't want to lose ground to those who do.	X		
The results of this specific challenge don't contribute much to my overall growth so cheating doesn't matter.			X*
I can't afford to flunk.	X		
Nobody gets hurt by what I do.	X		
The instructor should have been paying more attention so if I can get away with it, I will.	X		
I am not personally defined by the results of any specific test.			X*

*One of the harder things to understand about Kohlberg's classification system is that postconventional reasoning doesn't always lead to the most defensible moral behavior. The key to classifying postconventional reasoning is adherence to well-defined personal standards rather than conforming to societal norms (conventional) or avoiding unpleasant consequences (preconventional).

▼Exercise 4.7   CHARACTER BUILDING

CREATE: Imagine

This person needs to be sensitive enough to deal with witnesses and victims; tough enough to stay alive in the face of bombs, hired killers, and guard dogs; intelligent enough to break secret codes and outwit the criminal mastermind; and witty enough to be interesting and to find the humor in devastating situations.

Sample biography: Private eye Jo Hardison was a skilled detective whose distinguished police record *(nurture)* made her a natural at solving mysteries in the private sector. The eighth of nine children, she had developed some wily strategies to navigate her way in her crowded family *(nurture)*. Somehow Hardison still managed to get into trouble on a regular basis. Her father's harsh punishment tactics helped her develop the resilience and persistence *(nurture)* she used to cope with her most challenging cases. Her father's love of physics *(nature)* and her mother's quick Irish wit *(nature/nurture)* seemed to find a perfect outlet in Hardison's deft handling of evidence and clients. All of her siblings were successful in high-pressure, professional occupations *(nature/nurture)*, so Hardison always felt some extra pressure to do the job right *(nurture)*.

▼ Exercise 4.8 SEEING DOUBLE

CREATE: Design

There are quite a few possible hypotheses that you could have created. Whatever your hypothesis is, it should be stated as a question for which you could find an answer. Both the dependent and independent variables should be obvious from the question. Examples of possible hypotheses include:

- Is an individual's level of extraversion greater when raised in a family with more than four children?

- Is an individual less likely to be extraverted when raised in an urban community?

- Is an individual's level of extraversion higher when parents are also extraverted?

- Is an individual more extraverted when exposed to diverse educational settings in the primary school years?

The design that you outlined should take into account the fact that identical twins have the same genetic information and that environments include factors like socioeconomic status, family structure, educational opportunities, as well as the more obvious ones like geographic location and race.

Numerous ethical issues make such experiments impossible. It is not ethical to take children away from biological parents able to provide for their needs and assign them to new parents. It is not ethical to separate children who share strong biological and emotional ties that would prove supportive to their development. It is not ethical to place children into potentially less than ideal circumstances simply for the purpose of seeing what happens. It is not ethical to give couples or individuals children who are not their own and for which they may not be prepared and force them to raise these children. The list goes on and on. So, given these necessary ethical restrictions, what alternative experiments are there?

One alternative is to use animal studies. It is possible to take animals like voles, rats, mice, or fish that have multiple offspring at the same time and to give those offspring to different foster parents to raise. Those foster parents can live in different environments and have different resources at their disposal. Although there are limits on the conclusions that one can draw from such experiments, their results can be combined with other correlational and naturalistic observations of human experience to provide a more complete picture of the issue. Did you propose other alternatives?

Chapter

◀ **The Developing Person** ▶

▼**Exercise 5.1 WHEN BAD CHILDREN AREN'T BAD**
UNDERSTAND: Translate

Holiday Toys: Children under the age of 2 are most interested in exploring their world through their actions. Manipulating everyday objects is a great delight. What makes this example even more exciting is that this girl has recently discovered that objects exist even if she can't see them (object permanence). This makes the game of peek-a-boo a potential marathon event.

The Scary Boyfriend: This infant also has realized that things exist outside of his presence. In this case, he knows that this person is new and would much prefer to be with his aunt or other familiar caretaker. This stage is referred to as "stranger anxiety." This fear may be exaggerated by the presence of unfamiliar features, such as a mustache, but children in this stage can shriek at any person who is perceived as "not Mom" or some other familiar caregiver.

The Flying Bottle: This child has learned a simple cause-and-effect relationship and is delighting in experimenting with it. Not only does the bottle hit the floor every time he throws it, but Mom picks it up so he can do it again. This is lots of fun! This ability is a result of the infant developing object permanence. He can recognize that the bottle in his hand and the bottle on the floor are one and the same, but it can take a long time for him to see the connection between the two objects.

The Card Game: The younger sister has not yet developed the concept of conservation: the ability to recognize that the same number of cards exists regardless of arrangement. As far as the girl is concerned, if her cards take up more space, then there are more of them and she wins.

Juice, Please: This is also an example of a child who does not understand the concept of conservation. Even though the same amount of juice went into the bigger glass, she was happy because the glass looked bigger.

Twins' Toys: This is a classic example of egocentrism. Young children cannot perceive things from another person's point of view, so everything is as they see it. They are not able to understand how another person feels, only how *they* feel. Although giving the lecture may make the father feel better, it is unlikely that the children have sufficient cognitive sophistication to profit from his wisdom.

▼Exercise 5.2   THE SITTER'S DILEMMA

APPLY: Classify

The 9-month-old will be interested in games that focus on looking, touching, and putting things into his mouth. This might include watching a mobile, playing with stackable blocks, or eating Zwieback Toast. Because of a newly acquired awareness of object permanence, peekaboo is also a favorite game.

The 2-year-old will probably enjoy activities that allow her to explore her growing ability to use words and "make-believe." Many children of this age like puzzles; they have the motor skills necessary to put large pieces together and can anticipate what the picture will be. Games of pretend—house, store, princesses—will be a big hit. Telling stories and making up words with funny sounds should also keep her out of trouble.

The 5-year-old will enjoy many of the same activities as the 2-year-old. In addition to this, he will enjoy telling simple jokes and playing those games that don't require a long attention span; Candy Land, Chutes and Ladders, and Hi Ho! Cherry-O are all examples of board games that appeal to children of this age.

At 9 years, the oldest child will have more abstract reasoning skills and will enjoy games with complex rules. Monopoly will probably be a favorite, and her sense of humor will be quite sophisticated. Word and number puzzles might be appealing, as will some basic science experiments.

Activities that can be approached at many different levels are your best bet. Reading stories is a possibility; have the 9-year-old read to the younger children. Have the children make up their own stories. Each child can contribute an idea as you verbally tell the story, or the older children can make up stories to tell to the younger ones. You could even turn this into a play, with the older children acting and the infant and you serving as audience. If all of this fails, hit the kitchen. While the infant bangs pots and pans, and the 2- and 5-year-olds pretend to make a cake, you and the 9-year-old can find a simple cookie recipe that she can make while you supervise. Everyone will have fun, and you will end up with a bedtime snack!

As the younger children go to bed, the activities can become more complex and abstract. Instead of Candy Land, for instance, you could play Yahtzee or Monopoly. Instead of *Goodnight Moon* you might read *Charlotte's Web*.

▼Exercise 5.3   ON DEATH AND DYING

ANALYSIS: Relate

Note: These answers are samples only. They may overlap with the hypotheses you generate, or you may be able to derive other approaches not listed here.

Characteristics of the illness

Variable 1: Type of illness

Hypothesis: It is easier to sustain denial of impending death if symptoms develop gradually. Illness with sudden, dramatic symptoms may be easier to adjust to and accept than gradual-onset illness.

Variable 2: Amount of pain

Hypothesis: More painful terminal conditions produce reports of more intense anger than those found in less painful conditions. Conditions that involve greater pain may be more difficult to bear for the dying person and for the individuals in the support system.

Characteristics of the person

> *Variable 1:* Personality structure
>
> *Hypothesis:* People with stronger control issues in their lives might have a more difficult time moving beyond denial. Optimistic people may be more inclined to bargain, or they may more readily accept their own death, believing that it is a blessing.
>
> *Variable 2:* Gender
>
> *Hypothesis:* Men may demonstrate more visible anger responses to terminal illness; women may demonstrate more depressive responses.
>
> *Variable 3:* Age
>
> *Hypothesis:* Children may spend less time bargaining than adults spend.
>
> *Variable 4:* Religious belief
>
> *Hypothesis:* Some religions do not regard death as an enemy. Where death is regarded as a more natural part of life, perhaps we wouldn't observe the grief reactions described by Kübler-Ross at all.
>
> *Variable 5:* Experience with death.
>
> *Hypothesis:* Being present at the death of a loved one might influence a person to be more accepting of his or her own death.

Characteristics of the environment

> *Variable 1:* Social support
>
> *Hypothesis:* Those with a strong social support system are likely to demonstrate acceptance more quickly.
>
> *Variable 2:* Culture
>
> *Hypothesis:* Cultures differ in their responses to death. In cultures where death is seen as natural, people may show less anger about a terminal illness and the predicted death.

▼ Exercise 5.4 PIAGET MEETS SANTA CLAUS
ANALYZE: Compare/Contrast

What Are the General Characteristics of the Sensorimotor Stage Child?

In the sensorimotor stage, children have not acquired many meaningful concepts. Their primary activities involve experiencing and exploring the physical world and discovering the abilities and limits of their growing bodies. Sensorimotor stage children would not have learned the concept that Santa Claus represents.

On encountering Santa, what would the sensorimotor stage child

- *observe?*

On first encounter, Santa's image is likely to be discrepant with anything that is familiar. His image is a mass of bright red and white. He makes deep booming sounds. Santa's lap is soft and his beard tickles. If the child is receptive to the experience, the nature of the interaction will stimulate the child's senses, the basis of the sensorimotor period.

- *think and feel?*

Sensorimotor stage children think and respond to Santa Claus in different ways. Many identify this new acquaintance as distinctly strange (think about it—a huge, oddly dressed, hairy guy who breaks out in bellylaughs all the time) so that the first visit with Santa often ends in fright and tears. Other sensorimotor stage children may be drawn to the novel person. Their curiosity fuels interest and excitement as they experience their first ritual visit.

- *believe?*

Children in the sensorimotor stage have no relevant organizing schema to interpret Santa, so belief in his existence is not an issue.

What Are the General Characteristics of the Preoperational Stage Child?

In the preoperational stage, children have acquired some stability in their ideas about how the physical world works; however, their ideas may not correspond to physical realities.

On encountering Santa, what would the preoperational stage child

- *observe?*

In this stage, children have comfortably acquired the concept of Santa Claus if that tradition is part of their culture. They observe consistency in his attire and his demeanor. They observe his generosity and jolliness.

- *think and feel?*

Santa encourages children to behave well since he knows who's "naughty or nice." Children think Santa has the capacity to watch over them and evaluate their behavior. Parents rely on this phenomenon, sometimes invoking Santa's presence during the holiday season to encourage the preoperational stage child to behave. The preoperational stage child feels excited about encounters with Santa and may create obnoxiously long lists of wishes that she expects Santa to fulfill via his reindeer-drawn sleigh.

- *believe?*

The preoperational stage child truly believes in the physical reality of Santa. Santa lives at the North Pole? No problem. After all, that's where the toy workshop is. Besides, Santa can stay warm in his fur-trimmed red outfit and black boots. All elements of the cultural tradition make sense to the preoperational child, making this easy to believe.

What Are the General Characteristics of the Concrete Operational Child?

Children who begin to demonstrate concrete operations develop a much more accurate picture of operations in the physical world. Their cognitive skills improve, not just in conservation skills (for example, recognizing that mass doesn't change merely by changing an object's shape) but also in understanding causality and in developing reliable categorizing strategies.

On encountering Santa, what would the concrete operational child

- *observe?*

The concrete operational child begins to recognize inconsistencies in Santa's appearance. A concrete operational child might ask, *"How can there be so many Santas all over town?"* or *"Why are some Santas thin?"* More refined observational skills set the stage for disbelief in Santa.

- *think?*

As concrete operational children come to understand some physical realities about the world, other kinds of questions further undermine Santa's existence:

—How can Santa get to kids' homes all over the world in one night?

—How can reindeer really fly and pull a sleigh?

—Wouldn't there be a better place for Santa to live, especially since he's so old?

—Just how does Santa keep track of good behavior? . . . Hmm.

- *feel?*

Discovering principles of physical reality often represents a period of serious disappointment for concrete operational children. However, they may receive some compensation from making the transition to thinking as adults do around the holidays. They may experience new kinds of fun in actively assisting younger brothers and sisters in continuing their own beliefs.

- *believe?*

Before you know it, the concrete operational thinker is no longer willing to hang a Christmas stocking. Concrete operational children abandon their belief in Santa but may still believe that it is important to continue the holiday celebrations. After all, a concrete operational child, capable of conservation skills regarding number, would recognize that the number of presents might be reduced if traditional practices were abandoned.

How do these transitional experiences differ from the characteristics of the formal operational child and adult?

As children move into the *formal operations* stage, they begin to appreciate the cultural custom of Santa. They enjoy Santa as a symbol of seasonal celebration in keeping with their ability to understand abstract ideas. They recognize the importance of shared customs as a means of promoting cohesion in their families and in their culture.

▼Exercise 5.5   TEEN PREGNANCY
EVALUATE: Justify

1. However you approach this problem, you should take into consideration the biological, social, and cognitive issues of adolescence. Physically, people of this age become sexually mature. Girls develop breasts and have their first menstrual cycle, and boys experience their first nocturnal emission; both grow additional body hair. This process happens rapidly, generally over about two years. If it happens earlier or later than for others in the peer group, young people may feel uncomfortable about the changes. Reasoning powers continue to develop, and it is at this point that teenagers begin to be able to reason abstractly and to question the reason of others. As they develop their own sense of right and wrong, adolescents begin to try to separate themselves from their parents. Trying out different roles, changing one's appearance, and forming strong peer relationships are part of the job of the adolescent.

Many of these changes could explain higher-than-expected teen pregnancy rates. Because their bodies are changing so rapidly, teenagers may not understand how their new bodies work and how they can avoid pregnancy. Also, because their bodies look adult, adolescents often experiment with adult behavior as they try out different roles in an attempt to find a personal identity. Although their reasoning powers are improving, they may still not be able to interpret accurately abstract statistics or relate those statistics in a concrete way to their own actions. Finally, all of the above, when combined with the teenager's desire to separate from parents, means that teenagers are notoriously poor at seeking out answers to questions about sex and pregnancy prevention from reliable sources.

Adolescence is a unique developmental stage. The adolescent is not a big kid or a small adult. Any program that takes this into consideration and finds ways to create developmentally appropriate educational opportunities will have a higher rate of success than those that deal with adolescents as either big children or small adults.

2. You can make a case for many useful statistics. Make sure that you clearly state the rationale for your choice. For example, if you believe that using contraceptives is necessary to reduce the teen pregnancy rate, then looking at the numbers of teens having unprotected sex may be your statistic of choice.

▼Exercise 5.6   DEVELOPMENTAL DELIGHTS

CREATE: Design

These are only examples. Your toys and activities may be very different, depending on what potential relationships you saw among the different objects.

Objects: drinking straws, cardboard, large plastic cups, string
Children: 6 months: Make a caterpillar by alternately stringing straws and cups for the body and using the cardboard to make feet.

4 years: Fill the cups with water and blow bubbles through the straws; make it even more fun by blowing patterns of water onto the cardboard to make pictures.

7 years: Make a telephone, using the cups and string, and a telephone booth out of the cardboard.

Objects: 4-quart pot, spoon, measuring cups, sinkful of water
Children: 9 months: Turn the pot and cups over in the sink, and let the child beat on them with the spoon to make "music."

3 years: Play restaurant and wash the pot, cups, and spoon in the water; then make pretend soup.

10 years: Make spaghetti sauce from scratch and then clean up the mess (okay, the cleanup part is less fun).

Objects: 2 chairs, pillows, several books, large blanket
Children: 12 months: Put the chairs close together, with the pillows underneath. Practice climbing on the chairs. You could also play peekaboo with the books and the blanket.

2 years: Play preschool. Sit on the chair and read the books; then pretend it's nap time and sleep on the pillows with the blanket.

9 years: Make a fort out of the chairs and the blanket. Curl up inside with the pillows and read.

▼**Exercise 5.7   THE END OF THE STORY**

CREATE: Invent

Although yours is likely to be different, we provide a model of an obituary that neatly touches on Erikson's four adult psychosocial stages:

Miranda Jones passed quietly in her sleep at age 96 following a birthday celebration at the Happy Meadows Senior Center in which she was surrounded by loved ones. Surviving Ms. Jones were her son and daughter and their respective children (INTIMACY VERSUS ISOLATION). Ms. Jones retired after a successful career as an attorney (IDENTIFY VERSUS CONFUSION), a career in which she developed a reputation for fighting hard for her Legal Aid clients (GENERATIVITY VERSUS SELF-ABSORPTION). During her birthday party, she was reported to be in a great mood and frequently commented that if she had it to do over again, she would make very few changes in how to conduct her life (INTEGRITY VERSUS DESPAIR).

Chapter

◀Sensation▶

▼**Exercise 6.1 CROSSING THE THRESHOLD**

APPLY: Classify

- *"Learn While You Sleep:"* subthreshold
- *Sentry:* detection threshold
- *Father and child:* difference threshold
- *Potatoes:* difference threshold
- *Contact lens:* detection threshold
- *Music group:* subthreshold
- *Pajamas:* difference threshold
- *Hottest chili:* difference threshold
- *Cinnamon chili:* detection threshold

▼**Exercise 6.2 OCCUPATIONAL DESIGN**

PART 1: ANALYZE: Reason

Sensory Profile of a Garbage Collector

	Diminished Abilities	Average Abilities	Heightened Abilities
Vision			X
Hearing		X	
Smell	X		
Touch		X	
Taste		X	
Pain	X		
Balance			X

Explanation: An effective and efficient garbage collector would have refined abilities in balance and vision. It would be helpful in the short term if both pain and smell were diminished, though again these reduced abilities might cause trouble in the long term. Average performance in other sensory modes would be adequate for this job.

Sensory Profile of a Dessert Chef

	Diminished Abilities	Average Abilities	Heightened Abilities
Vision			X
Hearing		X	
Smell			X
Touch			X
Taste			X
Pain	X		
Balance			X

Explanation: Here is an occupation that requires finely tuned abilities in many areas. Dessert chefs need more than effective taste buds; they must also carefully attend to the visual impact of the desserts they create. A well-developed sense of touch will assist in guiding their actions in various cooking modes (such as beating a batter rather than just stirring it). The sense of smell can sometimes rescue creations before they are overcooked. A chef employed in a high-volume restaurant may need an especially keen sense of balance. On the flip side, pain resistance would be an advantage, so a diminished capacity to transmit feelings of pain would be helpful.

Sensory Profile of a College Professor

	Diminished Abilities	Average Abilities	Heightened Abilities
Vision			X
Hearing			X
Smell		X	
Touch	X		
Taste		X	
Pain	X		
Balance			X

Explanation: This profile may vary with the college professor's specific field; generally, however, only a few sensory modes need to be heightened in order to promote the most effective performance as a teacher. An acute sense of hearing and vision enable teachers to monitor student response to classroom activities. Balance is probably also an important mode as teachers move rapidly between activities and among students. Taste and touch are probably of little consequence. And pain? Teachers will tell you that grading a stack of essays can stimulate a variety of painful stimuli, so a diminished capacity to experience pain would be helpful in this job also.

PART 2: EVALUATION: Justify

This is one possible solution to the given sensory profile; with the many possible choices yours is probably different. Remember, a good explanation will show that you comprehend the purpose of each sense and their value for individuals in the occupation you choose.

Occupation: Ballroom dancer

Explanation: All dancers rely on balance to do their work, and this is even more important in dancing with a partner. Not only must one be aware of one's own balance and position in space, but also extremely sensitive to the cues of one's partner. Touch is an important part of balance and essential for being aware of and moving with a partner, so it would also help to have heightened awareness in this sense. Normal vision is necessary for navigating on the dance floor and moving in synchrony with a partner when not in physical contact, and normal hearing is necessary for hearing the music. A normal awareness of pain would allow this individual to be careful of injury, without being overly sensitive to the physical sensations inherent in this job. Taste and smell are unnecessary for a dancer and would serve little purpose.

▼Exercise 6.3 REACH OUT AND TOUCH SOMEONE

CREATE: Imagine

The only limits here are the limits of your imagination. However you design this new form of communication, it should recognize that the skin senses pressure and temperature. Perhaps you could communicate content using pressure, much like Helen Keller and her teacher would use the manual alphabet, fingerspelling words into each other's palm. Maybe touches on different parts of the body could mean different things. Emotion could be communicated using temperature changes; giving someone an ice cube could mean you are angry, whereas giving a warm cup of tea could mean you are happy.

Long-distance communication would need to rely on the same principles. Using something like a telegraph, one could send Morse code in a way that physically tapped out a message on someone else's hand or arm. Maybe computers could be used to control temperature and pressure changes in a way that allowed one to send a totally different type of email.

What did you come up with?

▼Exercise 6.4 IT'S A MATTER OF TASTE

CREATE: Design

Here is an example of a possible experiment. Although yours may be different, it should have all of the same components and demonstrate your understanding of how to design an experiment, as well as the basic principles of taste.
  Example:

- *Hypothesis:* Sweet tastes can be detected on all areas of the tongue.

- *Independent variables:* Areas of the tongue; sweet taste

- *Operational definitions:* Areas of the tongue—the tongue will be divided into four quadrants; sweet taste—a solution of 1 cup sugar in 1 pint water

- *Dependent variable:* Detecting sweet taste

- *Operational definition:* Being able to successfully label a taste as sweet, when given options of sweet, sour, salty, bitter

- *Brief description:* A subject (or subjects) is asked to identify tastes as sweet, salty, sour, and bitter. Plain water, the sweet solution described above, and diluted lemon juice are placed in unlabeled cups. The experimenter then uses a cotton swab to dip in the solutions and apply to different areas of the tongue. Each solution should be applied in different or random orders to each quadrant of the tongue. If sweet can be detected on all tongue surfaces, then the subject should be able to identify the sugar solution correctly in each quadrant.

- *Extraneous variables:* Subjects should not be able to use scent as a cue. Tastes should be applied to different areas within a quadrant. Different cotton swabs should be used each time. Subjects should not have a cold, and should have normal breathing/smelling abilities. Anything that would interfere with your results could be listed here.

▼ Exercise 6.5   PARTS IS PARTS

ANALYZE: Infer

How do the following entries compare with your lists? If forced to choose, which sense would you give up? Why?

Sense	Energy	Positive Consequences	Negative Consequences
Vision	Light	• Won't see painful, sad, or cruel sights • Won't see when others are making faces at you • Won't need to pay for sunglasses	• Won't see the flowers in the spring or the changing colors of leaves in the fall • Won't see your friends and family smile at you • Won't enjoy seeing the words on the page of a good book
Hearing	Air pressure waves	• Will get more sleep because you won't hear the loud music the neighbor upstairs plays at 2 A.M. • Won't hear your 8- year-old nephew practicing the violin • Won't hear the chalk squeak on the blackboard	• Will never hear the beautiful precision of a Bach quartet • Won't hear friends or family say "I love you" • Won't hear birds singing
Touch	Pressure Temperature	• Will save money because you won't need a coat in the winter despite the threat of frostbite • Won't feel the bruise after you've run into the coffee table • Won't feel the burn from the hot stove	• Will drop or break objects because you can't tell how hard you are holding them • Won't feel a friend hold your hand • Won't feel the exhilaration of jumping into a cold pool on a steamy hot summer day
Taste	Chemicals	• Won't mind eating cafeteria food • Won't notice the nasty taste of medicine • Will never know you have morning breath	• More likely to get sick because you won't know if food has spoiled • Will never taste a fresh strawberry • Won't be able to distinguish between vinegar and wine
Smell	Chemicals	• Won't notice the smell of garbage • Won't mind cleaning out the fridge because you can't smell last month's leftovers • Will never know if your partner has morning breath	• Will never think of Grandma when you smell cookies and bread baking • Won't appreciate the smells of a Thanksgiving dinner • Will never smell a Double Delight rose

▼Exercise 6.6   DO YOU HEAR WHAT I HEAR?

EVALUATE: Take Perspective

There are many different sides and perspectives to this issue, and it is perfectly reasonable for you to have developed a different opinion than others in your class. Your opinion may be informed by how much you value certain aspects of the hearing world, like music, and whether you have some personal experience with hearing loss or deafness or know someone who has. For more information about this debate, as well as information about the actual potential and risks of the cochlear implant procedure, you can begin with the following resources:

- The U.S. Food and Drug Administration (2014). The Benefits and Risks of Cochlear Implants. Available: http://www.fda.gov/MedicalDevices/ ProductsandMedicalProcedures/ImplantsandProsthetics/CochlearImplants/ ucm062843.htm

- PBS. (2007). Sound and Fury. Available: http://www.pbs.org/wnet/ soundandfury/index

- Hladek, G. (2009). Cochlear implants, the deaf culture, and ethics. Available: http://www.ohio.edu/ethics/2001-conferences/cochlear-implants-the-deaf-culture-and-ethics/index.html

▼Exercise 6.7   THE EYES HAVE IT

UNDERSTAND: Observe

How did it go? How did your experience compare to the experiences of your classmates? What factors seemed to be involved in successfully adapting to the altered visual experience?

Chapter

◀Perception▶

▼Exercise 7.1 CLIFF HANGERS

PART 1: UNDERSTAND: Describe

Infants, kids, chicks, kittens, and other babies could be using a variety of monocular and binocular depth to perceive depth. They include retinal disparity (binocular), convergence (binocular), relative size (monocular), relative height (monocular), linear perspective (monocular), relative brightness (monocular), and texture gradient (monocular). Other cues that can be used to perceive depth—such as interposition, relative motion, and relative clarity, all of which are monocular—are less likely to be potential cues in these experiments because the experimental conditions are not designed to give this information.

PART 2: CREATE: Design

Whichever cue you choose to discuss, your hypothesis should be stated as a prediction, and the experiment you design should allow you to control when a baby (of whatever species) receives the information about that cue. Be as specific as you can when you discuss how you will control your independent variables. Also, make sure that you are explicit in stating your dependent variable. For most experiments, the dependent variable will be whether the baby crawls or walks over the visual cliff. What extraneous variables will be important to consider?

Of the factors that could improve a baby's performance on this task, you should be able to discuss two: biological maturation and experience. The more physiologically mature a baby, the more developed the neural systems that process visual stimuli. A 1-day-old kid (baby goat) has more mature visual systems than a 1-day-old kitten. In addition, more visual experience stimulates better development of the neural networks within the visual system. Kittens and monkeys with limited visual experiences after birth did not develop the same sensitivity to visual stimuli as did those raised in a normal visual environment, even after the restrictions were removed.

▼Exercise 7.2   THE BIG PICTURE

APPLY: Illustrate

Selected Performance: Ballet

Figure-ground. The relationship of the prima ballerina to the other dancers is often one of figure-ground. Her movements are choreographed to be distinctive and different from the movements of others on the stage. The principle is also illustrated when the prima ballerina dances alone: She is the figure, and the scenery becomes the backdrop.

Proximity. Some choreography provides for smaller groupings of ballerinas placed strategically on the stage. We perceive them to be grouped due to their nearness to each other and the distance separating them from other groups.

Similarity. Grouping may rely on similarly constructed costumes or movements that appear to be the same.

Closure. Some elements of ballet introduce actions that demand a sense of completion. For example, a leap into the air must resolve in a return to earth. Some paired dancing steps exploit our expectation that the couple will come back together at some point if the dance is to be satisfying.

Continuity / connectedness. Our inclination to see smooth, continuous patterns is exploited in particular by choreography that creates fluid motion among dancers. For example, we may see a movement ripple through a dance line, as in the classic Rockettes' leg movements, and we perceive a strong impression of good form. We are likely to perceive dancers who are touching in some capacity as forming a meaningful subgroup.

Selected Performance: Football

Figure-ground. The players in the immediate vicinity of the ball will create the *figure* against the *ground* of the rest of the team. The ball becomes the focal point for your attention unless you happen to be following a preferred player on the team. In that case, your attention may shift to that player as the figure; the rest of the action will be the ground.

Proximity. Teams begin each play in proximity with one other—one team per side. Once the ball is in play, the good form of proximity is sacrificed. The quarterback is challenged to maintain a good "gestalt" in order to maintain the play as team members pursue their assignments in a chaotic field.

Similarity. Uniforms are a distinctive symbol of similarity. Regardless of team members' physical location on the field, their colors identify them as part of the group.

Closure. Each play represents the principle of closure. Once the ball is snapped, we anticipate how the play will end, whether the ball is galloped into the end zone or buried beneath a mountain of shoulder pads and cleats. The end of the play represents the good form of closure, regardless of whether we like the actual outcome of the play.

Continuity / connectedness. A well-executed play represents the principle of continuity. When the team is functioning well, each member contributes to the overall pattern that makes the play successful. More sophisticated fans recognize the role of all players in a successful strategy, demonstrating the continuity of each successful play. When plays are unsuccessful, the group members appear to be disconnected from one another. Signals are missed; errors are made. Despite other elements of grouping (proximity, similarity), the team may not appear to function as a connected whole.

▼ Exercise 7.3 CONTEXT CUES
APPLY: Solve

There is a wide variety of scenarios you could create that would influence what a person perceived in this situation. The best ideas will be those that include both internal and external factors. Here are some examples that can serve as models.

Vase only: If this slide were inserted in a series of slides given to art history students or archaeology students, both internal and external cues would encourage the viewer to see only the vase. In addition to the expectations one of these students has of viewing objects of art and/or pieces of pottery, seeing many other slides with these themes sets the external context as well.

Faces only: This one might be a little trickier. Imagine that the picture were hung in a gallery devoted to portraits of British royalty. Again, such a setting would provide both the external and internal contexts. It would also be helpful if the viewer were an expert on either Prince Philip or Queen Elizabeth. Perhaps you would present it to the Royal Historical Society to be part of its annual slide show.

Both vase and faces: Obviously, the primary consideration here is that the viewer know that the picture is reversible. If this is the case, then you could put the picture into almost any setting. You could also set the context so that the viewer might be open to looking closely at the picture—perhaps you could hang it in a room with various optical illusions, "Where's Waldo?" posters, or even computer-generated pictures-made-of-pictures posters.

▼ Exercise 7.4 CHAOS CONTROL
ANALYZE: Relate

If we weren't able to habituate, the world would indeed be a chaotic environment. Input from all sensory modes would be overwhelming. For example, our figure-ground relationships in the visual field would be problematic. Objects in the environment would all demand our attention as the figure, with few objects staying in the background. We would probably be dizzy from the competing demands of new stimuli constantly breaking through our awareness as new figures. Smells habituate with good and bad effects. Without habituation, every sweet swig of soda would taste equally pleasant. However, the unsavory smells of a "hygiene-impaired" classmate also wouldn't fade. Habituation is especially important to the senses of touch and kinesthesis. Imagine trying to study with complete and constant awareness of how high our socks are or just how many pounds we need to lose.

Without chaos management by our perceptual sets, we would have a challenging time formulating a course of action. As any experienced traveler can tell you, the challenge of a new environment requires vigilance because you do not have routines to fall back on. That confusion can be compounded when traveling in foreign countries where not only landmarks are unfamiliar but the customs may be different as well. Many people enjoy this assault on the routine; others find the challenge overwhelming. Without reasonable perceptual sets, life would be a constant surprise—and mostly not in a good way.

▼Exercise 7.5   THE CASE AGAINST ESP
EVALUATE: Assess

Example	Rating*	Alternative Hypothesis
You are driving along in your car and find yourself humming a pleasant tune. You turn on the radio and that very song comes on. You smile to yourself and think your ability to predict music on the radio is just a bit uncanny.		You may inadvertently narrow the field of available music selections through your listening habits. A song that runs through your mind may be played particularly often during the period in which you experience your uncanny ability. The amount of time you spend humming heavily played popular music probably far exceeds the time spent humming other kinds of music. For this reason you may occasionally "hit" the song about to be played, giving you the impression of extrasensory talent. You probably do not react with the same intensity when a song you are humming does *not* match the next one on the radio, so you become a victim of your own selective perception. To confirm the existence of this telepathic skill, a psychologist would ask if you could perform this event reliably from a wide selection of music or of music stations. That would constitute objective evidence of your extrasensory ability.
Brenda prides herself on being able to predict the gender of unborn children. Expectant parents eagerly sought her predictions until newer, less fallible medical technologies displaced her skills.		Brenda's chances of being right are 50 percent—not bad odds even in casinos. But does Brenda let people know when she does not predict accurately? Perhaps her reputation does not reflect those failures. She may truly enjoy her position as an adviser to parents-to-be, and she probably won't be reported to the Better Business Bureau if she errs. Oddly enough, even the fancier technologies supporting scientific predictions of gender are not 100 percent accurate.
Eugene is one lucky guy. Almost every month he wins something in the state lottery. His friends believe he must be clairvoyant.		As aggravating as lucky lottery players are for those who spend a lot of money in this manner, it does appear that some people are more frequent winners. How could this be? First, we need to look at the frequency with which people like Eugene play the lottery in order to report one instance of winning. If he plays every chance he gets, then cumulatively his chances of winning will be higher. He has virtually the same chance each time he plays, but the sheer volume of his lottery tickets will increase his opportunity to win. In addition, runs of luck are common in gambling situations. We can explain this occurrence statistically because even unusual events—like chronic winners—can happen. The trick is knowing when to quit, a feat as hard to accomplish as winning is in the first place.
Pat hates it when she gets those "ooky feelings." Her heart starts to race and she knows something terrible has happened, sometimes to a loved one but most of the time to a stranger whose bad luck is reported on television.		Does a disaster happen every time Pat has an "ooky feeling"? To understand this phenomenon, we need to examine how this problem is framed. Disaster happens somewhere on a regular basis. As broadly defined as Pat's skill is, she could probably report a disaster "hit" after watching the evening news. When the clairvoyant feelings prompt Pat to worry about specific loved ones, does she routinely report these concerns to verify her feelings? Or does she confirm that the feelings were present only after an unpleasant outcome is reported to her?

* Ratings will differ according to your personal beliefs that support or oppose the existence of ESP.

Continued

Example	Rating	Alternative Hypothesis
Bruce hardly studies at all and he gets superb grades. He claims he has a special ability to predict the kinds of questions instructors will include on exams. He brags that this ability saves him hours of study and earns him nearly a 3.5 grade-point average.		This explanation has several points of entry. First, Bruce may be quite good at guessing—but not because he has ESP. He may have refined his abilities to observe the professor and to infer the concepts and skills that will appeal most to the professor for exam purposes. (Students sometimes refer to this skill as "psyching out" the professor, despite mild protests from psychologists!) If you wanted to develop this ability, what kinds of indicators might help you pick out the most important ideas in the professor's lecture? Another explanation might be that one successful examination score does not constitute a reliable ability. *Samples of 1* represent suspicious evidence to most psychologists. Finally, has anyone seen Bruce's report card? He could be lying about his examination success, his grade-point history, and his ability to predict exam construction.
A magician claims he can identify the most pressing concerns among audience members. He asks each person to fill out an identical index card, stating his or her most serious worry of the moment. He collects the cards, raises one index card to his head, and—without reading the card—voices a specific concern. Then he asks, "Whose worry is this!" A shy woman in the middle of the room raises her hand and claims, "It's mine!" He examines the card to verify her claim. One by one, the magician then accurately identifies at least five more pressing concerns for astonished members of the audience.		Were you able to guess how this *illusion* might be accomplished? Magicians refer to this illusion as "one-ahead." A skilled magician merely places an accomplice in the audience. He palms (secretly removes) her index card to make sure that he will not randomly select this card from the pile and read it. When he selects an actual card from a real audience member, he holds it in front of his forehead but he actually reports the agreed-upon worry that his accomplice will claim as her own. He is then free to read silently the card he has held to his head and to report that worry after holding the next card to his head. While our attention is riveted by the accomplice's powerful acting job, we fail to observe that the magician is preparing himself to accurately identify all following cards.

▼Exercise 7.6 BREAKING THE CODE

EVALUATE: Critique

The main challenge is finding a good internet example of sleight-of-hand. If you assume that objects cannot disappear, then, instead of being amazed that the object is gone, you embark on a hunt to determine where the object went. It could be the start of a whole new career!

▼Exercise 7.7 ASSEMBLING THE ASSEMBLY LINE

CREATE: Plan

Anything that you do to facilitate shape identification and comparison would make the inspectors' job easier. For example, maybe you would color the conveyer belt so that it contrasts with the widget; which would make detecting the widget and identifying its shape easier. Perhaps you would have all objects facing the same direction as they move down the assembly line to facilitate shape comparison. Perhaps halting the conveyer belt at regular intervals would help people concentrate. Or you might send some obviously different widgets down the line to reorient people to the task. Taking regular breaks would also help concentration during inspection. The fundamental processes involved in this design correspond to *signal detection theory*.

Chapter

◀ Learning ▶

▼Exercise 8.1 POWERFUL CONSEQUENCES

UNDERSTAND: Translate

	Object and Action of the Consequence	Likelihood of the Behavior Recurring	Operant Principle Illustrated
Example: A young man notices his neighbor's trash can still out by the curb. He *brings it up and sets it* next to the neighbor's garage. The next day, the neighbor comes by with homemade cookies.	Retrieving a trash can (+) → and getting cookies (+)	Increases	Positive Reinforcement
a. A student *volunteers* to answer a tough question in class, and the teacher comments favorably on the quality of the student's contribution.	Answering a question (+) → getting praise (+)	Increases	Positive Reinforcement
b. A wife brings home flowers to her husband because of the special dinner he had *cooked* for her.	Cooking dinner (+) → getting flowers (+)	Increases	Positive Reinforcement
c. A child is sent to his room with no supper after *presenting a bad report card*.	Presenting a report card (+) → losing dinner (−)	Decreases	Punishment (See note below marked "a")
d. Dad and tot enter the checkout lane of the supermarket. When the child *screams* for candy, dad *pops a sucker* in her mouth to quiet her down.	Dad: Noisy conditions (−) → escaping noise (−) Tot: Screaming (+) → getting sucker (+)	Dad: Increases Tot: Increases	Dad: Negative Reinforcement Tot: Positive Reinforcement
e. A child *spills* milk all over the supper table, and Mom (having had a very bad day) swoops the child up from the high chair and spanks him.	Spilling milk (+) → getting a spanking (−)	Decreases	Punishment (See note below marked "b")

Continued

	Object and Action of the Consequence	Likelihood of the Behavior Recurring	Operant Principle Illustrated
f. A student has a terrible headache after an intense preparation period for a test. He *takes two aspirin*, hope to make it go away.	Being in pain (−) → taking aspirin and having pain go away (−)	Increases	Negative Reinforcement
g. Two children, who usually spend most of their time fighting, finally *play peaceably* over a coloring book. Dad peeks in and sighs, "At last, they are getting along." He returns to work without saying anything to them.	Peaceful play (+) → no consequence (0)	Decreases	Extinction (See note below marked "c")
h. As parents drive a spoiled child past a fast-food restaurant, she begins *screaming* that she must have french fries or she won't survive. The parents *surrender* and drive in for a large supply.	Parents: Tantrum conditions (−) → escape from the noise (−)	Parents: Increases	Parents: Negative Reinforcement
	Child: Manipulative crying (+) → french fries (+)	Child: Increases	Child: Positive Reinforcement
i. A teenager *whines* about having nothing to do. Dad gives him yet another lecture about all the stuff in his room and the good old days when he, the father, didn't have all that stuff but still managed to be happy.	Teenager: Whines (+) → Gets boring lecture (−)	Decreases	Punishment
j. A terrorist *applies an electric current* to the feet of a spy to make her *confess*. She tells him everything she knows.	Terrorist: Applies shock (+) → gets information (+)	Terrorist: Increases	Terrorist: Positive Reinforcement
	Spy: Pain from torture (−) → escape from pain (−)	Spy: Increases	Spy: Negative Reinforcement

Notes

a. In this example, the child's academic behavior was met with a negative consequence intended to discourage him from continuing at the same level of performance. Unfortunately, the consequence may influence only the behavior of presenting the report card, not necessarily the level of academic effort itself. Some children avoid punishing consequences by figuring out how to prevent parents from seeing their grades.

b. The spill was followed with physical punishment and the behavior may decline in the future. Or the child may just become afraid of making natural mistakes in front of Mom. Some spills are unintentional, and the commotion and embarrassment that follow them are naturally punishing. Parents may undermine their attempts to teach proper table manners if they don't distinguish between unintentional and intentional messes.

c. This dad really neglected his opportunity to strengthen appropriate playing behavior. By not offering praise, or a consequence of any kind, he missed an opportunity to reinforce peaceful behavior. The chronically warring children are not likely to be sustained and rewarded by the fun they have together, and so the mutual cooperative play is likely to extinguish rapidly.

▼Exercise 8.2   THE CLASSICAL CONNECTION
APPLY: Classify

The Troublesome Shower

Unconditioned response (UCR): pain avoidance

Unconditioned stimulus (UCS): boiling-hot water

Conditioned response (CR): fear and jumping

Conditioned stimulus (CS): sound of toilet flushing

The Water Show

Unconditioned response (UCR): fainting

Unconditioned stimulus (UCS): heat

Conditioned response (CR): dizziness

Conditioned stimulus (CS): organ music

The Trouble with Tuna

UCR: stomach cramps

UCS: tainted mayonnaise

CR: stomach turbulence

CS: sight of tuna fish and possibly the smell, taste, suggestion, and menu listing of and commercials for tuna fish. (Note the expansion of reactions, due to stimulus generalization, the tendency of similar stimuli to elicit aversive reactions.)

Captain Hook's Time Problem

CR: anxiety attack

UCS: croc bite

CS: clock ticking

UCR: pain from loss of hand

Note: Did the changed order of the classical conditioning components make your answers wrong? If you conditioned to the prior order, you may have linked the right components with the wrong labels. If your habit was disrupted by the warning, you may have not conditioned to the order in which the concepts were presented.

▼Exercise 8.3   CHEMICAL ENGINEERING
APPLY: Compare

This exercise is a tricky one. Operant schedules of reinforcement focus on a reward paradigm, meaning that the target organism responds to receive a reward (for example, a food pellet, electrical stimulation of the hypothalamus, access to a treasured object or activity). That definition is simple to understand in the abstract but, applied to the chemistry professor's desire to modify her student's study behavior, things get a bit more complicated. The vast majority of students in a class do not see a pop quiz as a reinforcement opportunity. If anything, hearing "put your books away" becomes a classically conditioned stimulus for the onset of conditioned fear, especially if you failed to prepare for that opportunity.

However, let's assume the student we are talking about is Harry Potter's good friend, Hermione Granger, who is widely known for her academic eagerness. Consequently, quiz opportunities are highly positive experiences that allow her to show off just how much she knows. Now let's examine how schedules of reinforcement using pop quizzes apply to the intellectually ambitious for whom such opportunities represent reward.

Requiring a quiz at the start of every class. This strategy represents a *fixed ratio schedule.* Every time a lecture happens, so does a quiz. Hermione is likely to study a lot, knowing the "threat" of a quiz will be realized in each and every class. If Hermione weren't so strongly motivated, her studying behavior would dramatically decline at the conclusion of the class. She would readily extinguish her test preparation behavior.

Requiring a quiz to be taken at any time on line before each class starts. The contingency is no longer fixed to the classroom hour but must be taken at some point during the week. Although Hermione decides when to self-administer the test, the conditions constitute a *fixed internal schedule.* Behaviorists have noted that responses tend to intensify toward the end of the interval, comparable to cramming the night before an exam.

Requiring a limited number of quizzes randomly through the semester. By making the quizzes hard to predict, the *variable ratio schedule* produces high rates of responding as well as behavior that is most likely to persist after the class is over. Variable ratio schedules produce behavior that is more resistant to extinction.

Requiring a limited number of quizzes anytime before the end of the semester. No teacher in her right mind would adopt this strategy. A *variable interval schedule* means that reinforcement could happen at any time. Students who are self-motivated would probably opt for taking a quiz in the context of the course coverage that provides the best input. Students who are less motivated would probably take all the quizzes during finals week, compromising the likelihood of their success in class.

▼Exercise 8.4 SELF-IMPROVEMENT REVISTED

We won't be able to address every human frailty you might have selected for this exercise, but we can provide a model for how the protocol can be applied. In this instance, we will use out-of-control eating.

How do the three learning frameworks apply to the problem of curbing overeating?

Observational Learning
It doesn't take too much exposure to advertising campaigns to recognize how much we may be influenced in a culture of indulgence. Good intentions can easily be sabotaged with a constant barrage of commercials touting the satisfying taste provided by your favorite foods.

Classical Conditioning
Food isn't just sustenance; through classical conditioning principles it takes on added significance. For example, think about the food that you would put in the "comfort food" category. Just thinking about eating your Mom's mac and cheese may give you a warm and fuzzy feeling through classical conditioning. Unfortunately, under stress we are likely to turn to comfort food to make the blues or the blahs go away.

Operant Conditioning
Virtue only goes so far. Distancing yourself from some of your favorite reinforcers is challenging to do when there aren't other reinforcers to build and sustain behavior. Dieters often feel a rush of success when they drop a few pounds but at the point where weight loss hits an inevitable plateau, the reinforcers drop away and the indulgent

behavior ramps up, sometimes causing the dieter to regain the lost weight and add a few pounds more. No wonder it is so hard to modify behavior.

How would we use the frameworks more effectively to modify overeating?

Observational Learning

We need to surround ourselves with successful models of restraint. Join a weight management group so that emotional support is available even during the rough spots such as the weight loss plateau. You will still be surrounded with tempting advertisements, but at least you will have positive emotional support to stay the course.

Classical Conditioning

Here is an ugly and impractical application of classical conditioning. Modify the comfort of comfort food by engaging in purposeful aversion conditioning. Eat mac and cheese until you feel nauseated and preferably regurgitate. Mac and cheese will lose its power to seduce you. (Obviously, we don't really recommend making yourself sick to accomplish your goal, but the example allows you to see how the framework could come into play.)

Operant Conditioning

It will help to do a better job of making reinforcers readily accessible to reward and sustain weight loss. It is best to use reinforcers that are not food related (for example, treat yourself to a movie, contact an old friend, buy an item you can wear now that you couldn't before).

Whatever your chosen target might be, recognize that you have a rich arsenal of learning strategies to help you achieve your goal.

▼Exercise 8.5   THE DISCRIMINATING DACHSHUND

ANALYZE: Infer

Pavlov's explanation: The tennis ball originally was a stimulus for play. Paired with the painful ant bites (UCS) the tennis ball became a conditioned stimulus (CS), which produced a response of avoidance. Avoiding balls that are similar in shape and size to a tennis ball demonstrates generalization of the response.

Skinner's explanation: The pain of the ant bites serves as an immediate and strong punishment, and decreases the preceding behavior of picking up the tennis ball. Skinner would state that other small balls became discriminative stimuli for pain. Large balls were safe; small balls were dangerous.

▼Exercise 8.6   LITTLE ALBERT REVISITED

EVALUATE: Take Perspective

Fear of Rats

Someone who believes that a particular fear is the result of classical conditioning will attempt to extinguish the response by weakening or eliminating the pairing between the CS and the UCS. In this case, treatment would consist of making sure that there were many opportunities for Albert to experience rats without loud noises. This approach stresses extinction as the main mechanism for dealing with Little Albert's fear.

Someone who believed in the operant conditioning model would provide rewarding experiences when Albert experienced rats. Treatment would include giving Albert things he liked or taking away things he did not like. This approach is sometimes referred to as counterconditioning.

With no intervention at all (and no further unhappy accidents with furry creatures), Little Albert's fear might naturally extinguish. However, when people develop fear of some dreaded objects, they naturally avoid circumstances that will bring them into close contact with the object. If Little Albert successfully avoided contact with furry creatures, then chances are good his fears would have been maintained throughout his life.

Maltreatment of Children

Is it inevitable that Little Albert might himself become someone who—through modeling—maltreats children when he grows up? No, it is not. Child abuse researchers suggest the risk for abusing children increases when a child experiences abuses, but it is not a given that an abused child will become an abuser. One negative model, even when it is an extreme model, may be dramatically outweighed by other positive models in the child's life.

▼Exercise 8.7   REINFORCING RHYMES
CREATE: Invent

It is hard to predict what kind of rhymes and revisions you came up with to illustrate learning principles. Was the learning mechanism (for example, negative reinforcement, punishment) obvious in your creative execution?

▼Exercise 8.8   A WORKING HYPOTHESIS
CREATE: Design

Hypothesis: Using a fixed-ratio schedule (paying for piecework) will result in more "royas" produced than will a fixed interval schedule (paying a weekly salary).

Independent variable(s): the type of schedule; either FR or FI.

Dependent variable(s): the number of royas produced.

Extraneous variables for which you would control: There are a variety of reasonable answers, including: experience of workers, length of shift, time of shift, working conditions, and so forth.

Basic experimental protocol: Randomly assign half of each shift during a one-month period to be paid based on either an FR or FI schedule. At the end of that month, the number of royas produced by each group will be counted.

Potential ethical considerations: There are a lot of things that we can do because this is only a pretend experiment. In real life, it would be unethical to pay people different wages for doing the same job. Pay for piecework in manufacturing plants was discontinued in the United States many years ago.

Chapter

▼Exercise 9.1 THANKS FOR THE MEMORY

PART 1: UNDERSTAND: Observe

PART 2: APPLY: Solve

Answers will vary. Evaluate your own answers by how much insight they give you into your own study habits and practices. Are you likely to change anything?

▼Exercise 9.2 STORY TIME

APPLY: Use

Anything goes! Here is one example: *Sally and Mike* went searching for *rental units* (parents) and met *Sam the ant* in the kitchen of one apartment. Not wanting to disturb the local fauna, they continued to look in an exclusive area known as Alphabet City. Driving down *E Lane* in their new *Van*, they saw a log cabin that reminded them of the one that *Laura* and her *sisters* lived in on *Little House on the Prairie*. Another house was shaped like a ship that *Christopher Columbus* could have sailed on. *"Uncle!"* they cried. "This is enough!" They finally asked for help from *Melissa and John*, who told them to go down *Grand Ave.* and look for a sign proclaiming *"Uncle Larry's Famous Farm,"* where they should turn left. After going past two baby goats *(kids) named Tisha and Devon,* they finally arrived at the perfect place to live and decided never to apartment-hunt again.

▼Exercise 9.3 THE MAGNIFICENT SEVEN

PART 1: ANALYZE: Infer

An encoding problem. A person would be unable to recall the name of a single dwarf if he or she had never properly encoded the fairy tale. People with this problem may simply never have heard the story, as might be the case if they had been raised in a culture other than the American culture. You can't recall details of a story you have never heard.

A storage problem. If a storage problem has occurred, people are likely to encode the target memories insufficiently. The seven names may have been misperceived and the wrong names may have been entered into storage. Upon retrieval, they would retrieve from memory just what they put in—the wrong names.

An interference problem. The part of the brain that is dedicated to the housing of fairy tales and fictional characters is a pretty crowded place. If people can't dredge up the right names, it might have been easy to substitute some new domestic partners for Snow White.

An insufficient-cueing problem. One minute was not very much time to recall all seven names. Some people might have been able to produce several accurate names if they had been given more time to tap into the context to make the associative network yield the right answers. Or perhaps there weren't enough story details to activate the proper associative network in the first place.

A repression problem. A horrifying experience with mean and evil apple-toting relatives or some hard days in the mines might make this recall task especially difficult. Anything that reminds you of such challenging times might block recall, according to this distinctly Freudian and controversial view of forgetting.

PART 2: EVALUATE: Decide

Answers to this part of the exercise will vary by individual. Regardless of which description you believed best fit your own situation, you should be able to identify the reason and link it to the ideas listed in the first part of the exercise.

▼ Exercise 9.4 ROSEANNE'S DILEMMA

ANALYZE: Compare & Contrast

Formulate one hypothesis that might explain how a real, traumatic, and previously forgotten event could suddenly be remembered: Most of the possibilities revolve around retrieval cues. Perhaps the person is in a unique context that is similar enough to the earlier event to provide a reminder about that event. An experience with an extreme mood (terror, exhilaration, overwhelming grief) could also serve as a prime for retrieving a forgotten memory. In such cases, however, the cue (emotion, context, or similar event) would be extreme or there would have been multiple opportunities for such remembering to have occurred earlier.

Formulate one hypothesis to explain how people could remember something that never really happened: False memories can arise for a variety of reasons. As demonstrated in the research by Elizabeth Loftus and her colleagues, the associations a person has with words used during questioning about specific events can influence a person's memory for that event. For example, a person questioned about how fast the cars were going when they smashed into each other will remember the speed of the cars as faster than a person asked how fast the cars were going when they bumped into each other. False memories can also arise when a person is given misinformation about an event, or if a person is asked to repeatedly imagine an event that never happened. In addition, it is possible to forget the source of the memory; to forget the context but to remember an event. It is very important to note that, because false memories "feel" like real memories, it may not be possible for the person who is remembering to tell, based on the strength of his or her emotional response or confidence, whether the event occurred.

Describe one strategy that might help distinguish between real and false memories: There is no solid evidence that any particular test or procedure can distinguish between real and false memories. As you may remember from your reading, early work with brain imaging techniques indicates that the left temporal lobe is active when remembering words that were actually spoken and not when inaccurately "remembering" words that were not spoken. This technique is not viable when working with events in the distant past, however. The best way to distinguish between real and false memories in eyewitness accounts is to use questioning techniques that do not provide misinformation or prime for certain types of recollections.

▼ Exercise 9.5   MAKING MEMORIES

EVALUATE: Take Perspective

There are many issues you could discuss here. A strong answer would recognize that basic tasks like answering the phone, doing dishes, and going shopping would be difficult or impossible for Patsy because of the many barriers that require explicit memory—knowing what objects are used for, where to put things away, how to get and prepare food, and so forth. She would need someone to teach her to perform all of these activities of daily living. Patsy also had some rather unusual limitations in her ability to rely on implicit memory, so physical, occupational, and speech therapy might be required for support as she relearned how to walk, tie her shoes, and speak clearly. In addition, there are the emotional challenges of making and maintaining friendships, participating in social and community organizations, and raising a family, if an individual does not know the people involved, their roles, the social structures, and culturally appropriate behaviors. Patsy would need support to help reestablish the emotional ties she had with family and friends and to deal with the extreme stress of living in a very frightening situation. Other family members would probably also need professional support as they assumed many of the roles that Patsy previously performed and as they discovered how Patsy's personality has changed. The key criterion for successful treatment is recognizing that true amnesia has the potential to rob the individual of basic functions, and that this will impact the larger family and social structures of which this individual is a part.

▼ Exercise 9.6   TOO MUCH OF A GOOD THING

EVALUATE: Assess

This answer is strictly personal. Those who are persuaded that mastering minutiae is a small price to pay for more consistent memory function would probably willingly take the memory-enhancing medication. On the other hand, those who find regular life to be fairly distracting would probably prefer to struggle along with the unadorned limits of their memory.

▼ Exercise 9.7   LOOKING AHEAD

CREATE: Plan

No two people will have the same answers or develop the same approach. Even two people with the same basic focus for the exercise—say, remembering material better for a test—may have two very different hypotheses about the cause of the inefficient memory process. One may decide it is a coding issue and develop a plan that works to improve coding efficiencies, while another may decide it is a retrieval issue and create more robust retrieval strategies. Whatever approach and plan you develop, we hope you took this as a serious opportunity to improve one aspect of your cognitive skill set.

▼**Exercise 9.8   CREATING CONTEXT**
CREATE: Design

Independent variable: The context in which the learning and recall occur. In this exemplar it would be the classroom and school cafeteria.

Dependent variable: Student performance. This could be measured in a variety of ways, but test score or number of correct answers are used here.

Extraneous variables for which she should control: Any variable other than the context that might affect student performance should be considered. A short list might include the type of material the instructor is teaching, the mode in which the material is presented (lecture, reading, lab), the time of day, and the type of test. A more complete list could also include things like the gender of the students, their majors, how they take notes, how many days they were present, and how many other classes they are taking this semester.

Outline of a basic experimental protocol: One idea would be to take a class and have half the students take the test in the classroom where the course is normally taught, and have the other half take the test at the same time in the cafeteria. The instructor could then compare the scores of the students who took the test in the classroom (same context) with those who took the test in the cafeteria (different context). Although this would give her the comparison she wants, it also leaves her with several questions. The most serious of these questions is: What if students don't do well in the cafeteria simply because it is the cafeteria and it is noisy, big, has tables instead of desks, and lots of interruptions?

A more sophisticated design would use two classes of students, one that she teaches in the classroom and one that she teaches in the cafeteria. The instructor would be careful to teach the same material over the same time period to both classes and to control the extraneous variables listed above to the best of her ability. She could then divide each class in half and have half of each class take the test in the cafeteria, and half take the test in the classroom. With this design, she has more information. Half of the students taking the test in the classroom learned in the classroom, and the other half learned in the cafeteria. At the same time, half of the students who took the test in the cafeteria learned in the cafeteria and half learned in the classroom. In this way she can determine if something unique about the setting causes any differences she finds. If all students who take the test in the cafeteria score lower than those who take the test in the classroom, for example, then she knows it is not taking a test in a different context that is the issue (because half of the students taking the test in the cafeteria are testing in the same context), but rather that something about the cafeteria impairs test performance. On the other hand, if the half of the students in the cafeteria who learned in the classroom *and* the half of the students in the classroom who learned in the cafeteria both score lower on the exam, then she can be fairly certain that it is the changing of the context that is responsible for the difference in performance.

By the way, it is very important to note that, although this scenario makes for great discussion, it is *not* ethical unless the students' grades are not affected. Knowingly placing some students at a disadvantage is not appropriate behavior in anything other than a research setting where students are not given grades. Instructors work very hard to encourage the success of all their students, not to hinder it!

10

Chapter

◄Thinking and Language►

▼Exercise 10.1 BASIC COMMUNICATION

UNDERSTAND: Explain

"Muh...muh...muh" ➡ Phoneme (Many a new mother mistakes verbal playing with sounds as carrying more meaning than originally intended.)

Second vs. First cousins ➡ Semantics (Rachel is trying to sort out the meaning of the **various family relationships.**)

"Waggy" ➡ Morpheme (Her label for her doll represents the smallest language unit that demonstrates meaning.)

"Goed to zoo" ➡ Overregularization. (Rachel applies structural rules about past tense inappropriately.)

"Throw me down" ➡ Syntax. (The more common syntax is "Throw the broom down to me.")

▼Exercise 10.2 IF WE COULD TALK TO THE ANIMALS

PART 1: UNDERSTAND: Explain

Examples of evidence supporting the viewpoint that animals have the capacity for language:

- Washoe's use of sign language to communicate, including the creation of new words
- The teaching of other chimps to use language without the intervention of trainers
- Lana's use of a computer equipped with word symbols

Examples of evidence challenging the viewpoint that animals have the capacity for language:

- Nim Chimpsky's trainers believe he is merely imitating his trainers.
- The apes' use of language is extremely limited.
- Their behaviors may represent the effect of operant conditioning.
- Interpreting language use may represent more of a human wish than an animal reality.

PART 2: EVALUATE: Justify

Answers here will vary depending upon how persuasive you find the evidence. To complete this portion of the exercise well, you should be able to discuss how you evaluated evidence for the use of symbols, syntax, and creativity.

▼Exercise 10.3   HEURISTICALLY YOURS

APPLY: Examine

Your answers to this exercise will be uniquely your own. No matter what situation you choose to describe, however, and no matter how accurate or error-prone the solution was, your description should recognize that the availability heuristic suggests that we rely on whatever you were able to remember quickly and easily. Your use of the representative heuristic should demonstrate how much we rely on prototypes to help us solve problems even if that reliance can lead us astray from time to time.

▼Exercise 10.4   THERE'S GOOD NEWS AND THERE'S BAD NEWS

APPLY: Illustrate

Have I Got a Deal for You!

You sell used cars. The best car on your lot has 100,000 miles on it. How could you describe this car to a prospective buyer to make the purchase more attractive?

Many used-car salespeople have opted to describe their products as *pre-owned* to reduce some of the tiredness associated with the term *used*. Another option you may want to examine is framing your description of the mileage in terms of the car's expected mileage over its lifetime. If this model can go another 200,000 miles, then 100,000 won't sound so bad.

Making the Grade

You're carrying six full classes. You've had a hard semester, and you are about to talk with loved ones about how things have been going. You've excelled in five courses, but you know you won't pass the other course. How do you talk about your experience in this difficult semester?

If your intention is to maximize a sympathetic response from your loved ones, then your wisest choice may be discussing the course that is giving you pain. If your intention is to gain their admiration for your hard work, your best bet is to focus on your success in the five courses and to minimize or omit the news about your most challenging course.

IRS Blues

You've just started working for the Internal Revenue Service. Tax specialists have developed tax brackets to assist in equitable taxation. Will you work with taxpayers by describing how much tax they will pay or by explaining how much income they will keep?

Most taxpayers aren't keen to surrender their money. Even so, they will probably find it easier to hear a description of the percentage of federal tax they will pay (for example, 28 percent) than to hear that they will be able to keep only 72 percent of their income.

Rain, Rain, Go Away

As a weather forecaster in an area that depends on the tourist industry, will you state your forecast as the likelihood of sunshine or as the likelihood of rain?

Your decision will probably depend on how routine sunshine is in the area. If rain is rare, you may want to forecast rain to prepare tourists to spend their vacation time better. If rain is a common occurrence, tourists may find it more encouraging to hear about the likelihood of sunshine, even if the chances are fairly slim.

▼ Exercise 10.5   MONEY IN THE BANK?

ANALYZE: Relate

You could use the availability heuristic to educate investors about the many ways that relying on remembered information is dangerous and how they can avoid making predictable mistakes. For example, just because you see some people making money in computer chip technology, or you saw an article on a successful and profitable computer chip company, doesn't mean that all computer chip technology investments are sound. You can explain that focusing on a particular company's past success rates, and separating a specific stock from the general category of stocks (for example, a particular medical technology firm rather than medical technology firms in general), would help your investors make more successful choices.

By understanding how overconfidence works, investors can be aware of the human tendency to explain away failures to confirm strongly held beliefs. Instead of ignoring the poor quarterly profit report of a particular company because "that company always does well," perhaps they will be able to see it as the first sign of a turnaround and then sell while its stock is still desirable.

Did you see these tendencies in your own money management experiences?

▼ Exercise 10.6   SEEING IS BELIEVING

ANALYZE: Reason

Many of the concepts in your text could help you explain how people still maintain beliefs in the face of contradictory evidence. Some of the more obvious include:

- *Confirmation bias:* We tend to look only for information that confirms what we already "know." This makes us less likely to question our judgment or look for an alternative explanation.

- *Availability heuristic:* We rely on information that is accessible and quickly remembered. This makes us more likely to rely on personal experience than on something that we've read or heard.

- *Overconfidence:* Because we seek to confirm the beliefs that we already hold and we explain away failures, we overestimate how accurate our judgments and beliefs are. This can contribute to the tendency to rely on our experience, rather than on the collective experience of others.

- *Belief bias:* This concept states that it is easier to see illogic when the conclusions run counter to our beliefs than when they confirm them. Because it is hard to doubt the validity of our experience, we often cannot see where the logic of our conclusions is faulty.

▼ Exercise 10.7   POOR JOHN AND MARY

EVALUATE: Assess

The solution to this riddle rests in a complete examination of your assumptions and inferences. We can solve the riddle if we first recognize that John and Mary are fish! The dog jumped on top of the table and knocked the fish tank onto the floor and broke it. The fish "drowned" by being unable to extract oxygen from the air. The chair added nothing; it was a decoy.

If you got stuck, you probably experienced a problem called *functional fixedness*, a condition in which we automatically make some assumptions about the elements of a problem, based on our own experience. For example, it was hard to avoid the image of John and Mary as humans in this problem because we don't often assign common human names to goldfish. If the problem specified that Goldie and Fin were found dead in a room, you probably would have had no difficulty solving the problem. Those names are commonly used in our language to communicate the *concept* "goldfish," just as John and Mary invoke the *concept* "human."

▼Exercise 10.8   ALEX, THE ACCOUNTANT

CREATE: Design

There is a variety of potential answers. One example is given below. A strong answer will express a testable hypothesis, provide operationalized variables, and clearly describe the experimental design.

Hypothesis: Alex can make comparative numerical decisions, using the concepts of greater than, less than, and equal to.

Experimental design: Alex will be shown a tray on which there are different classes of objects. He will be asked to compare any two classes of objects on the tray. For example, if there are blue blocks, red blocks, red rings, and blue rings on the tray, Alex could be asked to compare the number of red to blue things, or the numbers of rings to blocks. Questions should be framed so that some of them ask which has the most, some ask which has the least, and some ask which groups have the same number of objects. The independent variable is the comparative relationships (more, less, and equal to) and the dependent variable is Alex's response. If the hypothesis is supported, then Alex should be able to reply correctly to questions about these relationships at a level significantly greater than chance. It is important to remember that there are other things that can influence Alex's performance on this task. To be a good test of this ability, Alex must be able to distinguish among the objects presented on the tray and be able to group them into the flexible categories needed to answer the questions (for example, a red ring could be either a ring or a red thing). Alex also needs to be able to indicate his answer either through clearly spoken words or some other method that can be understood by any trained, objective observer.

If your hypothesis is supported, how might this task change our understanding of human language and thinking? If Alex can do this task, then presumably other animals can as well. How might this outcome affect our understanding of what it means to be human? How much of our sense of identity and value arises from our assumptions of intellectual superiority? There are no easy answers to questions like these. Consider discussing these issues with your classmates to see the range of perspectives and to expand your own understanding of what it means to think and use language, and how these are related to our definition of intelligence and humanity.

Chapter

◄Intelligence►

▼Exercise 11.1 EINSTEIN'S THEORY OF INTELLIGENCE

UNDERSTAND: Translate

The possibilities for letters are almost endless. As long as your letter takes one of the complex ideas in the chapter and explains in a way that would allow you and your grandmother to have a meaningful conversation about it, then you have achieved the objectives of this exercise. If your grandmother is still alive, why not send it to her? If she isn't, maybe you could send it to another older adult with a vested interest in your life.

▼Exercise 11.2 "CHARACTER"ISTICS OF INTELLIGENCE

APPLY: Illustrate

Character	Academic	Practical	Creative
Scrooge	Strong: His career as an accountant dictates good analytic skills.	Strong: His money-making abilities attest to his street smarts.	Weak: He conforms to conventions to an extreme degree.
Mary Poppins	Strong: Her tutoring skills are unparalleled.	Strong: She is interpersonally shrewd ("practically perfect") and skilled at solving problems.	Strong: Her strategies for child care reflect unconventional but successful solutions.
Sherlock Holmes	Strong: His detective career offered the opportunity to show off an impressive range of knowledge.	Strong: His problem-solving skills were legendary.	Strong: He adopted unusual costumes and creative approaches to catch criminals.
Winnie the Pooh	Weak: No sign of book learning for poor Pooh!	Weak: Poor Pooh works hard to "think, think, think" but such efforts are rarely successful; he often has difficulty figuring out how to do the tasks of everyday living.	Strong: Pooh usually takes an unconventional point of view in coping with the world.

Continued

Character	Academic	Practical	Creative
Don Quixote	Strong: Prior to his quest, Don Quixote was respected as a learned man.	Weak: Don Quixote's problem-solving skills were exquisitely unsuccessful.	Strong: Don Quixote's romantic and nonconformist view of the world was impressive.
Your example			
Your example			

What were your examples? Did you notice any patterns in either intellectual strengths or weaknesses of the characters you selected?

▼Exercise 11.3   BRAVE NEW WORLD

PART 1: APPLY: Classify

Five components that researchers often use to capture creativity include expertise, imaginative thinking skills, a venturesome personality, high intrinsic motivation, and a creative environment.

Given current evidence about personality, it would be reasonable to assume that there is a genetic component to a "venturesome" personality. It is probably also reasonable to think about imaginative thinking skills and intrinsic motivation having some very weak genetic component, as well as environmental components. The other aspects of creativity—expertise and creative environment—are probably almost entirely external or acquired through experience and are therefore best thought of as environmental influences.

PART 2: ANALYZE: Relate

If you are serious about wanting to perpetuate a desirable trait that has a genetic component, you will want to control breeding. In this case, one could increase the likelihood of producing children with venturesome personalities and imaginative thinking skills by encouraging (or requiring) those individuals possessing these traits to mate with each other. Another alternative would be to collect the eggs and sperm of the "best individuals" and then to implant the resulting embryo in a suitable host.

Arranging the environment in a suitable fashion can also help encourage the expression of creativity. In order to possess expertise, children will need extensive education in a broad range of subjects. Learning the techniques of imaginative thinking skills will also be important. Parents and teachers may be encouraged to teach children how to recognize patterns, see things from different perspectives and solve problems in a variety of ways (sound familiar?). Making sure that external rewards do not become the focus of work and providing students with supportive relationships should also help develop creative expression to its fullest potential. How would you feel about implementing such a program? Chances are, even if you value creativity and think that it is a desirable trait, you would not want to do everything listed above. Where do you draw the line and why? Discuss your answers with some of your classmates and try to establish a set of guiding principles for encouraging the development of desirable characteristics.

▼ Exercise 11.4   CHALLENGING QUESTIONS

ANALYZE: Reason

As with any complex set of questions, there is variety of possible answers. The advantages and disadvantages you describe will be based on your perspective on the educational practice under consideration, as well as your understanding of, and experience with, educational systems in general.

Some of the advantages that you might think of include the following: providing individualized attention to students whose needs might be different from the majority of students; providing students with a "safe" learning environment where their academic abilities are not obviously different from the rest of their peers; and increasing the likelihood that teachers will be able to use teaching methods appropriate to the more closely grouped abilities of the students in their classes.

On the other hand, you might also recognize some of the following disadvantages: students less likely to be academically successful will not be stimulated by their more talented peers, nor exposed to them as peer role models; all students will have limited experience with the true diversity of abilities and may find it difficult later to cope with diverse workplace and social settings; and resources may be unequally and unfairly distributed to the detriment of other groups of students.

As for the values that underlie such practices, you might identify success, education, individual growth, and efficiency. These do not always lead to the same set of actions but can compete and pull people in different directions. For example, strongly supporting the value of education would lead one to strive to provide education for all individuals, whereas valuing efficiency might lead one to want to focus educational resources only where they will "do the most good." Valuing success exclusively might support a practice of educating only academically talented individuals, but valuing the growth of the individual makes providing specialized education designed to build on each individual's unique strengths a priority.

▼ Exercise 11.5   IT'S ALL GOOD

ANALYZE: Categorize

CASE 1: Ronnie's Bad Grade

Inter-rater reliability could be the culprit. However, we also must factor in that the second reader did not receive training regarding the expectations the professor had for the assignment. The graduate student's lack of experience could contribute to some error in the second result.

CASE 2: Bruce's Dream Vocation

Predictive validity is a problem in this example. The test prediction generated a false negative, meaning it wrongly interpreted his skills as not up to the job, with regard to Bruce's prospects for a successful career as a CPA. Bruce was able to disprove the expectation with his successful career.

CASE 3: Joshua's Wobbly IQ

Children's IQ scores begin to stabilize around age 7. Therefore, the dramatic difference in the results of his two tests, which were separated by three years, could be attributed to a problem with *test-retest reliability*. We could speculate that some of the difference in the two test scores could be the result of at least one session having nonstandard testing conditions (for example, noisy environment, intrusive reviewer).

CASE 4: Darla's Test-Taking Terror

Technically, *split-half reliability* is established when test questions from a single test are randomly assigned into two halves and then correlated. The resulting correlation should be very high if the parts of the test cohere. However, we import the idea here to discuss multiple choice versus essay skills.

CASE 5: Angelina's Honors Dilemma

In this example, we have a significant mismatch that produces challenges about *concurrent validity*. Here is a proven scholar who has demonstrated she has the academic chops to be successful, but her results on the admissions test used by the honors program for selection would prevent her from taking on the additional responsibility.

CASE 6: Dr. Swenson's Misfire

Imagine how frustrating it would feel to invest time and energy trying to figure out a high-quality method to measure one construct only to discover that the test is unusable for that purpose. In this case, Dr. Swenson's investment failed the criterion of *construct validity*.

▼Exercise 11.6   WHEN TO TEST

EVALUATE: Justify

There are many possible alternatives. Strong answers will provide a clear rationale for each choice, recognizing that appropriate choices consider the relationships of the individuals involved and the tasks that each person will probably need to be able to accomplish in order to succeed within the context of those relationships.

▼Exercise 11.7   JUST TOO COOL

CREATE: Invent

Operational definition: This will vary depending on the target group you wish to define. Chances are good that your definition will include elements of practical intelligence or street smarts: knowing how to solve problems, knowing how to create a positive impression, using language that is current or cutting edge, striving to dress as a fashionable trendsetter.

Measurement strategy: The measurement strategy for each dimension that defines "cool" would differ. Regardless of the dimension selected, you would need to identify some "cool" judges and require them to adhere to the same criteria that define the dimension. Or perhaps you could develop scenarios in which various alternatives could be rated for the degree of "cool" demonstrated in the choice.

What's difficult? The prior two steps should make it clear that it is hard to come to a consensus about the operationalizing of a concept, let alone developing a strategy for its measurement. Because ideas regarding the definition are likely to be diverse, coming up with a reliable and valid way to measure this dimension may not be very feasible. Many people find the process of making comparative judgments among human beings distasteful, further complicating a very difficult task.

▼Exercise 11.8   TO RETEST OR NOT TO RETEST?

CREATE: Design

What is your hypothesis?

In experiments, we try to establish differences between groups. Therefore, an effective hypothesis would be that the use of test-preparation courses leads to a significant gain on a second taking of the GRE.

What is the independent variable?

The independent variable is presence versus absence of test-preparation training.

What is the dependent variable?

The dependent variable is GRE score, or the difference in the GRE score from first testing to second testing.

How will you assign volunteers to test conditions?

Volunteers would have to be assigned randomly to the two conditions: test preparation and no test preparation.

What elements of the experiment will you need to control?

- the amount of time between the original testing and the second testing
- the use of the same form of test for all participants
- the test conditions, which must be similar

Although listening to a powerful commercial and deciding what to do on the basis of the strength of testimony may be easier than searching for objective evidence, such a decision-making process doesn't represent good science. Controlled comparisons contribute more objective data to assist in making such an important decision.

Chapter

◀Motivation▶

▼Exercise 12.1 THEORIES OF MOTIVATION

UNDERSTAND: Compare

Behavior	Theories	Explanations
A human infant rooting to find mother's nipple	Instinct theory	This is a reflexive behavior that increases the likelihood of survival.
	Drive reduction theory	Hunger creates an aversive state that the infant attempts to relieve through behaviors that increase the likelihood that the mouth will come in closer contact with a food source.
Getting a glass of water when you are thirsty	Drive reduction theory	Thirst creates an aversive state which the person then works to diminish by behaving in ways that reduce the need.
Going for a walk when you are worried or restless	Drive reduction theory	The feeling of restlessness or worry creates an aversive state that is relieved with activity or a change of scenery.
	Arousal theory	The walk actually increases arousal, which gives the individual the energy to focus or deal with the cause of the anxiety.
Working on a difficult jig-saw puzzle	Arousal theory	Tackling the difficult task increases the intellectual stimulation of the individual in a way that is rewarding.

Behavior	Theories	Explanations
Studying hard to pass an exam	Drive reduction theory	The exam creates an aversive state of anxiety, which studying relieves.
	Arousal theory	Working hard to learn new material or to do well increases arousal because it is intellectually stimulating.
Crying when hurt or upset	Instinct theory	This is a reflexive behavior that increases the likelihood of survival by drawing the attention of others who could provide aid.
	Drive reduction theory	Physical or psychological distress aversively arouses an individual, who releases the excess energy by crying.
Developing a lasting, intimate relationship	Drive reduction theory	Sexual and reproductive needs build and an individual works to find a way to ensure that those needs can be met easily or conveniently in the future.
	Arousal theory	Long-term, intimate relationships with others are stimulating and therefore provide energy for the individuals involved.

▼ Exercise 12.2   NOW HIRING

APPLY: Illustrate

Human resource specialists recognize that individuals who are high in need achievement tend to be the best candidates for employment because they work hard, persist on challenging tasks, and respond to feedback effectively. They also demonstrate the capacity to delay gratification to accomplish long-term goals despite the lure of short-term attractions. Consequently, you should probably classify the human resources questions about whether each reflects a clear need achievement theme in the following manner:

Yes   Maybe   No   How long did you work at your last job?
The answer potentially reveals persistence.

Yes   Maybe   No   What awards have you won based on your performance?
To the extent that the competitions represent acknowledgment of serious application of time and talent, award histories provide a good reflection of need achievement.

Yes   **Maybe**   No   What do you like to do in your spare time?
Watching television endlessly doesn't reflect well on high need but some hobbies can reveal high need to achieve tendencies. For example, gourmet cooking, woodworking, and golfing would be some hobbies that showcase high standards, persistence, and intrinsic motives.

Yes   **Maybe**   No   What kind of coworkers appeal to you?
Identifying kind and pleasant coworkers rather than productive and hard-working colleagues as ideal might indicate some laxness in need achievement.

Yes   Maybe   **No**   What was the last book you read for pleasure?
Human resource specialists often include an off-task question to find out about personal interests in addition to work habits.

Yes	**Maybe**	No	Why do you want to work here?

"Having a regular paycheck" won't be reassuring to the person doing the hiring that you intend to be a hard worker for the company. On the other hand, answering the questions with long-term objectives that emphasize success examples can produce persuasive evidence that you are the right person.

Yes	Maybe	No	How closely do you like to be supervised?

Although high-need achievers respond well to feedback, their intrinsic motives can sometimes be undermined by close supervision. Self-starters don't need too much supervision to stay on track and get the job done.

Yes	Maybe	No	Would you prefer short-term assignments that are relatively manageable or a longer-term assignment that is more exacting?

High-need achievers prefer tasks of moderate complexity that have a reasonable likelihood of success.

Yes	Maybe	**No**	What kind of vacations do you like to take?

Similar to the question regarding your literary preferences, vacation options don't shed much light on need achievement.

Yes	Maybe	No	Have you ever been described as a workaholic?

Unfortunately, this question can capture those whose need achievement may have gotten out of control. The workaholic may have too much intrinsic motivation to work at the cost of personal and family relationships.

Yes	Maybe	No	Where do you hope to be in five years?

Low need achievers may not reflect strong motives to succeed in their answers. High need achievers are more likely to target advancement within the company to illustrate their hard work and dedication.

Yes	Maybe	No	What do you typically do when you receive constructive criticism?

Although no one relishes being told that he or she has fallen short of expectations, high need achievers recognize that an honest evaluation will help them accomplish their goals more effectively in the long term.

▼ Exercise 12.3   THE WEIGHT-LOSS COUNSELOR

ANALYSIS: *Reason*

Some possible answers:

Variable 1: Food intake

   Question: Approximately how many calories do you consume each day?

Variable 2: Genetic influence

   Question: Are other members of your family overweight?

Variable 3: Activity level

   Question: How much exercise do you get on a regular basis?

Variable 4: Social influences

   Question: Are you likely to eat more when you are alone or when you are in the company of others?

Variable 5: Diet history

> *Question:* Have you ever lost weight and maintained your weight loss successfully in the past?

Variable 6: Physiology

> *Question:* Do you seem to have a set point at which your weight can be more easily maintained?

▼Exercise 12.4   HUMANISTIC HISTORY

EVALUATION: Take Perspective

Obviously, we cannot anticipate the specific example you will use to demonstrate that the validity of Maslow's hierarchy of needs is questionable. A good example will describe an individual, or group of individuals, who behave in ways that suggest that their priorities of needs are different from those proposed by Maslow. Some of the examples often used to question his theory include examples of altruism—sacrificing one's safety or life for another—and cultural differences in need priorities. What example did you use? If possible, compare your example with those of your classmates. Can you identify any patterns or similarities in the examples used?

▼Exercise 12.5   YOU DON'T HAVE TO BE LONELY

ANALYSIS: Compare

To maximize appeal to potential partners from the parental investment theory, the following strategies would be most effective, even if these strategies don't actually reflect what the male or female truly wants.

For the male appealing to the female:

Ambitious, successful single male looking for a woman interested in building a family. Join me in an exciting life filled with interesting social opportunities that come with my high socioeconomic status.

For the female appealing to the male:

Superhot, sexually adventurous female interested in hooking up with a hot guy. No commitments, no strain, no worries.

In contrast, an honest ad would reflect the characteristics that support the gender-specific motives of parental investment theory.

For the male expressing an evolutionary imperative:

Hot women only need apply! If you are young, attractive, and careless with contraception, I'm your man!

For the female expressing an evolutionary imperative:

Home-oriented female looking for a home-oriented good provider. Must love children. Looks are not important, but bring copies of your bank statements and other financial data to facilitate a second date.

▼Exercise 12.6   HUMANISTIC HISTORY

EVALUATE: Take Perspective

Obviously, we cannot anticipate the specific example you will use to demonstrate that the validity of Maslow's hierarchy of needs is questionable. A good example will describe an individual, or group of individuals, who behave in ways that suggest that their priorities of needs are different from those proposed by Maslow. Some of the examples often used to question his theory include examples of altruism—sacrificing one's safety or life for another—and cultural differences in need priorities. What example did you use? If possible, compare your example with those of your classmates. Can you identify any patterns or similarities in the examples used?

▼Exercise 12.7 CHICKEN OR EGG?
EVALUATE: Justify

The job of an institutional review board is to ensure that all experiments are conducted according to the ethical guidelines of the discipline and institution, and that the participants are protected from undue harm or risk. In this case, there are several critical questions you would need to ask yourself:

- What is the benefit of this research?

- Is the research design appropriate? Is the experiment designed so that the data collected will ethically provide an answer to the research question?

- What are the risks to the participants? If these risks are significant, are they explained clearly to the participants? Are the potential benefits important and likely to justify the risks?

It is important to recognize that risks include more than simply the potential for physical harm. Because of the stigma often associated with homosexuality, there are potential social and emotional risks associated with participating in experiments of this type. In addition, the findings from the research could be used to push a political agenda that ultimately would be unacceptable or harmful to those who had participated.

If you, as an institutional review board member, decide that this research should be funded, you must explain how the research is of benefit and how participants can be protected from harm based on their participation in this research. If you decide not to fund the research in this area, your explanation should demonstrate how and why the risks outweigh the potential benefits. You may also decide that some research in this area seems feasible, while some does not. If this is your position, be as specific as you can about the criteria for funding. What is the dividing line between those experiments that will be funded and those that will not?

▼Exercise 12.8 THE CREATIVE CONSULTANT
CREATE: Invent

Some examples of possible answers:

Motive 1: Hunger
   Product name: Dee-Lish
   Advertising approach: The new toothpaste could be connected with images of people happily eating food and then just as happily brushing their teeth with a toothpaste that claims to taste as good as a banana split.

Motive 2: Pain avoidance
   Product name: Heavenly
   Advertising approach: The toothpaste itself could have some anesthetic quality to address the challenges of those with sensitive teeth. The scenes would emphasize the relief that could be gained from using the product.

Motive 3: Safety

Product name: Refuge

Advertising approach: This campaign could use dental visits in a mildly arousing depiction of the consequences of bad dental care. The campaign could stress prevention as a security measure. This might be especially effective for parents trying to increase their children's tooth-brushing behavior.

Motive 4: Love

Product name: Glow

Advertising approach: This campaign would target the dating crowd. Choosing not to use "Glow" should be linked to increased risk of not having an active love life.

Motive 5: Esteem

Product name: Peak

Advertising approach: Is there a way to link tooth-brushing behavior with the practices of high-status individuals? Could brushing regularly with this product confer some state of grace not available to other toothpaste users? Perhaps reduced cavities represent a type of hygiene achievement that most people can't manage; if so, a good dental record might confer a sense of being special.

All these approaches have been used to promote oral hygiene products. You may have difficulty choosing one approach over the others. The connection between hunger and toothpaste might be difficult to establish. Pain avoidance connections are tricky; potential buyers perceive them as too threatening, and they may form an uncomfortable connection with the new product. Nevertheless, advertising campaigns derive their success from imaginative approaches to the problem of selling an unexciting product. Do you think any of your approaches would work?

▼Exercise 12.9   THE DIET RIOT

CREATE: Design

There are several components of the physiology of hunger that you might wish to share with people who are interested in changing their eating behavior and/or weight. Hunger pangs are related to the contractions of an empty stomach (although there are also other factors involved). Using water and fiber to fill the stomach decreases the sensation of hunger pangs. Insulin and glucose are also related to feelings of hunger. Insulin decreases the availability of glucose, and decreases in blood glucose levels increase feelings of hunger. Maintaining a consistent blood glucose level will help decrease hunger sensations. It is interesting to note that body chemistry also affects one's choice of food. Some people crave sweet or starchy food when depressed or anxious. The carbohydrates found in these foods help raise serotonin levels and improve mood. Finally, it will be important to discuss the concept of a set point; the natural weight of an individual that the body works to maintain. When the weight drops below this point, feelings of hunger are triggered and the metabolism is slowed to help recover the lost weight. This set point can be changed by a slow and steady weight loss and by maintaining a realistically lower weight until the body becomes accustomed to its new "normal" weight.

There are also other, practical suggestions you can offer about healthy eating. Because some people are sensitive to external cues for eating, keep food out of sight. If it is not visible, people who are externally cued to eat are less likely to consume food when they are not hungry. Consider raising metabolism by increasing activity. Not only does this help build muscle and increase strength, it helps overcome the tendency for the body to decrease its metabolic rate when losing weight.

Because many individuals trying to lose weight have a negative image of their own bodies, and because such negative perceptions are one factor in developing eating disorders, it would probably be a good idea to share a little information about eating disorders with your clients. Eating disorders are becoming increasingly common as the cultural ideal portrayed in the media becomes more unlike the majority of women. Women who have low self-esteem; a high need to achieve; who come from a competitive and protective family; or have a family history of eating disorders, alcoholism, obesity, and/or depression are at higher risk for developing certain eating disorders. These women should be especially careful with their weight loss goals and plans and should be aware of where to seek help if necessary.

Chapter

◀Emotion▶

▼Exercise 13.1 TOURIST TRAP

UNDERSTAND: Translate

Description of behavior: One thumb is held up while the four fingers of the same hand are tucked into the palm.

Meaning: In North America, this is a sign that things are OK or that a person is hitchhiking. In German bars, this gesture will get you one beer. In Japanese bars, it may get you five. In Nigeria, if you use this gesture while hitchhiking you may be beaten by motorists, who will find your gesture extremely insulting.

Description of behavior: The index finger on the right hand is circling the right ear.

Meaning: In North America, this gesture signifies that you believe the receiver of the message may not be mentally stable. In Argentina, however, this gesture alerts you to the fact that you have a phone call waiting.

Description of behavior: An extended left hand appears to be offering an apple.

Meaning: The sender could be offering the apple as a gesture of friendship. Although this example looks harmless enough, woe to the tourist who uses it in Middle Eastern cultures. To use the left hand to offer anything in this manner, whether food or money, is considered a great offense. Why? Because the left hand is reserved for hygiene and is regarded as "soiled," and it should not be used in social transactions of any kind. Offering presents should be done with the "clean" right hand.

Description of behavior: Eyes are cast downward.

Meaning: In North America, a downcast glance represents a loss of self-esteem or shyness. In Japan and Korea, downcast eyes demonstrate respect.

Description of behavior: Head is moving from side to side in one plane.

Meaning: Head shaking substitutes for a negative response in North America. However, in Bulgaria, Turkey, and Iran, you've said "Yes." In India, you've said "Yes, I am listening."

Description of behavior: Forefinger and thumb are joined to form a circle.

Meaning: In North America, this behavior signals that "everything is OK." However, the gesture is interpreted very differently in other cultures. In France, you have implied that something or someone is worthless. In Japan, you've gestured for "coins." In Malta, Sardinia, Turkey, Greece, and Italy, you've implied an unfavorable comparison to some female body parts.

▼ Exercise 13.2   PINOCCHIO'S LEGACY

UNDERSTAND: Predict

Here is just a sampling of some possible outcomes of social behavior if lying prompted a swollen proboscis:

- People would develop a stronger value for honesty under all circumstances.

- People who tend to lie would increase their use of phone and e-mail so that their swelling would not be noticeable.

- People with lying tendencies might learn to speak back to back instead of face to face.

- We would start using metaphors that are nose-related, such as "honest as your nose is long!"

- A nose wardrobe? Perhaps a series of stylish covers coordinated with your clothing would catch on to hide the problem.

- People might pursue plastic surgery, not to enhance beauty but to alter the natural course of swelling.

Were you able to think of any other possible outcomes?

▼ Exercise 13.3   FORGET YOUR TROUBLES

APPLY: Illustrate

It would be impossible to predict all the wishes that might have been listed in this exercise; given this culture, however, it is easy to guess that many wishes were for improving material wealth. Research with lottery winners indicates that the adaptation-level principle holds true: The glow of newly acquired wealth is transient. However, the relative deprivation principle could be invoked to ward off this reaction. To invoke it, all you need do to feel happier about your current circumstances is to remember an earlier time when your resources were more limited. If no such time exists, perhaps you could envision some less fortunate circumstances that could occur. Dwelling on worse-case scenarios will make you feel better, perhaps even happier, for a short period of time.

▼ Exercise 13.4   EXPRESS YOURSELF

ANALYZE: Reason

Here are some suggestions about when it might be a bad idea to express an emotion:

Fear

- when you are giving a speech in which you are trying to be persuasive

- when expressing fear might communicate to a rival or opponent that you are weak

- when you are trying to model bravery for a younger person

Anger

- when the control of your anger might get away from you

- when there are unwarranted risks attached to expressing anger (for example, being angry at your boss, who is known for having little patience with complaining employees)

- when your anger might contribute to fomenting irrational or dangerous responses in a group

Sadness

- when there are proactive things you can do to relieve the sadness but choose not to
- when the larger context is a joyous one in which the expression of sadness might ruin or diminish the occasion

Happiness

- when the larger context is a sad occasion in which the expression of joy would be deemed inappropriate

▼Exercise 13.5   'CAUSE I'M HAPPY

ANALYZE: Categorize

Happiness Variable	Strong Relationship	Moderate Relationship	No Relationship
Being a parent			X
Love & marriage	X		
Social activity		X	
Personality	X		
Money			X
Age			X
Health		X	
Attractiveness			X
Work	X		
Genetics	X		
Intelligence			X

▼Exercise 13.6   A ROUSING WALK IN THE WOODS

EVALUATION: Choose

	Evolutionary (ET)	James-Lange (JL)	Cannon-Bard (CB)	Schachter Two Factor (S2F)	Comment
Which theory handles being in a good mood due to math performance?		X		X	Both JL and S2F provide for the perception of positive mood. JL predicts a different pattern of arousal than S2F predicts.
Which theory requires arousal as the first step in the sequence?	X	X		X	Only CB ties arousal to a simultaneous event; all other theories start with arousal.

Continued

	Evolutionary (ET)	James-Lange (JL)	Cannon-Bard (CB)	Schachter Two Factor (S2F)	Comment
Which theory fits best with fight-or-flight reactions?	X				Evolutionary theory is most explicitly tied to survival outcomes. A moderate case can be made for both JL and CB if recognition of emotion translates to escape or confrontation.
Which theory helps explain that the park ranger might be perceived as more appealing following his rescue activities?				X	S2F is the only emotion theory that emphasizes cognitive interpretation of emotional states.
Which theory invokes subcortical activity as an essential step?	X	X			Both ET and JL emphasize the role of lower brain centers in initiating emotion.

▼Exercise 13.7   HONESTY IS THE BEST POLICY

EVALUATION: Take Perspective

Possible answers:
An Owner's Pro-Use Position

Values: Protection of investment and profit

Arguments:

- Screening everyone would lift suspicion from those who don't deserve it.
- Employee morale would improve when the thief was exposed and fired.
- Polygraph testing is widely used in all kinds of American businesses.
- The privacy of all those who were questioned would be protected because no one else would know the results.
- The owner is volunteering to submit to the procedure and to be the first person tested.

An Employee's Anti-Use Position

Value(s): Right to privacy

Arguments:

- Federal laws limit the use of polygraph tests.

- The owner's widespread suspicion of the employees has already been a drain on morale.

- Those who can control the symptoms of arousal could fake the results and could therefore divert suspicion to other employees.

- Employee anxiety about the procedure itself might lead to *false positives*—innocent people who appear to be guilty simply because the procedure makes them highly anxious.

▼Exercise 13.8   WHAT IS THIS THING CALLED LOVE?

CREATE: Design

Some indicators of falling in love:

loss of appetite → loss of body weight

increased eye contact → increased time gazing at target

increased appetite → gain in body weight

inability to concentrate → minutes off-task

increased conversation → greater time on the phone or online

greater excitement → increased heart flutters

Why isn't the experience uniform?

No one really knows the answer to this one . . . yet.

14

Chapter

◀ Social Psychology ▶

▼ Exercise 14.1 PRIDE AND PREJUDICES

PART 1: UNDERSTAND: Compare

Although these ratings are uniquely your own, you can recognize from glancing over your list that it is highly unlikely you came through the experience with the capacity to maintain the claim that you have no prejudices. Sometimes prejudice can be favorable, meaning that you might be inclined to think more favorably about redheads as a group of people than they necessarily deserve just by having a certain hair color. On the other hand, negative prejudices can easily be generated and maintained. Your personal experience dictates the degree to which you have established positive or negative attitudes about distinctive groups of people based on one attribute, behavior, or social role.

PART 2: ANALYZE: Categorize

Your answers in this categorizing exercise will be driven by your personal experience, but the following provides some additional input about how the categories of origins of prejudice might pertain to the target group.

In-Group Bias leads you to confer advantages to people who are like you. Similarly, those who don't share your attributes constitute an out-group and that status automatically may make you less generous in your interpretations of their behavior. If you were a cheerleader or dated a cheerleader, you might be inclined to grant privileges to that group or at least cut them some slack. If you weren't a cheerleader, or worse, if a cheerleader treated you insensitively, then you are more inclined to be dismissive in your regard.

Scapegoating transpires when you escape responsibility by blaming others. For example, high school principals, who normally must deal with a range of student misbehavior, can easily be scapegoated as a means of minimizing the negative impact of a misdeed that brought a student to the vice principal's attention.

Social Inequality tends to exaggerate identification with socioeconomic groups and to promote prejudice for those who don't share your socioeconomic status. If you have never had life challenges that limited your family's capacity to provide for basic needs, it is easy to be prejudiced against Welfare Moms, as well as have unflattering attributions about their motives. On the other hand, if you have experienced dependence on governmental agencies to help your family survive, it is less likely that you would express negative judgments about a Welfare Mom.

Categorizing represents a cognitive shortcut. Rather than consider every single hunter on the planet, you simply generalize your conclusions about one or two hunters to everyone who chooses a gun-toting hobby.

Vivid Cases provide an extension of categorizing. You engage in categorizing a group of people with whom your experience is limited but when the expectations you hold are prominently shaped by a high-impact example. For instance, our expectations about flamboyance in preacher personalities can be influenced by watching evangelical pastors with well-bankrolled Sunday services broadcast on television.

Just World Phenomenon is a particularly divisive justification for prejudice. If we operate with the expectation that good things happen to good people and bad things happen to bad people, it may help us feel superior to those who have misfortune, that is, until something bad happens to us. A great deal of the animosity generated toward AIDS patients can be explained as a retreat to the unreal just world where the AIDS patient's illness is interpreted as retribution for an objectionable lifestyle.

▼ Exercise 14.2   DEAR ABBY

APPLY: Illustrate

Regardless of how clever or poignant your letter as Abby's substitute may be, your advice to the lovelorn is likely to have touched on the following principles:

Proximity

Research indicates that proximity breeds liking. Therefore, your advice should reflect stronger attempts to put Worried in closer proximity to his beloved. Since they attend different universities, he might consider transferring. Alternatively, he could increase his letter writing and phone calling to simulate his presence. Perhaps you can think of other ways to enhance his presence in her life—the more creative, the better.

Physical Attractiveness

Anyone aspiring to a serious emotional relationship spends time attempting to be as attractive a stimulus as possible. Part of the challenge in this simple advice, however, is that people differ in what they find attractive. Therefore, it may be useful to advise Worried to do some research on the tastes and preferences of his beloved. She may be wild about beards or turned off by extra weight. If he knows her preferences, he could tailor his energies to enhance attraction.

Similarity

You might advise Worried to find out more about his beloved's interests and leisure pursuits. What does she like to do? What interests does this couple have in common? What shared interests might create stimulating times together in the future? What could they learn from each other?

Arousal

A date to a horror movie or participating in some other highly arousing activity could help Worried in his campaign. In the presence of such activities, he could come to symbolize both excitement, indicated by the stimulating choice, and safety, reinforced by hugs, reassurance, and encouragement.

Equity

The principle of equity suggests that we tend to express our liking in relationships in which power feels fairly distributed. This suggests that Worried needs to carefully gauge his campaign so that he will not overwhelm his beloved but will offer some mild incentives to increase her involvement.

Self-Disclosure

Self-disclosure also needs to feel equivalent if the relationship is to feel balanced. When one partner shares too much too soon, the act can frighten and overwhelm the other person. On the other hand, sharing too little may cause alienation if it projects a remote quality. Worried would be well advised to show some restraint in his feelings until he has greater confidence that his beloved's feelings are similar.

Evaluate your comfort level in serving as Abby's substitute

This exercise concludes by asking you to consider the emotional consequence of using psychology to influence the behavior of others. Advising the lovelorn may have been easy for you. Or you may have felt uncomfortable about the degree of manipulation inherent in applying the principles of psychology to promote affection. Although control of behavior is often cited as a fundamental goal of psychology, many circumstances may prompt ethical concerns that limit psychology's applications.

▼ Exercise 14.3   THE SOUR GRAPES PRINCIPLE
ANALYZE: Reason

Dissonance Example #1: The Charming Math Teacher

Although you may decide to double your study efforts to impress your math teacher, the easier course of action is an attitude adjustment. You may be amazed to discover that the behaviors you originally thought of as charming now may seem over the top to help justify your satisfaction with your test performance. If somehow she becomes more problematic, then you don't need to face your poor performance or change your own study routine.

Dissonance Example #2: Paying Off Student Loans

Facing huge student debt is likely to temper your prior enthusiasm about the quality of your education. Actually, attitude change can move in both directions. You may begin to talk trash about the college to vent your bad feelings, but cognitive dissonance also predicts you could speak even more favorably about your education to justify the huge loans that await you after graduation. Of course, an extreme behavioral change is vacating college altogether so your debt load won't increase.

Dissonance Example #3: Lonelyhearts

What are your options to resolve the dissonance between a satisfactory academic experience and an unsatisfactory social life? You can minimize the importance of a social life while you are earning your college degree. You can fill the empty spaces with more study and tell yourself that you will make up for it when you graduate. On the other hand, you can make some behavioral changes and reduce the lonely feelings. Joining clubs, exploring online dating, and taking the initiative to ask people you like out for coffee are just some activities that you can undertake that may modify your lonely feelings.

Dissonance Example #4: Cram Regrets

Every bit of cognitive science suggests cramming is not a great way to learn, yet so many students forgo more systematic study strategies in favor of the all-nighter before the cognitive challenge. By sacrificing sleep, crammers often guarantee poorer performance, because the brain is simply not going to work as efficiently or creatively without appropriate rest. The best resolution of the dissonance created in this situation is to change your behavior. Go to an academic support center on campus and get some assistance in how to craft a manageable timetable to accomplish the work required and still have time for a social life. Unfortunately, most crammers adopt an illusion that somehow the inefficiency predictions just simply won't apply to them. They are just that good! The delusion is so powerful that it can often weather profoundly bad test scores, which crammers believe simply don't represent their true potential.

▼Exercise 14.4 FOR THE SAKE OF THE CHILDREN
EVALUATE: Assess

In each of the examples below, we offer a few suggestions; you may have been able to generate many other ideas related to the problem of reducing violence in children's schools.

1. Metal detectors at the school entrances:
   a. Related psychological concepts: signal detection, conformity, obedience to authority
   b. Positive criticism: provides a sense of security for students who are not tempted to bring guns to school; challenges students who intend to bring guns to school to be more creative in smuggling them
   c. Negative criticism: expensive and oppressive
   d. Predicted success: what is your opinion?

2. The requirement to wear school uniforms:
   a. Related psychological concepts: social stigma, conformity, obedience to authority, physical attraction through similarity
   b. Positive criticism: reduces the sense of competition among students on the basis of looks; reduces financial pressures for parents to provide their children with the most popular clothing; reduces the grounds on which students can be harassed for failure to conform to popular standards
   c. Negative criticism: reduces individual expression; superficial approach to reducing harassment of individual students
   d. Predicted success: what is your opinion?

3. Sensitivity training built into the curriculum:
   a. Related psychological concepts: empathy training, interdependence, appreciation of diversity
   b. Positive criticism: provides for safer expression of individual differences; encourages students to understand the consequences of their actions
   c. Negative criticism: may appeal only to a selected portion of the population of students; may be too superficial to address profoundly disturbed individuals in the population
   d. Predicted success: what is your opinion?

4. Holding parents accountable for the violent actions of their children:
   a. Related psychological concepts: scapegoating, attribution
   b. Positive criticism: might encourage parents to pay more attention to children who are showing signs of difficult adjustment
   c. Negative criticism: parents are not the only influences on their children's choices of personal expression
   d. Predicted success: what is your opinion?

▼Exercise 14.5 PEOPLE WERE STUPID BACK THEN

PART 1: EVALUATE: Take Perspective

When you are first exposed to Milgram's fascinating demonstration, it can be hard to empathize with what the participants did. Milgram orchestrated conditions so that individuals thought they were shocking a man with a heart condition in ways that might have harmed him. Yet, they continued to shock the participants when encouraged to do so by the experimenter at rates that no one predicted. Around 65 percent of participants complied with the authority's request. However, going through each stage of the sequence can confer a different level of understanding about the social pressures being brought to bear on the participants. The thoughts and feelings of the participants in Milgram's original study are relatively easy to describe. With each successive step in Milgram's procedure, their anxiety and confusion mount. The participants begin the experience believing they are about to undergo a demonstration in learning; they complete the experience with, at the very least, some concern that they may have harmed the other participant. Even Milgram was surprised by the degree to which the intensity of the situation encouraged obedience to authority. Although many students dismiss the applicability of the findings to themselves (saying, "I would *never* do that to a fellow human being!"), other more astute students recognize that the complex social situation set up the participants to demonstrate how the power of the situation could overcome their own good judgment.

PART 2: EVALUATE: Justify

In this section you will break apart all of the variables that may have contributed to the surprising outcome.

How Did the Setting Contribute?

The laboratory in which Milgram's demonstration was conducted was organized to promote maximum credibility. The institution at which the demonstration was originally run was Yale University, one of the most prestigious universities in the United States.

How Did the Behavior of the Learner Contribute?

The learner, actually the experimenter's confederate, also enhanced credibility of the experimental manipulation. He gave no indication of being in league with the experimenter and convincingly acted the part of an unlucky volunteer with heart problems, compromised by his random assignment as the learner.

How Did the Emotional State of the True Subject (The "Teacher") Contribute?

In most experiments, volunteers feel some nervousness at the outset of their participation. However, in this situation the anxiety didn't diminish; it continued to mount with each step of the demonstration. Milgram's original subjects demonstrated anxiety in their body language, hesitant speech, requests for clarification of the researcher's intent, and nervous laughter in response to the confederate's protests.

How Did the Teacher's Experience of Being Shocked During the Demonstration Contribute?

The teachers were exposed to a mild form of shock during the preparation phase of the experiment. The mild level was distinctly uncomfortable but was not painful. Such exposure probably added to the sense of relief the subject had when assigned to the teaching role rather than to the learning role.

How Did "Luck" Contribute?

The participant was assigned to be the teacher by a rigged flip of the coin, with the role of the learner left to the confederate. This assignment may have enhanced the teacher's obligation to follow through on the roles that fate had determined. Perhaps the teacher felt more justified in executing the orders since he believed he could just as easily have been assigned to the role of the learner, where he would have had to endure the discomfort of that condition.

How Did the Demeanor of the Researcher Contribute?

The demeanor and dress of the researcher were consistent with the command and power of an authority figure. The experimenter wore a lab coat and referred to himself as a "doctor." In addition, his approach to the experience was quite serious and businesslike. When teachers questioned the procedure, the researcher responded with assurance and authority that he "would take the responsibility" and that "the experiment must continue." His manner encouraged submission and dependence.

Were People More Stupid Back Then?

Probably not. There is a strong likelihood that under conditions of anxiety and confusion we look to others for answers and guidance. Sometimes obedience to authority may be an adaptive and appropriate action. However, Milgram's study underscores how potentially damaging the absence of critical thinking can be when there is a possibility of doing harm to others.

▼Exercise 14.6   BUT MY TEACHER MADE ME DO IT!

CREATE: Invent

Regardless of the norm you and your partner choose to violate, your description of the behavior that you attempted should be free from interpretation. What exactly did you do? What was the consequence? What was the context?

Attribution theory suggests that you (as the actor) and your partner will blame *external* forces (this assignment or your teacher) as the reason you broke the social rules. In contrast, the casual observer is likely to blame your unexpected behavior on your undesirable traits (for example, being crazy, rude, and so forth), creating an *internal* attribution for action. This distinction between the tendencies of actors and observers in explaining action is called the *fundamental attribution error*.

▼Exercise 14.7   HOW CAN I HELP?

CREATE: Design

Variables that might influence the decision to loan class notes include:

timing of request (say, immediately after class has taken place versus later)

evidence of requester's disability (for example, arm cast, crutches)

gender of person making request

proximity to exam

presence or absence of incentive (for example, promise to return the favor)

proximity in seating

depth of prior acquaintance

Select one variable and work with the following questions to develop an experimental design on altruistic behavior:

A possible hypothesis regarding "class note loaning behavior" is: Factor X (your selected dimension) increases agreement to loan class notes in college populations.

Participants in the study would be: College students

The dependent variable would be: The participant's decision to loan or refrain from loaning the requested class notes

A possible description of the procedure, including any elements that you would attempt to control, would address the following issues: This dimension depends on the variable you have selected to manipulate as the independent variable, but everything else must be standardized if you are able to state with confidence that any differences in results were caused by the independent variable.

What independent variable would you be testing, and why does this variable appeal to you? Did you select an independent variable similar to the one in the brainstorming list above or another factor?

Do you think the experiment would confirm your hypothesis? Some independent variables simply may not produce a robust enough impact to create a difference in the behavior of your experimental and control groups. What supports your level of confidence about your selected experiment?

Chapter

◄Personality►

▼**Exercise 15.1** **FREUD MEETS MOTHER GOOSE**

UNDERSTAND: Translate and Predict

Jack and Jill

Likely developmental stage at fixation: Latency

Justification: The assumption of labor performed with a person of the opposite gender. Initial forays into pairing off are met with danger and physical harm.

Adult personality structure: Freud had little to say about the latent influence on human personality; however, the rhyme might portend difficulties in getting along with the opposite gender.

Three Blind Mice

Likely developmental stage at fixation: Possibly the phallic stage

Justification: The innocent mice encounter a symbolically castrating force. In this case, they lose their tails rather than their genitalia.

Adult personality structure: Freud might suspect that the anxieties sublimated in this rhyme would be manifested in adulthood as struggles about sexuality and gender identification. In this case the strivings of a sexually overactive adult might represent some traumatic experience in the author's phallic development.

Mary, Mary, Quite Contrary

Likely developmental stage at fixation: Anal

Justification: Mary's overconcern with tidiness in her garden.

Adult personality structure: Perhaps the creator of "Mary, Mary" would be characterized by the classic anal-retentive personality: These individuals are preoccupied with order and neatness. Freud could also have made a case for an anal-expulsive personality: These slovenly adults disregard order and thrive on chaos.

▼Exercise 15.2   MATCHMAKER, MATCHMAKER
APPLY: Classify

a. *Conscientious + Conscientious:* A good match. A tidy house, promises kept.

Conscientious + Irresponsible: Not a good match. The irresponsible partner will forever be disappointing the conscientious partner. The irresponsible one may feel frustration at constantly having to apologize and make amends and fail at that, too.

Irresponsible + Irresponsible: A good match. Two irresponsible people may function well together, because neither will have high expectations for themselves or the other person involved.

b. *Stable + Stable:* A good match (but maybe a little boring . . .)

Stable + Neurotic: Perhaps a good match because the unstable partner can bring some variety and challenge to the relationship, if both the stability and the neuroses aren't extreme.

Neurotic + Neurotic: Probably not a good idea. Two basically unstable people may not be able to offer each other much support and may feed on each other's worries and fears.

c. *Extravert + Extravert:* An excellent match! The only risk is that two extraverts might compete with each other a bit for the attention spotlight.

Extravert + Introvert: Only a fair match. The strong social needs of the extravert might feel a bit threatening to the introvert, whose needs are to be more solitary.

Introvert + Introvert: A good match. Perhaps a little quiet, but a good match!

d. *Open + Open:* A good match. These two individuals will spend all their discretionary income on new adventures and travels.

Open + Closed: Not a good match. The stimulus-seeking adventurer may have to pursue activities without the recliner-bound partner.

Closed + Closed: A good match. In extreme cases, they can simply sit and look at each other; however, neither might make a good client, because registering for the service would be an unacceptable adventure.

e. *Agreeable + Agreeable:* A good match. This couple should be flexible enough in times of difficulty to find some common ground and celebrate many anniversaries.

Agreeable + Hostile: Some possibility for partnership, if the agreeable partner can compensate for the angrier, hostile stance of the other.

Hostile + Hostile: Not a good idea. This is a combustible combination that is not likely to be very satisfying for either partner.

▼Exercise 15.3   MASLOW'S DECLINE
ANALYZE: Solve

Criticism 1: The sequence in the hierarchy is too rigid.

The hierarchy should probably not be regarded as having rigid boundaries. There are simply too many examples that violate that rigidity. Artists who become immersed in their work, forgoing food and sleep, prompt a bit more flexibility than Maslow may have originally intended.

Criticism 2: Self-actualization promotes selfishness.

Pursuing optimal experience could be construed as selfish; however, self-actualization could also transpire through helping others. Seeking life enhancement doesn't rule out being involved with others as a vehicle for achieving peak experience.

Criticism 3: The hierarchy doesn't apply well outside western cultures.

One effect of the internet, whether for good, bad, or in-between, is that the world is becoming a bit more homogenous. Practices, customs, and foods from other cultures surface in western cultures just as the internet exports western culture all over the world. It is probably less clear in an internet savvy world that such a crisp dividing line can be drawn between the west and the rest of the world.

Criticism 4: The hierarchy may not apply well to subcultures within western culture.

Although there may be some specific examples that don't fit with the hierarchy, the vast majority of examples in western culture probably still adhere to the expectations of the hierarchy.

▼Exercise 15.4   ME ON THE RISE
ANALYZE: Explain

What are some possible factors than can explain the growth of narcissism?

A. Social media may influence more shallow outreach. The more friends, the better. That approach may lead to lots of acquaintances, but few in-depth relationships.

B. Socioeconomic resources allow people to buy things on credit, which means they can satisfy needs before they can pay for them.

C. The growth of the celebrity culture tends to reward those who know how to attract attention.

D. Narcissists simply find new admirers when old admirers wear out.

E. The rewards for narcissists who are successful (for example, models, rock stars) are substantial.

F. Nonnarcissistic people may simply fade into the background making narcissistic people more prominent.

Can you think of any other reasons narcissism is on the rise?

▼Exercise 15.5   YOU CAN'T CHEAT AN HONEST MAN
ANALYZE: Identify

There are many complications in research of this type. Most come from the number and types of factors for which the researcher must control, but some come from the topic itself. Most people have a great desire to appear honest, and so they do not act the same way during an experiment (when they know someone is watching) as they might in "real life." An individual's need to demonstrate socially desirable traits can make it difficult to examine traits that *aren't* socially desirable—like *not* telling the truth. Other difficulties include differentiating between when someone is telling a lie and when someone is mistaken or just plain wrong (naturalistic observation) and manipulating internal factors and factors about the other person (laboratory studies). What other complications did you think of?

Factors that might influence honesty can be loosely grouped into three categories: things about you, things about the other person(s) involved, and the situation.

Internal factors: Emotional state—fear, anger

Factors about the other person(s): Relationship to you—stranger, friend, family

Situational factors:

> number of people present
>
> risk involved in telling a lie
>
> risk involved in telling the truth
>
> impact of lie
>
> duration of harm

▼Exercise 15.6 RORSCHACH'S FATE

EVALUATE: Justify

Your answer should reflect some sensitivity to what you have at risk by agreeing to a Rorschach exam. If you have little to risk, it may be more reasonable to allow conclusions from a projective test to contribute to a personality evaluation. However, as the risk increases, for example, when custody of children is at stake in a court battle, it may be unwise to submit to a projective test. It is also a bad idea to have projective tests be the sole source of a personality evaluation. If you have little choice in how an evaluation will proceed, at the very least, you (and your attorney) should be aware of the scientifically questionable research support available on Rorschach testing.

▼Exercise 15.7 HOPELESS—OR NOT?

EVALUATE: Take Perspective

Freud's belief was that personality is determined. In fact, Freud believed that personality patterns may be fixed as early as age 6.

Skinner also believed that the behaviors that constitute personality are determined. However, he stressed that the causes are strictly environmental.

Rogers believed in a nondeterministic view. He believed human development potential is strong at any age if the conditions are suitably nourishing.

Maslow also was nondeterministic. His humanistic background supported the optimistic view that people can change if conditions are favorable.

▼Exercise 15.8 PSEUDOSCIENTIFIC PERSONALITY EXPLANATIONS

CREATE: Invent

The Stock Spiel

The stock spiel needs to appeal to generalities about personality. The spiel should not be so specific that it enhances your chance of being wrong, nor should it be so negative that it will alienate the person whose character you are trying to describe. The following examples, adapted from astrological predictions, can serve this purpose well:

- You are hardworking, although you sometimes labor without getting attention from others who should notice your work.

- You are generous, sometimes giving when you can ill afford the gift.

- You really enjoy a lively party, but you may find more pleasure in a quiet evening at home.

- You appreciate nature and are surprised at how others take nature for granted.

- You've had some big disappointments in life, but you are able to bounce back without much delay.

- You sometimes feel frustrated by the foolish choices of others, but you are usually patient in the face of this frustration.

Would anyone reject these descriptions as characteristic of their own behavior? If such descriptions are universal, how effective can they be?

Inferences from Physical Cues

The following examples indicate the kinds of cues that would help you determine other "facts" to add to the personality description.

A wedding or engagement ring can serve as the basis for describing challenges in a relationship with a "significant other."

Type of clothes may suggest whether the individual has a formal or casual style; of course, uniforms provide even stronger hints about the kinds of frustration the individual may encounter professionally.

Nail and hand grooming may offer some tips about the person's profession or hobby.

Physical traits, such as gray hair, wrinkles, or acne, can offer hints about particular kinds of stresses that correlate with developmental stages of life.

The format of a check used to pay for your service can hint about values or style. For example, is the check computer-generated, or does it have frolicking kittens displayed prominently?

The type of transportation, especially the type of car, can suggest general aspects of socioeconomic class.

Chapter

◀ **Psychological Disorders** ▶

▼ **Exercise 16.1   HOW MUCH CRAZY?**

UNDERSTAND: Explain

Although some of the answers are debatable, the following grid represents one possible interpretation of how the behavior meets or does not meet criteria for abnormal behavior.

Type of Behavior	Is It Atypical?	Is It Maladaptive?	Is It Dangerous?	Is It Personally Distressing?	Does It Meet the Criteria for Abnormality?
Making obscene phone calls	Yes	Yes	Yes	No	Yes
Shoplifting	Yes	Yes	Yes	Maybe	Yes
Flaming others on the internet	No	Maybe	No	No	No
Hearing voices when no one is around	Yes	Yes	Possibly	Yes	Yes
Avoiding picnics for fear of snake encounters	No	Yes	No	Maybe	Yes
Cheating on course examinations	No	Yes	Yes	Maybe	Maybe
Hitchhiking	Yes	Maybe	Maybe	No	No
Starring in a reality television show	Yes	No	No	No	No
Serial killing	Yes	Yes	Yes	Maybe	Yes
Feeling too blue to get out of bed	Yes	Yes	No	Yes	Yes

Although some of the judgments are debatable, completing the matrix should provide practice with the framework that psychologists use when they determine whether or not a behavior constitutes disorder. Obviously, the more boxes checked, the easier it is to defend a judgment that a behavior is abnormal.

▼Exercise 16.2   AND THE WINNER IS. . . .
APPLY: Illustrate

Some performances and their corresponding disorders

Disorder	Performance	Film
Schizophrenia	Jessica Lange	*Frances*
	Winona Ryder	*Girl, Interrupted*
	Natalie Portman	*Black Swan*
Antisocial personality	Jack Nicholson	*One Flew Over the Cuckoo's Nest*
	Kathy Bates	*Misery*
	Michael Douglas	*Greed*
	Patty McCormack	*The Bad Seed*
Narcissistic personality	Dianne Wiest	*Bullets Over Broadway*
Borderline personality	Glenn Close	*Fatal Attraction*
	Cate Blanchett	*Blue Jasmine*
Cognitive deficits	Cliff Robertson	*Charly*
	Juliette Lewis	*The Other Sister*
	Tom Hanks	*Forrest Gump*
Obsessive compulsive disorder	Jack Nicholson	*As Good as It Gets*
Alcoholism	Jeff Bridges	*Crazy Heart*
Dissociative identity	Joanne Woodward	*The Three Faces of Eve*
	Sally Field	*Sybil*
Autism	Dustin Hoffman	*Rain Man*

▼Exercise 16.3   LOVE AND WORK
APPLY: Solve

Personality Disorder	Key Features	Possible Occupation	Possible Partner
Narcissistic	Grandiose, self-important	Actor, teacher	An enthused audience
Avoidant	Hypersensitive	Any job where there is limited performance feedback	Someone with low standards for a partner
Schizoid	Eccentric, bizarre	Artist	Another artist

Continued

Personality Disorder	Key Features	Possible Occupation	Possible Partner
Borderline	Unstable in mood and decision	Author	Someone with stable moods and decisions
Antisocial	Impulsive, nonempathetic	Car salesman, politician	Someone easily duped
Paranoid	Suspicious, vigilant	Spy	Probably no one!
Histrionic	Attention or crisis seeking	Emergency room worker	Someone calm might help neutralize the melodrama.
Dependent	Submissive	Military serviceperson	Someone who is dominant
Obsessive-compulsive	Preoccupied with rules and order	Librarian	Another librarian
Schizotypal	Isolated, humorless	Computer code writer	Another schizotypal

Although the matchmaking adventure feels a little frivolous, it highlights an important point that was essential in the last revision of the DSM; that is, personality disorders, as other diagnostic categories in the DSM, should be thought of as a continuum rather than as dichotomous situations. Individuals with weak disorder influences may be quite functional in the right workplace and with the right partner who can compensate for his or her shortcomings. Making effective vocational and partner choices can underscore Freud's wisdom particularly as it relates to those experiencing the negative effects associated with personality disorder.

▼Exercise 16.4   THE END

ANALYZE: Investigate (Part 1)

The following are examples of questions that could be helpful in evaluating the severity of depression.

- Have you ever felt like this before?
- How long have you been down?
- What kinds of things are bothering you?
- Are you religious?
- What are you hopeful about?
- Are you physically healthy?
- Are you suicidal?
- Do you have a plan?

The list of questions is relatively easy to generate, but depression and suicide are surprisingly difficult to discuss. Our reluctance to pursue these topics may be linked to the fear that we could put the idea in someone's head if that person has not considered suicide. This fear is probably unwarranted. Most depressed people feel a sense of relief when the topic is introduced and is followed by assistance in securing the services of a mental health professional.

EVALUATE: Choose (Part 2)

Mitchell is suicidal, and you correctly identify his intentions

Advantages: You can help him get treatment, and his depression may be alleviated.

Risks: He may initially be upset with you.

Mitchell is not suicidal, and you correctly identify his intentions

>   *Advantages:* You will have avoided a confrontation that would have exposed your worrying nature.

>   *Risks:* You may lose the opportunity to show support for a friend who, although not suicidal, may be suffering.

If you confront Mitchell and verify his suicidal intention, you are correct. This step can lead to professional intervention and the possibility that he can get treatment to keep him safe. If you fail to confront him and he is not suicidal, there is no loss. Both of these conditions represent "hits" in decision theory terminology.

Mitchell is suicidal, and you don't correctly identify his intentions

>   *Advantages:* There is very little, if any, advantage in this situation.

>   *Risks:* You could lose your friend, and you could be left with a lifetime of regret for not acting on your suspicions.

Mitchell is not suicidal, and you don't correctly identify his intentions

>   *Advantage:* You demonstrate your support and concern for a friend.

>   *Risk:* You may appear foolish or overconcerned.

The "misses" have fairly serious consequences. If you confront Mitchell and he intends not to harm himself, your risk lies in his interpretation of your confrontation. He may be touched by your concern, thereby deepening your friendship. Or he may be alienated by your overconcern, causing strain in your relationship.

Far worse, however, is the "miss" in which you ignore your accurate suspicions. If you do not act on your fears and Mitchell commits suicide, you not only will have lost a friend but also may be saddled with regret about the path that you didn't take.

What would you do in this situation? Reviewing these options may help you determine the safest course of action when confronted with the serious depression of a friend or a loved one. Perhaps the best way to reduce your own regret involves mentioning your concerns about the possibility of suicidal intentions to your friend when you feel worried about her state of mind. If you are wrong, the risk will be small. A friend with hurt or irritated feelings at least has the opportunity to get over feeling disturbed. On the other hand, a seriously depressed friend may not be around for long if you overlook the opportunity to demonstrate your sincere concern and your support.

▼Exercise 16.5   I'M JUST NOT MYSELF TODAY

EVALUATE: Criticize

Although the evidence from PET-scan activity on the brains of persons with multiple personality disorder is compelling, there is a flaw. The challenge involves the absence of appropriate control subjects in the original design. Apparently, when normal individuals are asked to complete an activity during a PET scan but also to try to do so pretending to be someone else, their brain patterns show differences that parallel those of individuals with multiple personality disorder undergoing the same task. At the very least this finding suggests that the capacity to manipulate different areas in the brain may be under voluntary control. We still don't have good evidence to suggest that different patterns of brain activation contribute to multiple personality disorder. It will be very interesting to monitor what happens in this controversial area as we apply emerging technologies to the problem of establishing the validity of multiple personality disorder.

▼Exercise 16.6 THE LABELING CONTROVERSY

EVALUATE: Justify

The Rosenhan study is a valid test of the problems associated with labeling

Supporting arguments:

- There are real cases of individuals who have been misdiagnosed and who have experienced difficulties getting out of institutions.

- The kind of symptoms reported by the pseudopatients were realistic for patients who ask for emergency treatment at in-patient settings.

- The pseudopatients acted normally after admission. How closely could the hospital staff have been watching them if they did not notice this normal pattern?

- The pseudopatients took notes about their experience. How can hospital staff justify not attending to this behavior as a possible source of treatment information?

- All pseudopatients reported that they were treated in similar ways, despite the fact that they were in different hospital settings.

Can you think of other arguments that support Rosenhan's conclusions?

The Rosenhan study is not *a valid test of the problems associated with labeling.*

Supporting arguments:

- Expectations of hospital staff members are based on their collective experiences. Clients who report auditory hallucinations are likely to fit the patterns associated with schizophrenia, a condition that usually warrants long-term, intensive care.

- The ethics of the research designer are questionable since the pseudopatients are presenting a pattern that is rarely seen.

- Can anyone verify that the pseudopatients actually acted normally while they were hospitalized?

- It may be wiser to err on the side of greater protection for individuals whose behavior is questionable than to take risks by denying treatment to those whose symptoms suggest that they need care.

Can you think of other arguments that could be used as criticisms of Rosenhan's conclusions?

▼Exercise 16.7 THE END IS NEAR (AGAIN)

EVALUATE: Take Perspective

Doomsday preparation offers us an opportunity to apply historical perspective taking to diagnostic practice.

a. Most diagnoses of excessive doomsday responsiveness would fall in the paranoid personality disorder or obsessive-compulsive personality disorder category. You may want to review the characteristics of these problems in your text to see the relationship between stockpiling and these Axis II dysfunctions.

b. The nondisordered person probably finds predicted disasters laughable and takes no steps to prepare for worldwide disruption. The mildly disturbed person would probably think the predictions would be wrong but probably put in a supply of water and may have celebrated the new year at home "just in case." The moderately disturbed person is more likely to lay in sufficient supplies in case of disaster. The seriously disturbed person begins to use disaster planning as an important framework for making business and life decisions; this person might stockpile supplies and shift resources to safer places. The extremely disturbed person will demonstrate "monomania" as disaster concerns become central to his or her waking life prior to the start of the new year. Significant energies would be devoted to stockpiling, reading expert predictions, making plans for recovery, and telling friends. Based on this continuum and the reality that none of the serious predictions came to pass, where would you draw the line of diagnosable disorder on the continuum?

c. Should dire predictions come to pass, then those who ignored the "obvious" signs of impending doom could have been diagnosed as suffering from hysteria. Of course, this assumes that there was a viable social/medical structure left to do the diagnosing!

▼Exercise 16.8   ALL I NEED IS AN AGENT!

CREATE: Invent

The *DSM-5* is rife with possibilities from which you might select material for your creative writing exercise. It is probably easy to see how challenging life might become for a person having to make accommodations around the symptoms described for any of the disorders you might have selected. Keep in mind as you develop your plot lines that the challenges are not isolated to the individual receiving the diagnosis. Families and friends often feel victimized by the existence of serious psychological difficulties. This fact might help you develop a rich story line that you can share with others in class.

Chapter

◀Therapy▶

▼Exercise 17.1 HOW DOES THAT MAKE YOU FEEL?
UNDERSTAND: Translate

Statement	Options
1.	"Tell me about your earliest memories from childhood.": Freudian
2.	"What were the consequences that happened after you punched your boss?": Behavioral
3.	"Rank order the things that frighten you from 'least' to 'most'.": Systematic desensitization
4.	"Let's explore how your role as a daughter, mother, and wife might influence the problem.": Feminist therapy
5.	"Have you been having recurring dreams?": Jungian therapy
6.	"In what ways do you think you have fallen short of your ideals?": Humanistic therapy
7.	"Pretend that your grandmother is sitting in the chair over there and tell her how you feel.": Gestalt therapy
8.	"You have developed a very powerful mental set that you are a loser.": Cognitive therapy
9.	"If you can refrain from losing your temper, you'll get two red stars.": Token economy
10.	"Let's try to figure out how your feelings of inferiority might be linked to your family.": Adlerian therapy

▼Exercise 17.2 EVEN DOMESTIC ENGINEERS GET THE BLUES
APPLY: Solve

Psychoanalysis
This framework would focus on the contributions of early childhood experiences and the way they shape adult behavior. The therapist would focus on revealing unconscious forces and reducing neurotic choices. The advantage of this framework is the benefit gained by focusing on patterns that have developed through life. The main disadvantages are probably the expense of such intensive therapy as well as the potential for antifemale bias in the treatment.

Ellen could find herself committed to long-term intervention to address the unconscious conflicts that influence her adult choices. Her current unhappiness in the family would be seen as an extension of early fixations and losses in her own development.

Person-Centered Therapy

This treatment approach would focus on the quality of self-concept and self-esteem. The therapist would try hard to listen and reflect the main issues, offering unconditional positive regard about the difficulties expressed by the client. For individuals whose distress is the result of diminished self-esteem, this approach is well tailored. For individuals who seek more direction from therapists, this approach will be frustrating.

Ellen's general distress may be linked to issues of low self-esteem. The therapeutic intervention would focus on her definition of what feels unsatisfying in life. The therapist would offer reassurance but minimal direction in designing a new path for Ellen.

Aversive Conditioning

Aversive conditioning addresses excesses in behavior by reconditioning pleasurable but undesirable activities to take on new aversive qualities. This approach is best implemented when individuals experience disturbing impulses as the source of their pain. The specific conditioning process is cost-effective, but it requires fairly well-defined symptoms to be effective.

Ellen's symptoms may not be specific enough to embark on a counterconditioning procedure. Her unhappiness feels diffused, so it may be difficult to implement this procedure with her.

Cognitive Behavior Therapy

The primary focus of this intervention is to examine the relationship between cognitive interpretations and behavior. The therapist examines the client's expectations and the learning experiences that encouraged the development of those expectations. The therapist may assign homework to help the client to rehearse different patterns of behavior. This approach has clear advantages for those with strong motivation; however, there may be some disadvantage if no distortion in perception or cognition can be identified.

Ellen's sense of self-defeat lends itself to this framework. The therapist would try to determine what her self-image is and how she arrived at such a low point.

Drug Therapy

As the name indicates, this type of therapy focuses on relieving symptoms by prescribing medication. It is used for a variety of conditions that present symptoms of anxiety or depression. When the client and medication are matched carefully, relief of symptoms can be quite rapid, even dramatic. However, there are some risks of long-term dependence and possible side effects. Medication can be expensive, but so can long-term therapy when undertaken without the benefit of medication that could be helpful.

Ellen would probably be a good candidate for medication to relieve her depressive symptoms.

Family Therapy

Family therapy focuses on the family as a system. Sometimes the symptoms of one family member can signify serious problems in the family system. Bringing the whole system into the therapy situation can uncover and heal problematic dynamics that are likely to affect more than just the target client. Families can be stabilized, thereby reaching new levels of understanding that prevent further damage to family members. However, some disadvantage lies in defining mental health concerns as a family systems issue when the origin of the problems may be much more individual.

It is unclear from the case description how much of Ellen's distress is the result of her role in her family. However, family dynamics are certainly influenced by the amount of strain manifested by one of the key caretakers in the family.

Electroconvulsive Shock Therapy

Shock treatments are still used in situations where depression is unrelenting and does not respond to less severe treatments. Relief from symptoms is not guaranteed, but if it occurs, it is rapid. The significant risks of memory loss accompanying this therapy have led to protests by many former patients who have felt damaged by this intervention.

Ellen's distress does not warrant such severe intervention at this time. If multiple interventions are unsuccessful, shock might be considered. However, it is usually reserved as a last resort.

Which framework would you select for Ellen?

Based on the information available in Ellen's case study, we can eliminate aversive conditioning, psychoanalysis, and electroconvulsive shock therapy. Each of the remaining therapies—person-centered, cognitive-behavior, drug, and family—could make meaningful contributions to relieving her depressive symptoms. Each therapy offers a unique approach to defining and treating her symptoms.

▼Exercise 17.3   FLAG ON THE PLAY
APPLY: Predict

Principle 1: Therapists must maintain confidentiality about client disclosure.

What would happen if the therapist violated this principle?

Clients might not necessarily know that confidentiality has been breached; however, should the therapist unwisely share details with family members, even if the impulse was intended to be a helpful one, the client should have difficulties in disclosing details in the future for fear these will be leaked to others who might use the information to place the client at a disadvantage.

Principle 2: Therapists must offer the least restrictive alternative for treatment planning.

What would happen if the therapist violated this principle?

If therapists intervene with too heavy or intrusive a strategy, the client's own capacity to evaluate progress is likely to initiate concerns about being required to do too much or to do something too soon. In addition, intensive therapies that require more time or resources aren't guaranteed to work more effectively. If a less intrusive therapy is a better choice, then something more intrusive will cost more money and will most likely be less effective.

Principle 3: Therapists must warn individuals who have been targeted for violence by their clients.

What would happen if the therapist violated this principle?

This violation predicts especially ugly outcomes. If a client threatens the well-being of a boss, family member, or some other identifiable figure in the client's life, the therapist must alert the target to the potential for danger. By failing to adhere to this ethical constraint, the therapist technically could be responsible for an injury or death of the target if the client's plan was sincere. This ethical regulation actually was initiated by a legal case lodged against a therapist who failed in his duty to warn.

Principle 4: Therapists must allow their clients full access to their treatment records.

What would happen if the therapist violated this principle?

A client who has an interest in seeing what the therapist records about their sessions has full rights to see those records. A therapist who refuses to grant that right is likely to lose the confidence of the client and possibly lose the client altogether. Being too protective about records suggests that something may be wrong or that the therapist hasn't been completely forthcoming about the conclusions drawn about the client and his or her progress. Despite the rights that clients maintain access to their records, most clients don't inquire; however, if the clients want to see the records, it is their right to do so. It is also their right to go shopping for a new therapist who is not so secretive.

Principle 5: Therapists should encourage clients to participate fully in treatment planning.

What would happen if the therapist violated this principle?

Many clients enter therapy rather passively. They expect to present their stories and then the therapist will magically deliver some insights that will make things better. They may not realize that they have rights to ask questions about justification of treatment planning and to assume a more active role in collaborating with the therapist. Clients who want to participate in planning are unlikely to stay with therapists who are not collaborative, thereby insuring that those therapists are more likely to end up working with passive, unquestioning clients.

▼Exercise 17.4   NOT SO CLEVER HANS

ANALYZE: Reason

If you wanted to design an effective outcome study on treatment effectiveness, here are the variables that might be pertinent:

1. How similar were the clients' psychological disturbances?

2. What was the length of treatment for the problem?

3. How were therapy dropouts classified? (In Eysenck's original study, dropouts were assumed to be and counted as "unimproved.")

4. What was the therapeutic orientation of the therapists?

5. Who was paying for treatment?

6. How experienced were the therapists?

7. How motivated were the clients to pursue change?

8. How satisfied were the clients with their treatment?

9. At what point was the measurement of symptom reduction completed?

10. Who offered the report of symptom reduction—the client, the therapist, or a third party?

As you can see from the number of variables that can complicate good controlled observation, producing a definitive outcome study is a challenging research problem.

▼**Exercise 17.5   WHO'S WHO AMONG THERAPEUTIC PROFESSIONALS**

ANALYZE: Categorize

	Clinical Psychologist	Counseling Psychologist	Psychiatrist	Social Worker	Counselor	Psychiatric Nurse	Marriage & Family Therapist
Who is in training the longest?			X				
Who is most likely to administer psychological tests?	X	X					
Who would you most likely find working in a school system?		X		X	X		
Who deserves to be called "Dr?"	X	X	X				
Whose treatment would be the most expensive?			X				
Who would be the most reluctant to work on an individual outside of the individual's system?				X			X
Who would most likely pay attention to feelings as the dominant information to guide therapy?				X			X
Who would provide care in hospital settings?	X		X			X	
Who works with children?	X	X	X	X	X	X	X

▼Exercise 17.6 THERE MUST BE 50 WAYS TO LEAVE YOUR SHRINK
EVALUATE: Choose

Below are several possible indicators that might help you determine when it is time to fly solo. How do these compare with the five alternatives you generated?

- Other people recognize that "there is something *different* about you."
- Other people don't recognize that "there is something different about you."
- You find yourself scrambling for things to talk about in therapy.
- You run out of funding.
- You find yourself quoting your therapist too regularly at social gatherings.
- You develop greater patience for human frailty.
- You have a strong sense of *déjà vu* in the treatment room.
- You know everyone in the waiting room by name (including their diagnoses and prognoses).
- You don't wonder about what your therapist would want you to do when confronted with a personal problem.
- You no longer have the impulse to call your therapist and brag when something goes well.
- You can comfortably disagree with your therapist without fear of reprisal or rejection.
- Your therapist falls asleep in session.
- *You* fall asleep in session.

▼Exercise 17.7 WHO'S GOT THE CHECK?
EVALUATE: Take Perspective

Arguments against equal access/improved funding:

1. Equal access in the form of a national health care plan would prove to be enormously expensive and taxpayers cannot afford this kind of burden.
2. If we provide increased mental health support, we undercut the will of the individual to solve his or her own problems.
3. This kind of system might be easy to abuse for malingerers (that is, people who are not really ill but attempt to exploit circumstances by pretending to be ill).
4. The effectiveness of therapy hasn't been sufficiently proven.
5. We already provide sufficient access to mental health care through community centers.
6. Increased access may not motivate individuals who need help to find their way into good mental health care.
7. I've never needed therapy so I think it is wasteful to have to pay for coverage I am unlikely to use.
8. The effects of therapy may make people too soft to survive in a difficult world.

Arguments in support of equal access/improved funding:

1. Improved access to mental health care may not cost more because earlier attention may reduce the severity of disorders and the length of treatment required.

2. Nearly everyone suffers mental health strain at some point, so coverage is reasonable because it parallels other physical health problems covered by insurance.

3. There is sufficient scientific documentation of the effectiveness of therapy.

4. People do not have any control over the conditions that produce severe disorder; a humane society takes care of those who are in need.

5. Equal access to mental health care might reduce the stigma attached to seeking care and encourage those who need it to take advantage.

6. Good therapists can identify malingerers and address the problems that might cause them to malinger.

7. Although there are services available to those without resources, the quality of care may be questionable because most services of this type are currently underfunded.

8. Therapy should instruct a client in how to become more self-sufficient, which should strengthen rather than weaken the client's character.

▼Exercise 17.8   OUT, DAMNED SPOT
CREATE: Design

What is your hypothesis?

Your new intervention produces faster and more effective relief than is obtained with other known interventions for compulsive hand washing or with no treatment at all.

What is your independent variable?

Type of therapy (your new treatment versus one or more other treatments versus a no-treatment control group).

How will you assign subjects to treatment conditions?

Random assignment among the treatment and control conditions will help eliminate alternative explanations. Perhaps the subjects could also be matched for type and severity of problem.

How will you measure your dependent variable?

By the frequency and intensity of anxiety attacks, as indicated by the number of episodes of hand washing.

What other elements will you need to control in order to rule out alternative hypotheses?

You will need to ensure that the participants receive no other treatment that might pose an alternative explanation for symptom reduction. Creating a standard environment for the duration of the study would also clarify the role of the independent variable.

If all proceeded as planned and you obtained the results you intended, would your study offer proof of the superiority of your treatment?

No. Psychologists generally avoid the notion of *proof* in connection with experiments about human behavior. The constraints of the experimental format limit the scope of our conclusions. In this case, your study *demonstrates* superiority over the other treatment conditions, but it does not prove it.

Chapter

◀Stress and Health▶

▼**Exercise 18.1   BETWEEN A ROCK AND A HARD PLACE**

UNDERSTAND: Translate

Going to the Dentist to Have an Aching Tooth Repaired

Type of conflict: Approach-avoidance

Your stress-intensity rating: This, of course, is unique to you. No attempt will be made here to predict this rating.

Choosing Between Chocolate-Chocolate Chip and Rocky Road Ice Cream

Type of conflict: Approach-approach

Discovering That Your New and Very Attractive Dating Partner Has Bad Breath

Type of conflict: Approach-avoidance

Choosing Between a 7 A.M. and 8 P.M. Class

Type of conflict: Avoidance-avoidance

Deciding Between a One-Week Vacation at Disney World and a One-Week Camping Trip in the Mountains

Type of conflict: Approach-approach

Choosing Between Breast Removal and Chemotherapy After a Diagnosis of Breast Cancer

Type of conflict: Avoidance-avoidance

Selecting One of Two Highly Rated Colleges That Have Admitted You

Type of conflict: Approach-approach

As a Vegetarian, Being Asked Whether You Want Steak or Ribs

Type of conflict: Avoidance-avoidance

Deciding Whether to Buy a Low-Priced, Beautiful Used Car That Needs a Major Repair to Its Engine

Type of conflict: Approach-avoidance

Having Plastic Surgery to Correct a Bump on the Bridge of Your Nose

Type of conflict: Approach-avoidance

▼Exercise 18.2   MY SCREW-UP PROFILE

APPLY: Illustrate (Part 1)

EVALUATE: Prioritize (Part 2)

Your answers will be distinctly your own, but we offer some personal examples to illustrate how things can go awry.

Maladaptive Coping Strategy	Your Personal Example	Consequence
Giving Up/Learned Helplessness	Abandoning a plan to stay healthy through Zumba because I didn't like the new teacher	About 10 extra pounds over the course of a year!
Blaming Yourself	Working on a group project that wasn't successful because I didn't exert effective leadership skills	Feeling bad about the group's failure substituted for taking more effective action to fix the problem
Aggression Against Others	Engaging in hostile driving tactics when thwarted on the road	Honking vociferously at a person with high potential for road rage can be dangerous.
Self-Indulgence	When things don't go my way, I head to Starbucks for a chai tea latte with nutmeg.	So that's where the 10 pounds came from!
Use of Defense Mechanisms	My favorite is *denial*. I'm particularly bad about accurately interpreting body signals that should get professional attention.	Because of my sluggish responsiveness about health, I end up going to the doctor when the problems are much harder to fix.
Avoidance	When a colleague causes me pain, I strategize about how not to spend time in his or her company.	I end up skipping events I might like to attend to avoid the painful colleague.
Passive-Aggressive Tactics	I "forget" to run a promised errand, because other demands trumped its importance.	Whoever I disappointed may exercise some revenge tactics of his own.

Priorities:

Most Regularly Used Bad Strategy: Self-indulgence. Happily, I don't overindulge in alcohol or drugs, but all the remaining indulgences take a toll on self-discipline.

Least Regularly Used Bad Strategy: Aggression against others. My core values tend toward peacemaking rather than stirring things up through physical or verbal means.

▼Exercise 18.3 STEP ON THE GAS
ANALYZE: Classify

Your answer will depend on the particular stressful situation you describe. Regardless of the situation, however, you should be able to identify and articulate the three stages Selye proposed. The first is the alarm reaction, in which the sympathetic nervous system is suddenly activated by the detection of the stressor. You should be able to identify the point at which you first identified the stressor and your immediate physiological reaction. During the second phase you cope with the stressor, and the sympathetic nervous system remains aroused to provide energy and protection against illness. Perhaps you spent a couple of weeks without much sleep while you made arrangements for a funeral or stayed with a sick friend and worked a full-time job. The final stage, exhaustion, occurs when the body's energy is depleted. During this stage your resistance to illness is diminished and energy levels are low. Maybe you had the experience of getting sick during Christmas vacation after a week spent studying all night for finals.

In terms of minimizing the negative effects of such experiences, knowing about the final stage of lowered resistance might be the most helpful. By recognizing that you will be more susceptible to disease or depression during this time, you could arrange to get some extra sleep, take vitamins, or have friends stop by to encourage and support you. Eating healthy foods and getting sleep during the second stage might also help by reducing your body's need to draw upon reserves of strength and lessening the exhaustion that follows.

▼Exercise 18.4 CUSTOMIZED STRESS ASSESSMENT
EVALUATE: Assess

You could pick any target population and think through the stressors most likely associated with the status or developmental challenges. For the scenario we provide, we share stressors experienced by professors. As a model, we think it might be interesting for you to consider the hardships experienced by those who stand behind the podium.

Proposed Stressor	Proposed Rating	Rationale
1. failure to achieve tenure or promotion	75	Getting rejected after investing several years at a university is hard on the ego and pocketbook.
2. 8:00 class assignment	30	I am not a morning person. I don't function well until mid-morning.
3. confronting students about plagiarism	45	Meetings that don't go well can turn into time sinks in administrative follow-up.
4. managing scholarship and grant deadlines	35	Projects have inflexible deadlines that if missed mean a lot of wasted effort.
5. getting ready for classes	10	You just never know if you have prepared enough.
6. coping with colleagues whom you fundamentally dislike	25	Committee meetings can be dreadful if they are filled with contentious behavior.
7. parking woes	20	Parking troubles afflict faculty and students alike.

Continued

Proposed Stressor	Proposed Rating	Rationale
8. managing paper flow	30	Staying organized and managing not to lose papers can be a sanity threat.
9. working with project partners who don't pull their fair share of the load	25	Do you confront the social loafer or do extra work without the confrontation? (Note: avoidance-avoidance)
10. threat of looking incompetent before a class	40	Very few things are harder on the sense of self-competence that making stupid mistakes or feeling humiliated in front of students.

▼ Exercise 18.5   THE GAME OF LIFE

EVALUATE: Justify

Again, your answer will depend on how you perceive the events listed. No matter which events you selected, however, the impact of the catastrophic event will be different if it occurs when you are 8 years old instead of when you are an adult. Predicting exactly how the experience will be different is difficult because of the great variation among individuals. Although an adult has more responsibilities and more decisions to make, adults also have more coping skills and strategies. An 8-year-old is old enough to understand what is happening but generally not experienced enough to have developed successful ways of dealing with the event in question. Because the child may not have the capacity to see the challenge in relation to the threat, and because personal health habits are not fully developed, the 8-year-old may be more likely to be ill. On the other hand, children are less aware of consequences of events and actions and may not recognize the seriousness of the event in the same way as an adult would. In this case, the adult is more likely to be ill.

▼ Exercise 18.6   HEALTHY LIVING

EVALUATE: Take Perspective

As a person who tends toward health, you see this as a challenge and opportunity for personal growth. With children going into college, you know the extra money will come in handy, and you have always thought you could do this job well. You discuss the pros and cons with your entire family, and many of your friends, and you, your children, and husband sit down to plan out exactly what it would take to get everyone where they are supposed to be and to make sure all the work around the house gets done. During the two weeks when you are thinking about and discussing your options, you continue with your normal lifestyle. You still take your evening walk every night after dinner and you spend time on the weekends with friends.

On the other hand, you may see this promotion as a problem; a threat to your current comfortable lifestyle. You could use the extra money, of course, but the travel seems like an insurmountable obstacle. After all, the kids have after-school activities and events and there is no way your husband can manage everything while you are gone. You don't want to ask your family if they are willing to make this sacrifice, so you spend a lot of time by yourself, thinking about how you might make it work. You also spend time wondering what will happen if you can't do the job as well as you think you can. After all, you've never done it before, and maybe you don't have the skills you think you do. During this two-week contemplation period, you are more quiet than usual, forgoing your usual activities, and comforting yourself with home-cooked pies and desserts.

▼Exercise 18.7 ENHANCING IMMUNE FUNCTION

CREATE: Design

There is a variety of extraneous variables which you could try to control. One of the primary concerns would be the individual's previous experience with medication. In order to test your hypothesis, individuals would need to have successful experiences taking oral medication in the past. This would establish the pairing between taking pills and increased immune function. Another concern would be making sure that the individuals taking the placebo in their coffee were as convinced that they were taking medication as the individuals taking pills. If they suspect that they are not receiving the medication being tested, then they will probably not follow through with the regimen, and you will lose your comparison group. You would also be interested in the more "normal" extraneous variables like age and the severity of the illness.

If the two placebo groups are different, then you might conclude that immune enhancement could be classically conditioned through the pairing of the biochemical effects of certain medications with the actions of taking the medication. However, you would not be able to draw any conclusions about other effects such pairing would have on the person's long-term health. That would require a different and more involved set of experiments and longitudinal studies.

Placebo groups—groups of people who think they are getting the treatment being tested, but who are given a neutral substance to compare their performance with those who do receive the real treatment—are frequently used to demonstrate the effectiveness of a given medication or treatment. Such methods are often the only way to determine the effectiveness of new medications and treatments or to compare their effectiveness with other, more established procedures. The use of such groups comes under debate, however, because it means that some of the participants do not receive treatments that are potentially helpful and may be denied an opportunity to overcome their barriers to a healthy life. Even when the placebo group receives the real medication once its effectiveness has been demonstrated, some people argue that this delay is unethical. They believe that any potentially helpful treatment should be offered to all. What do you think about this issue? Do you think the benefits of using a placebo group outweigh the potential harm, or do you think that "proving" the effectiveness of a treatment should take second place to offering potential help to individuals who need it?

▼Exercise 18.8 HEALTHY EXECUTIVES

CREATE: Plan

A strong stress management program will include opportunities for aerobic exercise, relaxation, and development of social support networks. In this type of environment, on-site programs would probably be the most effective because the employees don't have the time to go elsewhere to participate. For the same reason, the exercise programs should be short (maybe 30 minutes) and offered frequently during the day and every day of the week. This would increase the likelihood that employees could find times that fit their schedules, even if those schedules changed from day to day or week to week. There should also be opportunities for the employees to learn simple relaxation techniques that could be performed at their desks or in their offices. Some of this information could be handed out in the form of brochures and pamphlets, and brief classes or in-office sessions could be used for quick demonstrations of the techniques. For those who have the time and interest, biofeedback might be an option, but in this fast-paced environment it is probably too time-intensive to be successful. There are multiple ways in which employees could be encouraged to develop support networks. Simply taking part in one of the classes may provide people with an opportunity to converse and form new friendships. Hosting lunchtime discussions on various topics might also provide people with a chance to get together and talk about common interests. One possibility that would allow people to talk about problems related to work is to set up a mentoring program that pairs new employees with more experienced individuals. There is a multitude of possibilities; the important thing is to recognize the need for all three components.

Working with teachers would be very different from working with investment executives. Teachers have a much more predictable schedule with larger blocks of time potentially available for programs or classes. It might make more sense to offer exercise classes after school, three days a week, for example. You could expect more people to attend each class, and the classes themselves could serve as social groups. Teachers often work in groups or teams and may already have social networks in place. Instead of working to help them develop new networks, you might spend more time helping them identify and use the networks they already have in place. Relaxation techniques would need to be more suited for the public setting of the classroom or teachers' lounge rather than the privacy of an office. Shrugging shoulders or turning one's head from side to side would probably be okay; lying on the floor and lifting one's legs over one's head would probably not be okay. It might be more reasonable to offer biofeedback to this group than to the executives; the equipment and space might be more readily available in a school setting than in an investment office. What other differences did you think of?